day trade online

day trade online

CHRISTOPHER A. FARRELL

John Wiley & Sons, Inc.

New York • Chichester • Weinheim • Brisbane • Singapore • Toronto

Library of Congress Cataloging-in-Publication Data:

Farrell, Christopher A.   1973–
    Day trade online / Christopher A. Farrell.
      p.   cm.
    ISBN 0-471-33120-1 (alk. paper)
    1. Electronic trading of securities.   2. Stocks—Data processing.
  I. Title.
  HG4515.95.F367   1999
  332.64'0285—dc21   99-10248

Printed in the United States of America

10 9 8 7 6 5 4 3 2 1

*To my brother Peter, whose vision,
enthusiasm, and unswerving
support helped to make a lifelong
dream come true.*

CONTENTS

PREFACE

It's 9:00 Monday morning, and I awake to the sounds of my alarm clock. I couldn't be happier: It is the beginning of another trading week. I roll out of bed, "commute" into the next room, and turn on my computer. The work week has begun.

But this is not your typical 9-to-5 job. There is no office to go to, no car pool, and no "good mornings" to co-workers. There is no boss in the next room. I don't produce a product, nor do I sell one. When people ask me what I do for a living, I pause. In fact, I don't really "do" anything. There are no clients, no projects, and no deadlines. There are no co-workers, no staff, and most of all, no friends. I am known by account number only. I am in total isolation. The entire day I may not see or speak to another soul. The work is extremely intense. The pace is fast. In many regards, this is warfare. It is a job unlike any other in the world.

Sometimes I do feel guilty. I am 25 years old and I answer to no one. My day is spent in the comfort of my own home. People may criticize what I do, but on a good day I can make more money in a single afternoon than most of them may make in three months, without ever leaving the house. Still, I am not providing a service to anyone. Is the world a better place because of what I do? Sometimes I don't think so. Very few people understand. They think it's gambling: I tell them it's not.

I am a day trader. My job is to buy and sell stocks for a living. I do not work on Wall Street. My seat is not on the floor on the New York Stock Exchange, it is in cyberspace. This is rarefied air. These are untested waters. I am among a new breed of entrepreneur and this is a new frontier. But do I have what it takes? Mentally, am I strong enough? I've been doing this for almost two years. In the past I have made very good money. But the past is for cowards. And there are no guarantees. Today I must make money.

It is now 9:30. The bell has rung and the stock market is open. I take my seat at the table with the world's biggest banks, brokerage firms, and mutual funds. The chess match has begun.

The explosive growth and low cost of online trading has created a new class of investors who can make a living buying and selling stocks over the Internet in a way once reserved for Wall Street's most powerful brokerage firms and investment banks. The goal of this book is to provide a one-stop, comprehensive overview of how to make a successful living, whether full-time or part-time, by day trading over the Internet. We will examine all aspects of this new and untested area, from what it takes to get started, to the dangers and pitfalls of using online brokers, to an in-depth analysis of which trading techniques work and which don't.

The information provided here will reveal closely held and profitable short-term trading secrets that can only be learned from having worked on one of Wall Street's trading floors, combined with the real-life experience of someone who makes a living trading over the Internet. Quite simply, this is information that most stockbrokers, financial planners, and everyday investors do not possess. With this in mind, the emphasis is on simplicity. The best and most successful traders are those who keep things simple. This is a book on trading, not investing. Therefore it is written in a practical, nontheoretical manner for the reader who might have little or no investment experience, but only the desire to learn more about one of the most exciting and profitable businesses of the next millennium.

For me, day trading is an obsession. I absolutely love what I do. In this book, I hope to share that excitement with you. I am 25 years old. Since graduating from Colgate University in 1995, I have never wanted to do anything with my life but trade. I felt then, and I feel now, that trading is and will always be the most lucrative job on the face of the earth, *if and only if you know what you are doing.*

I began my career out of college working for two large brokerage firms: first for Olde Discount in Detroit, then for Gruntal and Company on Wall Street. At the age of 22, I was trading literally millions of dollars of the firms' capital. It didn't take long to learn how Wall Street made its money. There was a system in place, and there were traders such as myself whose sole job it was to exploit that system for profit. That's when I came to the realization that the knowledge I had, if used the right way, could make me substantial amounts of money. I also decided I had wasted enough time making other people rich.

This was around the same time online trading was beginning to come into its own. The landscape of investing was changing, and thanks to the Internet, trades were becoming extremely cheap. It was slowly becoming clear that it was no longer necessary to work on Wall Street to participate in this game. The rules were changing, and the Internet was the key.

That was all I needed to know. For me, this was the opportunity of a lifetime, and I wasn't going to waste another minute. At the age of 23, I left Wall Street and began an exciting journey that has led me to write this book. I moved back home to upstate New York, bought a computer, renovated my old bedroom into a home office, and began trading full-time for myself. From that old bedroom, I have traded over 15 million shares of stock over the Internet (almost $400 million in transaction value) since I started. My hedge fund, the Farrell Preferred Stock Arbitrage Fund, LP, returned over 65 percent in its first year using these methods. There is really no other way to put it: The trading strategies mentioned in this book work, and they work well.

And the lessons I have learned along the way are invaluable. Over the last two years I have made money and I have lost money, but I have enjoyed every step of the way. In this game, if you can weather the storms, ride out the inevitable ups and downs, limit your risk, and have confidence in your own abilities, you will prosper. You always have to remember that what you are doing is truly special. The job of the Internet day trader didn't even exist 10 years ago. I have been fortunate enough to be able to make a very good living in a way that many people can only dream of. And I wouldn't change that for the world.

ACKNOWLEDGMENTS

This book is not merely a chapter in my life, but the culmination of a lifetime of experiences. I owe a tremendous debt of gratitude to all those people who, often in unforeseen ways, made the completion of this book possible. Life is very short, and I am aware that, if you are lucky, the opportunity to thank the people who have had a positive influence on your life may come only once. For me, this is it, right here, right now. This is a rare chance for me to reflect back on my life and to express my appreciation to those who helped me reach this point.

First, on a professional note, I want to thank my editor, Pamela van Giessen, for all her help and guidance in making this book possible, for having faith in me and my abilities, and for trusting and believing in the ideas of a 25-year-old first-time author before even one page of the book was written. In addition, many people behind the scenes at John Wiley & Sons, including Mary Todd, have worked hard to make this book a reality.

On a personal level, I must first thank my parents, who in their love and uncompromising support have sacrificed so much over the years to get me to this point, especially to get an education at Colgate. In addition, no one will ever know the risks my parents took on my behalf to help make the Farrell Preferred Stock Arbitrage Fund, LP, a reality. Thanks, Mom and Dad.

To my brother Peter, for believing in my crazy dream when no one else did: Thank you for knowing the great enthusiasms, frustrations, risks, and emotions that are a part of going out on your own and trading for a living, and for never leaving my side through the entire process.

To my grandmother, Nana: Thank you for teaching me so much about what is important in life. To my grandfather, Papa: Your wisdom instilled in me a love and respect for the stock market at a very young age. To my extended family—all of the Farrells, Van Burens, Fitzpatricks, and Phillips: Thank you for your support and guidance, and for all the good times over the last 25 years.

Thanks to the people who have been there since day one, including Jesse Fogarty, Matt Hanvey, Brennan Perkins, Mike O'Heaney, Gordon McLean, Mark Garcia, Jim Egan, Scott Audlin, Andrew Guernsey, and Kate Macrae.

Thanks to the members of the Christian Brothers Academy Class of 1991, and to coaches Cliff Lehman and John Ashley and my teammates on that exceptional track and field team which, in retrospect, is exactly what earned me a scholarship to Colgate.

To all my friends at Colgate University, and especially the brothers of Delta Upsilon Fraternity, thank you for making my time at Colgate the best four years of my life.

Thanks to the people I have had the pleasure of working with over the years, especially my boss, mentor, and friend on the preferred stock desk at Gruntal, Art Bruno. Thank you, Art, for teaching me so much about trading, for instilling in me the knowledge and wisdom of someone who has survived for the better part of 30 years on Wall Street, and for setting the example of honor and integrity in a business that often does not reward those virtues. Also, a special thanks to my friends on the trading floor at Gruntal, especially John Maguire and Lisa Marchese.

Thanks to the guys who were there when it all began on the trading floor at Olde in Detroit back in the summer of 1995, who had the guts to uproot and relocate from all parts of the country to downtown Detroit in search of one thing—the promise of riches. To the members of that team: I salute you for knowing what it means to truly take a risk. That was an experience I will not soon forget.

And last, in memory of my fraternity brother Kyndle Mongeon, Colgate #70, "The Best": To Kyndle's family, we have not forgotten.

day trade
online

INTRODUCTION

Swimming with the Sharks

I see the ads on television. Open an account and your first trade is free. Trade as many shares as you'd like for one flat fee. Free real-time quotes. Free market research. Trade stocks. Trade options. With the click of a mouse. It's that easy. Anyone can do it. Do people really know what they are getting themselves into?

I think back to my time on Wall Street. Does the little guy really have a chance? There are sharks in these waters. They lie under the surface. You can't see them. You can't hear them. You don't even know they are there. But they are. And this is their turf. Whether you like it or not, they are swimming with you. And they are lightning fast and always hungry. If you are not careful, they will eat you alive.

But sharks are not always bright. They act on impulse. And, yes, they can be fooled. Do you really want to know how day traders make money? By taking food right out of the sharks' mouths. That is how I make my living. It's all a matter of being alert. Long-term investors have always managed to stay away from sharks. They are patient. But, in the financial world, you can't make a living as a day trader by being patient. No, you must swim with the sharks. That is where the money is.

Day trading is a skill, nothing more. And the more skill you have, the more money you will make. It's that simple. Some people are able to make millions trading stocks, while others find out in matter of months that they can't make a dime. Part of the skill is knowing how the system works, and the other part is exploiting it. That's what Wall Street has been doing for over 100 years, at our expense. But times have changed. Today, we live in a new age in which the playing field has finally been leveled.

There is no doubt about it, online trading is catching fire. And Wall Street is taking notice. In the matter of a few short years, the Internet has changed the very landscape of investing. The online trading revolution has begun. The walls have come down. Trading stocks has never been cheaper or more accessible. Against this backdrop, a new breed of entrepreneur—the internet day trader—has emerged. Internet day trading—the practice of buying and selling stocks over the Internet for quick profits—can be one of the most lucrative jobs on the face of the earth. It is also one of the most misunderstood. Regardless, it is the wave of the future. And it is here to stay.

The allure of day trading is strong. Everyone with an interest in the markets, it seems, wants to trade. And who wouldn't? If you are successful, there is no greater, more profitable, or more enjoyable job anywhere. But there are risks. The stock market is more volatile today than at any time in history. Markets move suddenly and without warning, creating and destroying wealth in ways the majority of market participants simply do not understand. In the rarefied air of stock speculating, fortunes can be made and lost in a matter of seconds. The naive and inexperienced will quickly learn that it is not a place for the faint of heart. Still, many people would love to trade for a living, if only they knew how.

Day trading is not gambling, however. If you want to play blackjack, go to Las Vegas. Personally, I hate to gamble. *The key to day trading is to trade only when the odds are in your favor.* It's that simple. Profits are awarded to those who act the most quickly and seize the opportunities. Literally every minute of every trading day, there are an infinite number of opportunities to make quick profits, if and only if you know what to look for. That is where the skill comes in. You have to know when to act and when not to. And you always have to be on guard.

Wall Street can be a dangerous place if you are not careful. There are sharks in these waters. They are the best traders in the world. They control the market, they set the odds, and they don't like day traders. The sharks make their living by trading against you, and you make your living by trading against them. The only problem is that the odds are on their side. This is how it has always been. They are better equipped, faster, and more knowledgeable. And they certainly don't like to give their money away, especially not to you. It is a fact that the system is geared toward your failure. Wall Street earns its money at the expense of the investing public. You have to recognize this. Many factors come into play to stack the odds of quick success against you. The system is not perfect, though. Through knowledge and experience, you will overcome the odds. Eventually, with the right tools and training, you will able to beat the pros at their own game. That is when the profits roll in. But you are truly on your own, and you must be prepared.

That is where I come in. It is my hope that I can help prepare you for the jungle that lies ahead. Trading for a living is hard. Trading for a living over the Internet is even harder. There are so many challenges, so many issues, and so many obstacles that confront you. And there is but one reward: Money. If you are successful, it can be more money than you ever dreamed of. I make a living by trading over the Internet. Follow my example. The profits are there: You just have to go out and take them.

The Internet is only one facet of the game. For the online day trader, the Internet is both a best friend and a worst enemy. You have to know how to use it. You must also understand that it has flaws. There is no cheaper way to trade. Period. Not even on the floor of the New York Stock Exchange. But this comes at a cost. And you have to trade accordingly.

And that is only the beginning. You have to know what to trade, and you have to know when. Buy or sell. Listed or NASDAQ. Timing is everything. You have specialists, market makers, and program trading to deal with. You have late fills, gap openings, and margin calls. The bid-ask spread. Trading halts. System crashes. Even SOES bandits.

Venturing into this jungle unprepared is a recipe for disaster. I will prepare you. I will be your guide and this book will be your trail map. You will learn about:

1. Trading on New York Stock Exchange and the role of the specialist
2. Trading on NASDAQ and the role of the market makers

3. How to beat the specialists and the market makers at their own game

4. Which trading techniques work and which don't

5. Which stocks to trade, and which to stay away from

6. What to look for when screening a group of stocks for a single trade

7. What it takes to get started in online trading

8. The dangers and pitfalls of using online brokers

Most importantly, when you are done with this book, you will be able to look at 10 different stocks and know exactly which to trade at that precise moment, what price to enter the buy order at, and why. You will be able to apply this knowledge to every single stock you screen, because although the situations may change, the fundamentals of successful day trading remain the same.

There are some things only experience can teach. You will come to know yourself and your limits very quickly. Trading is a mental profession. Your emotions will be put to the test. You will go through mood swings like never before in your entire life. Anger, frustration, elation: You will feel it all. Your heart will beat fast. Your head will throb. You will have trouble sleeping at night. Sometimes you will find it hard to keep your composure. In the world of trading, living with anxiety is par for the course. So is making and losing a few thousand dollars in a week.

In addition, very few people will appreciate the day-to-day challenges you face. The 9-to-5 world will not understand. How can it? You are speaking a different language. Other people earn their paychecks by working for someone else. You earn yours working for yourself, from the comfort of your own home, in what at times feels like a high-stakes game of poker. No one is ever going to give you a pat on the back and say, "Job well done." In fact, there are probably some people who would rather see you fail. But you know that going in. Sympathy is not what you are looking for. You are in this game for the money.

No one ever said trying to make a few hundred thousand dollars a year would be easy. There is always a price to be paid. The beauty of this business is that a six-figure income is an attainable goal. There is no one or nothing to stop you. You make the decisions and you are the boss. Best of all, you keep every single dime you make.

So the journey begins. The road to riches awaits you. Follow me and travel lightly. There are only four things you will need: trading capital, good instincts, a flair for risk, and a love of money. Good luck, and may the gods of trading be with you.

SECTION I

The World of the Day Trader

The online day trader is after one thing: the quick kill. But the day trader's job is much different than people think. Day traders are not investors, they are traders. What does this mean? It means that long-term trends and market conditions do not concern them. Reading The Wall Street Journal *cover to cover is not their job, nor is studying graphs, charts, and research. None of these things will put food on their tables. Neither will listening to brokers and analysts, nor knowing every fact, rumor, and tidbit about the market. In fact, day traders may not even know anything about the stocks they trade. They may not even know the names or lines of business of the companies— because they don't have to. In this game, knowing too much will not help you, it will hurt you.*

This is the short term, and the only thing day traders should be concerned about is the next five minutes. Yet, they know exactly what they are doing. Every trade they make is a precise, well-calculated move. The goal: to get in, to make a profit, and to get out, as quickly and as safely as possible. Welcome to the world of the day trader.

CHAPTER 1

The Baptism by Fire

Preparing the Uninitiated
for Their First Trade

Do you want to get your head handed to you on a platter? Do you want to get your eyes ripped right out of your skull? Unfortunately, that is the inevitable fate of too many first time traders. Why? Because they make the classic mistake of thinking day trading is that easy. It is not. The market is like a wild beast. Sometimes the beast is asleep, and sometimes it is awake. Regardless, you must have a respect for its power, because the beast doesn't care about you, your money, or your livelihood. Yet the only way to make a living buying and selling stocks is to fight this beast, head to head, nose to nose. If you want to be a day trader, that is what you must do. But everything you have ever learned about investing won't help you now. The short term is an entirely different world, on a different planet, with different rules. The people who excel here are a rare breed, and the way they make their money may surprise you. Second to second, minute to minute, this is a battle. And when there is a battle, there are casualties. Who will prevail? The one who is best prepared; the one who knows the risks; the one who knows when to fight and when to run.

It is often said that the market will humble those who do not respect its power. There are many day traders who enter the financial arena for the first time without having any respect for or real understanding of the system or of the risks that are involved. These people will only last so long before the market inevitably crushes them. Before you risk even a single penny of your trading capital, you must understand what you are getting yourself into. Good day traders can make literally tens of thousands of dollars in a single day. But any time you can make that kind of money, there is also the chance, however slight, that you can lose that kind of money as well. Most likely, this will not happen, but if you let your guard down, beware! You have to proceed cautiously. With that in mind, I will do everything possible in this book to make sure you are properly prepared before you make your first trade. And when you do finally "pull the trigger" for the first time, it is my hope that this book will have given you everything you need to successfully compete in the world of stock trading.

Figure 1.1 is a picture of my computer screen on a typical trading day. What do you see here? What can you make of this chaos? To the uninitiated, this is like an alien world, where the inhabitants speak a different language. But to the day trader, this screen is a bird's-eye view of a battlefield—of a war. And it is a war filled with opportunities, filled with emotion, filled with danger. Fear and greed. Risk and reward. What are they fighting over? Over gold, over wealth. But who is fighting whom? You can't see the players; you don't know who they are. All you see are numbers. But you know a struggle is going on. For-tunes are won and lost every single second of every single day, throughout Wall Street and throughout the world, on battlefields just like this one. And, to the well-trained day trader, this battlefield has within it extraordinary opportunities for profit *if you know what to look for.* When you are finished with this book, you will know exactly what I'm talking about. You will also know precisely how to take this information and profit from it.

What is the key to making a living as a day trader? To answer this question, you have to look to Wall Street for answers. Wall Street is bet-ter at the business of making money than any other industry in the world. Look at the large brokerage firms, banks, and trading firms. How do they make their money? What is it they do to generate billions of dollars per year in profits by trading stocks? Where is the money com-ing from? I will devote a good portion of the next few chapters to answering these questions. Why is this important? Because as a day trader, you are doing the exact same thing with your money as Wall Street does with its money. Understanding how the system works is the

Figure 1.1   The battlefield.

	Symbol	Last	Change	Volume	Bid	Ask	Bid Size × Ask Size
	$INDU	9124.53	+68.48	DOW			
	$SPX	1159.58	+6.97	S & P Index			
	$@CCO	1921.16	+1.48	NASDAQ Comp			
	SP8Z	1162.5	+3.80	S & P Futures			
	$TYX	5.21	−0.33	30 year treasury			
	ZB8Z	$128^{29}/_{32}$	$+^{22}/_{32}$	30 yr bond futures			
1	AA	$80^{5}/_{16}$	+1	777,400	$80^{1}/_{8}$	$80^{5}/_{16}$	5 × 2
2	ADF	$9^{13}/_{16}$	$+^{1}/_{16}$	31,300	$9^{13}/_{16}$	$9^{7}/_{8}$	9 × 7
3	AXP	$104^{1}/_{16}$	$+2^{11}/_{16}$	1,473,700	$103^{7}/_{8}$	$104^{1}/_{8}$	41 × 100
4	NMK	$15^{1}/_{16}$	$-^{1}/_{16}$	201,500	15	$15^{1}/_{8}$	10 × 5
5	BA	$43^{7}/_{16}$	$+^{5}/_{16}$	2,418,900	$43^{3}/_{8}$	$43^{7}/_{16}$	65 × 20
6	EE	9	$-^{1}/_{16}$	58,000	$8^{15}/_{16}$	$9^{1}/_{8}$	140 × 2
7	CAT	$48^{1}/_{16}$	$+^{1}/_{4}$	967,000	$47^{15}/_{16}$	$48^{1}/_{16}$	100 × 25
8	GRT	$15^{1}/_{8}$	$+^{1}/_{16}$	72,300	15	$15^{1}/_{16}$	10 × 10
9	KO	$72^{7}/_{16}$	$+1^{1}/_{16}$	2,480,700	$72^{3}/_{16}$	$72^{7}/_{16}$	33 × 24
10	DIS	$28^{3}/_{8}$	$+^{1}/_{16}$	4,736,300	$28^{3}/_{8}$	$28^{7}/_{16}$	600 × 20
11	AMZN	$241^{5}/_{8}$	$-6^{1}/_{4}$	3,465,000	$241^{1}/_{8}$	242	1 × 2
12	EK	$76^{1}/_{8}$	$-^{1}/_{16}$	1,096,400	$76^{1}/_{16}$	$76^{1}/_{8}$	38 × 1
13	XON	$71^{5}/_{8}$	$+1^{3}/_{4}$	3,825,600	$71^{9}/_{16}$	$71^{11}/_{16}$	19 × 20
14	YHOO	201	$-4^{1}/_{4}$	3,425,600	201	$201^{1}/_{2}$	1 × 12
15	GM	$72^{1}/_{16}$	$-^{1}/_{2}$	2,338,800	$72^{1}/_{16}$	$72^{3}/_{16}$	10 × 10
16	GT	56	$+^{7}/_{16}$	438,400	$55^{15}/_{16}$	56	19 × 3

Real-time data courtesy of Paragon Software, Inc. (InterQuote), 1-800-311-1516, www .interquotc.com.

first step in sccing how to exploit it for profit. And exploiting the system is the only way it is possible to make a living as a day trader.

Once you get a little insight into how Wall Street works, we will then formulate a specific strategy on understanding how stocks actually trade. The emphasis in the beginning is on the inherent disadvantages that face the day trader who trades over the Internet. We will spend a good deal of time on the mechanics of the market maker system, the specialist, and the bid-ask spread. This will lay the groundwork for formulating the differences between trading New York Stock Exchange (NYSE) stocks and National Association of Securities Dealers Automated Quotation (NASDAQ) stocks.

Finally, we will get down to the task at hand: day trading. I will use a conservative approach, starting with low-volatility stocks like utilities and closed-end funds, before venturing into the volatile, high-risk, high-reward domain of the Dow stocks, technology stocks, and other momentum plays. This way, you will become acquainted with the principles of day trading in areas that are safer, instead of jumping headfirst into the volatile sectors of the market.

When you finish with the book, you will see that day trading is far different than you first thought it was. It really doesn't have anything to do with the kind of investing you see, hear, and read about in the media. Surprisingly, you really don't need to know the markets that well, and you certainly don't have to spend hours doing research and studying charts. But that is what makes day trading so interesting. To be honest, I find the economics of the market to be a bit dry. The mechanics of trading, however, are far from dry. Day trading is a dynamic and vibrant phenomenon. That is what makes me look forward to getting up every morning.

CHAPTER 2

The Golden Age of Internet Day Trading

The markets were going haywire that day. With the click of a mouse, I sold. The fill report came back. I breathed a sigh of relief. I was out. Five thousand shares sold at 8. A $4,000 profit in only 18 minutes. This was my best trade ever: I had never made this much money this quickly in my life. Finally, I had hit a home run. And there was no need to press my luck. I didn't want to trade for the rest of the day. I turned off my computer and got out my golf clubs. My workday was over. It was 9:48 A.M.

We live in a very special time. The Internet has changed the way we work, live, and interact. The flow of information is faster today than at any time in the history of the world. And nowhere is it faster than in the financial markets. The stock market of today is a far different place than the stock market of five years ago. We are witness to a revolution in the world of finance that began only a short time ago. The general public is fascinated with the stock market. As a society, we can't seem to get enough: The sheer numbers of financial Web sites, online trading firms, and news shows devoted to the markets stand as testament to this. Over the last few years, the bull market in stocks has made investing a dinnertime topic in many middle-class households for the first time. The investing obsession is now forever ingrained in mainstream

America. And the Internet has played a huge role. The result is that the individual investor is much more educated today than ever before. The necessity of depending on stockbrokers for advice and information is fast becoming a thing of the past. More and more each day, people are taking financial matters into their own hands. And, while the old paradigm is fading into the background, a new breed of speculator has emerged: the online day trader.

This is the backdrop for the explosion in online trading that has occurred in the last two years. There are now over 80 online brokerage firms competing for the 5 million individual accounts that now trade actively over the Internet. By the year 2000, it is estimated that that figure will have grown to over 10 million online accounts.

In many regards, this is a golden age for Internet day trading. In today's world, conditions are ideal for the day trader. Low commissions, a fair regulatory environment, and technology that allows someone in Alaska to have the same split-second financial information as a trader on the floor of the New York Stock Exchange are but a few of the reasons. Thanks to the Internet, information travels so quickly and efficiently that the day trader can witness and react to tiny, second-to-second price fluctuations in stocks that in the old days would go unnoticed. This enables day traders to make quick $\frac{1}{16}$-, $\frac{1}{8}$-, and $\frac{1}{4}$-point profits in less time than it takes to make a phone call, allowing them to capitalize on opportunities created by markets that can change drastically in just a few seconds.

It has not always been this way. For decades, the world of stock trading was dominated by a select few on Wall Street. The best and most profitable traders all held seats on the New York Stock Exchange. In the past, this was a necessity. These insiders had a virtual monopoly on financial information. Markets moved too fast for those who did not have the same access to quick trades and timely information that the floor traders had. If you were not on the floor of the exchange, you were on the outside, plain and simple. To make matters worse, only a privileged few could afford the high price of owning a seat. Day trading required a tremendous amount of money and resources just to compete. And the playing field was not level. The individual investor did not stand a chance in this environment. That is why, back then, the idea of the individual day trader competing on the same field with the Wall Street giants was unheard of.

In those days, the high commissions alone prevented most individuals from doing any stock trading. There was no such thing as discount brokers: Full-service brokerage firms were the only means for the individual to invest. If you bought 1,000 shares of a stock, you might pay a few dollars per share for the order. Imagine buying 1,000 shares of IBM and paying a $2,000 commission! The stock would have to move several points just to break even. And that doesn't count the commission you'd pay on the way out as well. There was simply no way to trade under these circumstances. If you were in the market, you had to have a long-term perspective. That was the only way.

But times have changed. Thanks to online trading, day trading is now feasible for those with limited resources and a small amount of trading capital. The individual trading from home now has access to the same profits the Wall Street brokerage firms have been making for decades. And the day trader is not at a real disadvantage for being at home. Online orders can be executed in as fast as one second and cost as little as $5. By monitoring a real-time quote screen, the active day trader can literally make a living on the same small profits—¼s, ⅛s, and even ¹⁄₁₆s—that make the large trading firms millions of dollars per year.

But that does not tell the whole story. Though Internet day traders have advantages today that they have never before had in trading, they are still at a slight disadvantage compared to the "real" players in the marketplace, namely the market makers and the specialists. The Internet day trader is on the outside, not the inside. Successful day trading requires an acceptance of this reality. To make a living trading, you have to gear your whole strategy around this fact. This will become clear as you get further into the book.

The trading strategies outlined in this book encompass a wide area of the universe of stock speculation. With this in mind, I am reminded that the financial world is vast. This book will touch on many subjects, each important in its own right. I write from experience, and I only write about things that I think will affect your bottom line—trading profits. Along the way, your understanding of how the game really works will deepen tremendously. You must be patient and give yourself time to understand these concepts. To the beginner, they are not easy. But they will come with time. And the better you understand them, the more profitable you will become.

Here is a summary of the major themes of the book:

1. In the short term, the stock market is inefficient, irrational, and imperfect. The system is flawed and can be exploited for quick profits.

2. Wall Street earns its profits at the expense of the investing public, by trading against its customers.

3. Day traders earn their profits at the expense of Wall Street, by beating it at its own game.

4. The system is flawed because in stock trading, as in a casino, the odds are always with the *house*. Over the long term, the house always wins.

5. The house in this case is the Wall Street firms who control the trading in stocks. The house always wins because of a mechanism called the *bid-ask spread*.

6. Because of the bid-ask spread, it is very difficult for day traders to be consistently profitable by betting against the house—trading against the Wall Street firms.

7. Day traders should only trade when they have an edge, when the odds are in their favor. And the only time the odds are truly in their favor is when they trade with the house, by being on the same side of the trade as the Wall Street firms. This is called *exploiting the bid-ask spread,* and it is the way day traders take food out of Wall Streeters' mouths.

8. Unlike the casino, the New York Stock Exchange has rules in place that allow individual traders to bet with the house. This gives traders the same edge and access to profits that the Wall Street has always had. This is *buying on the bid* and *selling on the ask.* The investing public is generally not aware that these rules exist. The public's ignorance of this rule is the key to the day traders' profits.

9. By exploiting the bid-ask spread, day traders are able to make consistent, low-risk profits even in stocks that don't move. The stock does not have to go up or down for day traders to make money.

10. The fact that day traders can make money in stocks that don't move means they don't have to trade volatile stocks to make a living. They can make just as much money trading slow-moving stocks such as closed-end funds, utilities, and real estate investment trusts.

11. In NASDAQ, the market makers have a huge advantage over the Internet day traders. Thus, trading NASDAQ stocks requires a slightly different strategy.

12. The online brokers are in the business, directly or indirectly, of trading against their customers. That is why the trades are so cheap. This further amplifies the fact that the house always wins.

So how do you trade with the house? A major portion of this book will be devoted to answering that question.

THE HOUSE EDGE

The basic premise of day trading is that you are attempting to make a living by profiting off tiny inefficiencies in the stock market. In layman's terms, this means buying stocks and reselling them to someone else at a higher price. The best trades are the ones where you resell the stock for a profit seconds after you buy it. So how is this possible? The markets do not give away money. Especially not to the day trader. It's because the markets are inefficient and the system can be exploited for profit. It's that simple.

Day trading is a zero-sum game. The profits you make come directly at the expense of someone else. Sometimes it's at the expense of the market makers, sometimes at the expense of the investing public. Nonetheless, if you know what to look for, the profits are there for the taking—and if you don't take them, someone else will.

Day trading, like many other lucrative professions, is an extremely competitive business. The profits certainly don't come easy. The only way to prosper in this environment is to have an edge in the marketplace. But the system does not give you the edge. So the only way to gain the edge is to exploit the system in some way. Without an edge, you don't stand a chance.

Let's draw an analogy to the casinos. In 1996, over 30 million people visited the casinos in Las Vegas, leaving behind over $2 billion of their hard-earned money. How did this happen? The casinos did not steal the money. It's because of something called the *house edge,* a slight and virtually invisible statistical advantage the casino has over its gambling guests. Every single transaction the casino engages in is the end result of exhaustive mathematical research to determine if the risk the house is taking is justified. Not a single penny of the casino's capital will be risked unless the odds are in the house's favor.

The key to success is that the casino doesn't get greedy. Its owners are perfectly content with paying out a majority of their profits and only keeping a small percentage for themselves. They do not do this because they like to give their money away. They just know that if you stay at the blackjack table long enough, chances are you will leave with less money than you came with. Over time, this house edge will destroy even the best recreational gambler.

But as strong as the house edge is, there are some people who have devised ways to overcome it. If you ask the pit bosses who poses the biggest threat to the casinos' earnings, they would all undoubtedly say that card counters are among the most dangerous. This is because these blackjack hustlers beat the casinos at their own game. They do this by raising their bets as the odds tip in their favor. By counting cards, a player is able to gain a slight statistical advantage over the dealer in predicting which cards will be dealt next. This edge becomes more exaggerated and more profitable the longer the gambler stays at the tables. There are numerous people who make a living by doing this. These are the true professional gamblers.

The only problem with this line of work is that the casinos prohibit card counting. The casino managers are not stupid. They are not about to give their hard-earned money away to people they consider card cheats. In fact, Las Vegas spends millions of dollars per year to protect itself from these "parasites." Consistently profitable blackjack players will last only so long at the tables before the casinos pull the plug. Well-known professional card counters can't even set foot in the large casinos without being asked to leave. Many have to resort to disguises just to go unrecognized long enough the make their profits. They are the most despised people in the gaming industry. It's funny how the casinos devote so much energy to preventing a practice that can essentially be taught and used by anyone sitting at the blackjack tables.

Yet these are the same casinos that welcome you and me with open arms. Every single service the Las Vegas casinos provide is aimed at keeping you at the tables. From the free drinks to the 24-hour room service to the fresh air that is pumped into the gaming rooms, you are made to feel as comfortable as possible. The casino is open 24 hours a day, but you can't find a clock anywhere. That way you are unaware of the time you have spent on the tables. This all revolves around the premise that, unless you have an edge, the longer you gamble, the less likely you are to win. The Las Vegas skyline was built with the hard-earned money people like you and me have left behind at its tables.

There is another industry where the edge is more subtle and less understood, but produces the same results—Wall Street. Did you ever wonder how Wall Street is able to make so much money year after year? Whether or not the great financial institutions would like to admit it, and whether or not the general public is aware it is happening, the Wall Street brokerage firms do to the individual investor exactly what the Las Vegas casinos do to their gambling patrons. In the gaming world, the house edge is probability. In the world of investing, the edge is known as the *bid-ask spread*. In the financial markets, the effects of the house edge are more dangerous. These forces go unseen, unfelt, and undetected by the ordinary investor, especially in a bull market where the feeling is that everyone is making money. But the house edge has always been there. While the casinos deal in craps, roulette, and blackjack, Wall Street deals in stocks, bonds, and commodities.

In many ways, the successful day trader carries the same persona on Wall Street as the blackjack hustler does in Las Vegas. Day traders' profits are made by exploiting the system. The system they exploit is controlled by forces much more powerful than the individual trading over the Internet. The Wall Street establishment that sets the odds does not take kindly to the intrusion of the day trader. As the casinos will do anything and everything possible to destroy the card counters, so will the Wall Street market makers do all in their power to prevent the day trader from being profitable, because the profits the day trader makes come directly out of the market maker's pocket. Like the unpopular guest sitting at the poker table with a weak hand, you must recognize that, as a day trader, the odds are inherently against you and there are many people who will revel in your failure. The key to profitable day trading is to recognize this fact, and, like the card counter in blackjack, to trade only when the odds are in your favor.

The great thing is that throughout the trading day there are an infinite number of times when the odds are in your favor. In the short term, the markets are irrational and incredibly inefficient. The markets are moved by fear and greed. This creates a tremendous opportunity for quick profits, if you know what to look for. The secret to success is to take the clues the market gives you and use them to interpret the intentions of the other players. With the odds in your favor, you can beat the players at their own game. To do this, you need to understand the components of Wall Street's version of the house edge, known as the bid-ask spread.

THE BID-ASK SPREAD

I remember the first time I ever visited Wall Street as a child. I recall feeling awestruck by the sense of wealth and power: I could feel it in the air. Did you ever wonder how this wealth is created? How do the large trading firms afford to pay the rent on those high-rise buildings in New York's financial district, which is some of the most expensive corporate real estate in the country? How do they afford to pay their top traders multimillion-dollar salaries? The money is earned at the expense of the investing public. As you know, the essence of the stock market is a difference of opinion. For every buyer, there is a seller. The large banks and brokerage firms make a sizable percentage of their profits by taking the other side of customer orders. When the customer buys, one of these financial institutions is usually on the other side of the trade. The key is that, like a used car dealership buying and selling cars, the trading firms buy low and sell high, skimming a few cents per share on the trade. Contrary to popular belief, Wall Street does not make its money by hitting home runs on huge one-time gains. Like the casinos, it makes its money on small, consistent profits of $\frac{1}{16}$-, $\frac{1}{8}$-, and $\frac{1}{4}$-point gains. This is done through the market maker system and the mechanism known as the bid-ask spread.

The market maker system is the glue that holds the financial markets together. Basically, the market makers are the intermediaries in the buying and selling of stocks. On the New York Stock Exchange and the American Stock Exchange (AMEX), market makers are known as *specialists*. Each individual stock has one specialist who is its sole market maker. On NASDAQ, the market makers are the numerous firms that trade in the stock. There are several market makers for each individual NASDAQ stock. The various exchanges have slightly different methods, rules, and systems for trading stocks, but the underlying principles are inherently the same. The role of the market makers is to maintain an orderly market.

The recent high-profile merger between the AMEX and NASDAQ exchanges will undoubtedly bring certain changes in the rules that govern the trading of stocks on those exchanges. For the purposes of this book, we will assume that the traditional trading rules specific to each exchange are still in place, because it would be impossible to speculate with accuracy as to what those changes will be in the future.

When it is said that specialists *make a market,* it simply means that at all times and under all circumstances they are both buyers and sellers of the stocks they trade. There is always a price at which specialists will buy stock from the public and sell stock to the public. They are always risking their own money to take the other side of your trade. If you want to buy 1,000 shares, the specialist will sell you 1,000 shares from his or her own account. If you want to sell, the specialist will be there to buy the stock from you, assuming there is no one else in the market. This is another way of saying that he or she is adding liquidity to the market by buying when there are no buyers and selling when there are no sellers. The specialist does this by keeping an inventory in the stock. This is essential to ensuring that stocks can trade freely.

But there is a catch. Specialists do not provide this service for free. The price at which a specialist sells stock to you is always going to be higher than the price at which he or she buys it from you. Consider this a price markup for maintaining an inventory in the stock. This markup is what enables specialists to skim the $\frac{1}{16}$s, $\frac{1}{8}$s, and $\frac{1}{4}$s all day from the order flow. The more trading volume, the more money they make. So how is this legal? It is very simple. The specialists are risking their own capital by maintaining an orderly market, and as such, are exposing themselves to a substantial amount of risk. The risk they take is what justifies the compensation they receive. Imagine being forced to buy stock during a time when large mutual funds are dumping the stock. This is like trying to catch a falling knife. Even worse, imagine having to sell stock to fill an influx of buy orders on a stock that is going through the roof. Either case could easily steamroll the market makers, leading to huge trading losses.

Acting as a market maker is a very risky and dangerous job. Yet, most of the time, the trading firms involved in this part of the business are able to make huge profits. How is this possible? Through the bid-ask spread. As we said, to maintain an orderly market, the market makers must always make a market in the stock they are assigned to, by setting a price at which they will both buy stock and sell stock simultaneously, even if they don't want to do either. Obviously, they will buy cheaper than they will sell. This is called *keeping a two-sided market.* The market makers are risking their trading capital to ensure that investors will always receive a fair execution, buy or sell. This guarantees that, so long as customers do not put limits on their prices, at some price their orders will be executed. The specialist system is the grease that keeps the stock market running smoothly. When the markets are quiet, this does not seem like such a big deal. It is when the markets are volatile that the market makers really earn their paychecks.

As we said, market makers do not provide this service for free. They must be compensated for the risk they take. For this reason, they are not expected to simultaneously buy stock from the public and resell stock to the public at the same price. It is simply too risky to expect this. Why would anyone risk his or her own capital not to make any money? Capitalism doesn't work that way. Thus, market makers are allowed to maintain a spread in the stock. This means that the price at which they will buy from the public is always going to be slightly lower than the price at which they will sell stock to investors. This is no different than the used car dealer who buys a vehicle for $5,000 on a trade-in and resells the same vehicle for $6,000. The $1,000 profit is the dealer's "cost of carry" for the risk of taking on inventory. There is no guarantee that the dealer will be able to resell the car, so the profit is justified. Instead of a car, the market maker will buy IBM at 105 and sell it at 105⅛. The buying price is known as the *bid*. The selling price is the *ask*. And the difference between the two is the *spread*.

The spread is determined by how volatile the stock is. When it is said that the spread is wide, this means that the difference in price between where the market makers are buying and where they are selling stock to the public is large. The more volatile the stock, the wider the spread. This is justified because the specialists are unsure of the future direction of the stock. The wide spread is the market makers' only way to protect themselves in the event the stock moves against them. The markup or spread between where the market makers buy and sell might be as wide as $1 in some volatile stocks. This means that, even if the stock doesn't move, the market makers might be buying from the public at $99 and selling at $100. This means they're making $1,000 for every 1,000 shares bought and sold. But there is no telling in which direction the stock is going. It could be on its way to $110—or to $90. Even the specialists don't know. Remember, the market makers *must* provide liquidity in a stock at all times. This means that, even if they don't want to, they are forced to be the buyer of last resort if they can't match the public sell orders with buyers. In volatile markets, this usually means that market makers accumulate large positions when the stock is falling (if there are all sellers, and the market makers are the only buyers) and get short the stock when it is running (if there are all buyers, and the market makers are the only sellers). Even the best traders cannot turn a profit under these circumstances. In most cases, the market makers will suffer substantial losses under these market conditions.

There are times when the opposite is true. The most profitable time for market makers is when the stock is trading in an orderly manner. This allows them to make a few cents per share without much risk. For example, in a $25 stock, this would be done by buying from the public at 25 and selling to the public at 25⅛. The spread is 12.5 cents, or ⅛ point. If the stock doesn't move and the buying and selling is equally distributed, the market maker will have made 12.5 cents per share on each trade. Imagine how much is made if the stock trades over 1 million shares per day: That's a $125,000 profit. This is justified because, even though the stock isn't moving, there is always a certain degree of risk involved in making a two-sided market. Suppose bad news comes out about the stock; the selling pressure could inundate the market maker. That is the risk market makers must take. Over the course of a year, it is the house edge of a few cents per share that compensates them for the few times they suffer huge losses. That is how a few cents per share can translate into millions of dollars in trading profits in the course of a year.

Another way to look at the bid-ask spread is as a form of *risk premium*. Imagine that the stock, instead of moving in one direction, is trading in a choppy manner. This is generally how volatile stocks trade. Under these conditions, the market makers must keep the bid-ask spread wide to protect themselves from the onslaught of day traders and speculators who will try to profit in the event the market makers are "off their market." Most of the time, the wide spread makes it very difficult to "pick off" the market maker. Because the profit the day trader makes usually comes at the expense of the market maker, market makers will not just give their profits away. Their only defense is to make it as difficult as possible for day traders to predict movement in the market makers' stocks.

As you can see, the bid-ask spread is the market makers' advantage over the investing public. So where does this leave day traders? In the best of all possible positions. Even though the specialists and market makers have the advantage, and even though they set the odds, the playing field is more level today than at any time in history. This is because the regulatory agencies are protecting the interests of the individual investors. Luckily, in the eyes of these agencies, even day traders is considered individual investors.

Let's be honest. Wall Streeters would get away with everything they could if there were nothing to stop them. But there is something to stop them. There are rules in place that force specialists to give priority to customer orders over their own. On the New York Stock Exchange, these rules essentially let day traders take the same side of the trade as specialists in filling customer buy and sell orders. This allows day traders to trade just like specialists and to gain all the advantages of the house edge by participating with the specialists in taking the other side of customer orders. This enables day traders, like specialists, to make a living on ¼s, ⅛s, and ⅟₁₆s on the investing public's order flow.

As you can see, day traders are in a very precarious situation. They rely on their own abilities to beat Wall Street at its own game. Although day traders have the rules on their side, they are able to exist, survive, and prosper only as far as their trading ability takes them, because the odds are not with success, but against it. Day traders are going up against much bigger forces possessing deeper pockets and more information. But, that should not faze you, however. The game is difficult, but it is not without rewards. Undoubtedly, you have seen the colossal amounts of money Wall Street firms are capable of making in a single year. This same reward is there for you as a day trader. It is just a matter of going out and staking a claim to it.

SECTION II

Introduction to Day Trading

The day trader's job is to grind out $\frac{1}{16}$s, $\frac{1}{8}$s, and $\frac{1}{4}$s throughout the course of the trading day. This is done by buying stocks and reselling them for profit minutes—even seconds—later. By limiting their risk and only trading when the odds are favorable, day traders can make thousands of dollars per day on these tiny profits, regardless of whether the stock market is up, down, or flat.

As a day trader trading from home over the Internet, you must realize that there are much faster players in the marketplace than you. These people have faster executions and better access to market moving information, putting you at a substantial disadvantage when mere seconds are the difference between winning and losing trades. To make a living at this game, you must utilize trading strategies that eliminate this inherent edge the faster players have.

CHAPTER 3

Trading 101

The Mind-Set of an Online Day Trader

What exactly do day traders do all day? How do they make their money? The answer would surprise most people. Most of the time, it is not the high stakes game of poker that people on the outside think it is. Remember, successful day traders are not gamblers. They understand the nature of risk, but that does not mean they blindly throw their trading capital at each and every stock that comes up on the quote screen. Nor do they base trading decisions entirely on hunches, gut feeling, or instinct. If they do, over time they will not last. Why not? Because when trading is your livelihood, there is no margin for error. No profits, no paycheck. That is why there is no room for gamblers.

THE DAY TRADER'S DISPOSITION

Before you make your first trade, you must understand the nature of the markets and the special role of the day trader. Day traders serve one and only one function: They are middlemen in the buying and selling of stocks. As middlemen, day traders are not worried about the same things as investors. How is the market doing? What will it do over the next few days, weeks, and months? Is the stock market overvalued, undervalued, or fairly priced at these levels? Which stocks are good investments right now? Day traders couldn't care less about any of these issues. Why? Because they are not concerned about the next six months, they are concerned about the next six minutes, and even the next six seconds.

Think of how successful middlemen operate. It doesn't matter what they are buying and selling—stocks, bonds, cars, stereos, or coins—the product is not what is important. Middlemen should not care if the goods they are buying are expensive or cheap. Only one thing matters: selling the goods at a higher price than they were bought for. That is all middlemen are ever concerned about. So long as they can do this, they will put food on the table. The same is true of day traders.

So what exactly are day traders looking for? What do they see that no one else sees? Day traders are looking at one thing: supply and demand. In the short term, the stock market is very inefficient. Second to second, minute to minute, it is in a constant state of flux. When the stock market moves in any one direction, it is to rectify an imbalance between buyers and sellers. For every buyer, there is a seller. When buyers and sellers agree, the stock trades. When they don't, the market readjusts its prices until they do agree. It's that simple.

Within that framework, day traders look to make tiny profits on these microscopic supply and demand imbalances. How big are these profits? $\frac{1}{16}$, $\frac{1}{8}$, and $\frac{1}{4}$ point—as little as 6.25 cents per share. How do day traders do this? By being temporary buyers when the market needs buyers, and temporary sellers when the market needs sellers. This may seem to go against common sense. But remember, day traders are nothing more than middlemen. Day traders make a living by taking the other side of the buying and selling of the general public.

A few words must be said about the profits day traders make. Day traders do not make a living on huge one-time gains. Instead, they are after razor-thin profits. These profits don't seem like much, but they may add up to hundreds of thousands of dollars at the end of the year. Small profits keep day traders in business. What is the secret? The key is to trade at high volume—2,000 or 3,000 shares at a time. A profit of $\frac{1}{16}$ on 2,000 shares is a profit of $125 before commissions. If you do that eight times per day, you will make yourself $1,000.

THE BROKERAGE COMMISSIONS

In my own experience, I may do up to 35 trades in a single day. This means that in the course of one trading day, I may spend upward of $350 on brokerage commissions regardless of whether I turn a profit. Online trades cost less than $10 at most firms, and this low cost is absolutely essential to the day trader's livelihood. But that does not tell the whole story. It's the cost of doing business. When I make this many trades in a day, I must ensure that I am turning a profit. Think about it: If I break even, I will have lost $350 in transaction costs.

My point here is simple. If they are to be successful, day traders have no margin for error. To make a living at this game, they must be right many more times than they are wrong. If not, they will starve. That is the reality of trading for a living, and it is exactly why I pick and choose my trades very carefully. I only like to place a trade when I know my chances for profit are very good. I do not have the luxury of being able to take a roll of the dice by buying and selling any stock that moves, not if I want to make a living. Over the long term, this will not put any money in my pocket. Remember, this game is not about luck, it is about skill.

NEVER ATTEMPT TO OUTSMART THE MARKET

If there is one thing you must have as a day trader, it is respect for the power of the market. You should never attempt to outsmart the market, because in the end the market always wins. What does it mean to outsmart the market? It means believing you are right and the rest of the investing world is wrong. This arrogance is very dangerous. The market is a reflection of the collective wisdom of the investing public. A bad stock is usually cheap for a reason. And a good stock is expensive for the opposite reason. Day traders have no business disagreeing with the market. If they are not humble, the market will humble them.

So, if day traders are not outsmarting the market, how can they buy a stock and sell it seconds later for a profit? It is because, in the short term, the market is inefficient. Day traders are not looking to disagree with the stock prices the market sets. They are not in the business of advising others as to the merits of a particular investment. They are merely temporarily stepping in, when conditions warrant, to fill the short-term gap between supply and demand. It's that simple. As we have said, day traders are middlemen, and nothing more.

But there is another dynamic to this as well. Day traders are not the primary middlemen in the buying and selling of stocks. Wall Street is filled with middlemen. When day traders trade, they are always stepping on someone else's toes. Each and every profit they make is a profit right out of the pockets of the other middlemen in the game of buying and selling stocks. This is the nature of the business. It is a very competitive and dangerous occupation, because day traders are not ever on safe ground. They must be aware that they are operating on enemy turf at all times. If they want to trade for a living, they do not have a choice. This is what they must do. As a result, day traders live in constant fear of the environment they are trading in. And there is only one way for day traders to combat this fear: to trade only when the odds are in their favor.

THE PRE-OPENING RITUAL

Your livelihood as a day trader depends on constantly finding situations that meet your criteria for temporary supply-demand imbalances. The beauty of the market is that these situations are everywhere. You just have to know where to find them. So what do you look for? The search begins even before the market opens.

The stock market opens at 9:30 A.M. eastern time, but my day begins about 30 minutes earlier. I usually get up around 9:00 A.M., and the first thing I do is turn on *Squawk Box* on CNBC to get an idea of what the markets are going to do that day. You may be surprised to know that I do not get up at the crack of dawn and comb through every section of the financial newspapers, nor do I hang on every word that is said on television about the markets. Why not? Because doing so will not put one single penny in my pocket.

MAKING SENSE OF THE CHAOS

As a day trader, you are going to be inundated with financial data. Our culture is fascinated with the day-to-day movements of the markets. *The Wall Street Journal, Investor's Business Daily,* CNBC, *Moneyline,* and numerous other publications and television shows constantly bombard us with the latest news, press releases, and conflicting opinions of the investing community, reported in a way that mimics a sports announcer calling a college football game. The media seem to love the volatility of the market, reporting every sharp sell-off as if it is the start of a 1929-style crash. Part of the skill of trading is to sift through this data and to make sense of the chaos. Too much information makes it very difficult to trade. The conclusion I drew years ago is that the majority of this information can be disregarded, because it will not lead to profitable trades.

This is because the markets are fueled by an inherent difference of opinion. At every given point of every given day, you will be able to find two opinions that are exact polar opposites. If you listen to the analysts and read enough stock research, it will seem that at every price, every stock is both a buy and a sell. This constantly changing tide of opinion can be a good measure of the prevailing level of fear in the market-place, but it is always slightly behind the curve. Markets move faster than the media can report. The news is old the second it is reported. But, ironically, it is this confusion that creates the buying and selling imbalances. And, as you know, these supply-demand imbalances are precisely what puts money in the day trader's pocket.

As you will learn when you get further into this book, online day traders are in an unusual situation. The conditions around them make it very difficult for them to be consistently profitable. How am I able to make a living as a day trader? Because I only trade when the odds are in my favor. I can tell you, if you blindly buy and sell every stock you are watching, over the long term you will lose money. Remember, this is your livelihood. You do not want to leave anything to chance. You have to pick and choose your opportunities carefully.

For me, picking my opportunities carefully often means that I trade stocks in areas overlooked by the rest of the trading and invest-ing community. I will show you that you do not need a stock to move to make money trading it. This means you can find temporary supply-demand imbalances in stocks that do not make the headlines. This is where the real gold mine lies. How do you get to the gold? By beating Wall Street at its own game.

I have really come to despise trading the same markets as the herd. The herd loves the glamor stocks, the market leaders, and the high flyers. I hate them. I find it very difficult to gain the edge, because there are too many other players involved. The competition is simply too fierce, and the Internet execution is too slow. If you are going to survive as a trader, you have to do everything you can to eliminate the disadvantage you face by trading from home. Often this means resisting the herd mentality that seems to prevail in the hot stocks.

THE SLOW EXECUTION

The biggest disadvantage faced by online day traders is the speed of their execution. Of all of the traders in marketplace, day traders placing their trades over the Internet have the slowest execution. This is an inevitable fact of life when trading over the Internet: There will always be faster players in the market than you. The problem with trading the high-profile stocks is that the whole investing world is watching them simultaneously. You are seeing the same exact things as everyone else. When it appears to you that the stock is headed higher, it appears that way to everyone else as well. So you find yourself in a race with the rest of Wall Street to get your buy order in as fast as possible—and anytime you are in a race with Wall Street, you will lose. You will get filled at the worst possible price, and you will always feel as though you have been robbed. Inevitably, you will lose money. This is the reality of trading glamor stocks over the Internet.

You must put the "slow" execution in context. When I say *slow,* I do not mean it in the absolute sense. I mean it in the relative sense. Most online market orders will be executed in less than two seconds. Two seconds may seem like lightning speed to the novice; however, in the world of Wall Street, two seconds is a lifetime. Remember, when a stock is in demand, only a limited amount of shares are for sale at each price level. The window of opportunity may be less than one second. The order that arrives first buys the stock at the best price. If your order takes even an extra second, the stock might be gone, and you will be forced to pay a higher price. This split second could mean the difference between a $1,000 profit and a $1,000 loss. And no matter what you do, the reality of online trading is simple. There are traders on Wall Street who can buy and sell stock faster than you can type in the stock symbol on your order entry screen.

After a while, you will learn the hard way that this slow execution prevents you from making certain trades. It will change the way you approach trading stocks when you see the difficulty in trading high-volatility stocks profitably. You do not have the luxury of the precision, split-second trade execution the faster players have. Why not? Because you are only paying $10 for the trade. Cheap trades come at a cost. And that cost is a lousy execution. That is the trade-off: When you are trading from home, you will not be able to buy and sell at the precise moment the herd does. If you are smart, you will quickly learn to trade high-volatility stocks only on special, rare occasions. As your experience grows, you will begin to lean toward safer areas and stocks that you find easier to trade—a natural progression for any smart trader. When you do trade high-volatility stocks, you will pick and choose your opportunities carefully.

THE INFORMATION VACUUM

The point I am trying to make is that if you refrain from trading the high-profile stocks, you will not have to worry obsessively about the news, charts, or overall markets. Everything you need to make your trading decisions can be found within the parameters of your real-time stock quote. Look at Figure 3.1. This illustration contains everything you need to know to make a quick trade. You won't need to waste time looking at news or reading pages of research. In the sort term, none of that makes one bit of difference. Remember, this is the short term. As a middleman, you are looking for one thing: a temporary supply-demand imbalance. And you will be able to detect that imbalance simply by the way the stock trades. Bid, ask, bid size, ask size: Nothing else is needed. You just have to train your eyes to detect this information. That is what the investing public does not understand.

This is the wisdom of short-term trading. If you are looking to get in and out of a stock in only a few seconds, you do not need to know anything other than the stock's real-time quote to make your decision. Ironically, in the ultrashort term, this means you can trade in a virtual information vacuum. Why? Because the bid-ask spread tells all. You will have your hand on the pulse of the supply and demand in the stock. You will react to things before anyone else does. That is all you need to know.

Table 3.1 shows a typical day's trades. Over the last two years I have been able to amass a track record similar to this one. I typically turn a profit on at least 8 of every 10 trades I make. And it doesn't matter what the overall market is doing. I can make money in an up, down, or flat market. How? By limiting my risk by only trading when the odds are in my favor. Any day trader could make 1,000 trades in a day if he or

Figure 3.1 Your real-time stock quote contains all the trading information you need.

	Symbol	Last	Change	Volume	Bid	Ask	Bid Size × Ask Size
	$INDU	9124.53	+68.48	DOW			
	$SPX	1159.58	+6.97	S & P Index			
	$@CCO	1921.16	+1.48	NASDAQ Comp			
	SP8Z	1162.5	+3.80	S & P Futures			
	$TYX	5.21	−0.33	30 year treasury			
	ZB8Z	$128\frac{20}{32}$	$+\frac{22}{32}$	30 yr bond futures			
1	GCH	$7\frac{3}{8}$	$+\frac{1}{16}$	54,500	$7\frac{3}{8}$	$7\frac{7}{16}$	5 × 58
2	UDR	$10\frac{13}{16}$	$+\frac{1}{16}$	31,300	$10\frac{9}{16}$	$10\frac{11}{16}$	18 × 8
3	WEC	30	$+\frac{1}{8}$	145,600	30	$30\frac{1}{8}$	25 × 14
4	NMK	$14\frac{7}{8}$	$-\frac{1}{16}$	102,400	$14\frac{3}{4}$	15	10 × 5
5	SUNW	81	$+\frac{1}{2}$	1,134,000	$80\frac{15}{16}$	$81\frac{1}{8}$	65 × 20
6	EE	9	$-\frac{1}{16}$	58,000	$8\frac{15}{16}$	$9\frac{1}{8}$	140 × 2
7	CAT	$48\frac{1}{16}$	$+\frac{1}{4}$	967,000	$47\frac{15}{16}$	$48\frac{1}{16}$	100 × 25
8	MO	54	$+\frac{1}{16}$	5,686,700	54	$54\frac{1}{8}$	10 × 10
9	KO	74	+2	1,340,000	$73\frac{3}{4}$	74	24 × 54
10	AMAT	$38\frac{7}{8}$	$+2\frac{1}{8}$	4,736,300	$38\frac{3}{4}$	39	3 × 4
11	AMZN	248	+3	2,354,000	$247\frac{3}{4}$	$248\frac{1}{4}$	1 × 2
12	EK	$75\frac{1}{4}$	$-\frac{1}{16}$	1,320,000	$75\frac{1}{8}$	$75\frac{1}{4}$	22 × 1
13	XON	$71\frac{5}{8}$	$+1\frac{3}{4}$	3,825,600	$71\frac{9}{16}$	$71\frac{11}{16}$	19 × 20
14	YHOO	198	$+3\frac{1}{2}$	2,567,000	198	$198\frac{1}{2}$	1 × 2
15	GM	$72\frac{1}{16}$	$-\frac{1}{2}$	2,338,800	$72\frac{1}{16}$	$72\frac{3}{16}$	10 × 10
16	GT	$55\frac{1}{2}$	$+\frac{3}{8}$	234,000	$55\frac{1}{2}$	$55\frac{3}{4}$	12 × 3

Real-time data courtesy of Paragon Software, Inc. (InterQuote), 1-800-311-1516, www.interquote.com.

she wanted to. But, in the end, that is not going to help him or her earn a paycheck. It is not the amount of trades that separates the winners from the losers. It is the percentage of trades that were profitable.

It is important to note the kind of trading that I do. My bias is toward trading for $\frac{1}{16}$s, or *teenies.* A $\frac{1}{16}$-point profit is only 6.25 cents per share. But I have been able to make a living on $\frac{1}{16}$s. If you are going to trade for $\frac{1}{16}$s, you must trade at least 2,000 shares at a time to overcome commission costs. Remember, a teenie on 2,000 shares is a $125 profit, but it is only $105 after commissions, with typical online commissions of $10 to buy, $10 to sell. In addition, if you are going to be buying and selling in lots of 2,000 shares, you must make sure that the stock is sta-

Table 3.1   My Daily Trading Log.

Bought 3,000 ADF 12 Sold 3,000 ADF 12¹⁄₁₆	+187.50
Bought 2,000 IF 4 Sold 2,000 IF 4¹⁄₁₆	+125
Bought 2,000 ADF 12¹⁄₁₆ Sold 2,000 ADF 12⅛	+125
Bought 2,500 EDL 25⅝₆ Sold 2,500 EDL 25¹¹⁄₁₆	+312.50
Bought 2,000 EE 9¹⁄₁₆ Sold 2,000 EE 9⅛	+125
Bought 2,000 EE 9¹⁄₁₆ Sold 2,000 EE 9¹⁄₁₆	EVEN
Bought 1,000 HWP 58 Sold 1,000 HWP 58⁷⁄₁₆	+437.50
Bought 3,000 NMK 15 Sold 3,000 NMK 14⅞	−375
Gross Profit for the Day	+937.50
Less Trade Commissions	−160
Net Profit after Commissions	+777.50

ble. You do not ever want to lose ½ point or more when trading big blocks of stock. That is precisely why I like to trade "boring" stocks. These are not the stocks making headlines, but headlines don't matter. I can make low-risk teenies all day without the rest of the trading world noticing. The key is that the stock does not have to move for me to make money in it. Why doesn't everybody else notice? Because they are too busy trading the glamor stocks, like IBM, Intel, and Microsoft.

There are certain rare times, however, when trading the high-profile stocks is warranted. This is why I do take a little time before the market opens to glance at the headlines in *The Wall Street Journal* and *Investor's Business Daily*. I do not spend more than five minutes reading the financial papers, because I am looking for only two things: good news and bad news. Good news and bad news alike are mechanisms for creating large supply-demand imbalances in the market. And when there are large supply-demand imbalances, the middleman can make large profits in a very short period of time.

BUY ON BAD NEWS, SELL ON GOOD NEWS

I have found that one of the best ways to profit from what you hear in the news is to be a contrarian. If you prefer to trade stocks that make headlines, sometimes it is better to buy on bad news and sell on good news. There is one stipulation: These trades must be done at the open of trading. This may seem contrary to common sense. From a day trading standpoint, you will be far more successful buying a stock at the open that has a very negative article in the paper than you will if you buy one that has a positive spin. This is because the markets will price-in all available information immediately. The general public will react by dumping shares with reckless abandon at hearing bad news. This amounts to an overwhelming amount of market sell orders at the open, which must be paired with buy orders. This is one example of an extreme supply-demand imbalance, and is precisely where the middle-man should step in. The opening trade will usually be where the selling pressure is most intense. What the general public does not understand is that this phenomenon is exactly what creates a market bottom. In many cases, this will be the stock's low trade of the day. Alert day traders will be buying on the low of the day, and hopefully selling the stock minutes later for a nice profit. How are they able to make a profit? Again, by buying when the market needs buyers, and selling when the market needs sellers.

Stocks will react to good news by opening significantly higher on a buying imbalance. For day traders, buying stock at the open on good news is a surefire way to lose money. This is the same as selling on bad news at the open. While that created a market bottom, the influx of buy orders on good news usually creates a market top. As middlemen, day traders must be on the other side of this trade. If the public is buying, day traders must be selling. As a rule of thumb, day traders should never be on the same side of a trade as the general public if the news moving the stock has been fully disseminated. By the time stocks open at 9:30 A.M. eastern, most stories have had several hours to reach the investing public.

These are both extreme cases of situations that can make the alert day trader substantial amounts of money in a very short time. But these kinds of trades are not the norm, they are the exception. Most of the time, the trading I do is far less exciting, far less glamorous. Some people might even consider it boring. If I want entertainment, I go to Las Vegas. To put food on my table, I go where I can make a profit. Often this means going where the rest of the world isn't looking: low-volatility stocks, stocks that don't move, stocks that are not in the headlines. This is my livelihood, and I take it very seriously. Every so often I have to remind myself of one simple fact: I am not in this game for the excitement. I am in it to make a living.

A FEW WORDS ON NEW YORK STOCK EXCHANGE VERSUS NASDAQ

It is my personal preference to trade New York Stock Exchange-listed stocks (and an occasional American Stock Exchange stock) rather than NASDAQ stocks. Ninety-nine percent of my trades involve NYSE-listed stocks. Why? It has to do with the way stocks trade on the different exchanges. My rule of thumb is that it is much easier to trade NYSE stocks profitably than NASDAQ stocks, if you are trading from home over the Internet. This is because the rules in place on the New York Stock Exchange are much more friendly to the online day trader than those on the NASDAQ exchange. To put it another way, if you are in the business of trying to beat Wall Street at its own game, you have to choose the environment that best allows you to do this. Without question, that environment is the New York Stock Exchange, so long as you are using online brokers and trading from home.

How can the beginner tell the difference between the two when choosing stocks? If the stock has a one-, two-, or three-letter symbol, it trades either on the NYSE or the American Exchange. If it has a four- or five-letter symbol, it is a NASDAQ stock. For the purposes of this book, you should refrain from trading NASDAQ stocks, because most of the time the odds of success are stacked against you. There will be rare times when the odds will be in your favor, and we will mention those in later chapters.

CHAPTER 4

The Day Trader's Arsenal

Choosing and Using Online Brokers, Real-Time Quote Systems, and the Home Office

As a day trader, you will learn very quickly that part of the online trading experience is dealing with headaches. The second something goes wrong, you will realize how much your livelihood is dependent on the reliability of your online broker. There is nothing more annoying and frustrating than those times when you cannot place a trade because the system is down. Late fills, system crashes, back office problems, commission overcharges, and trade discrepancies are all an inevitable part of life for the online day trader. And they always seem to happen at the worst possible time, when your money is at risk. You must prepare yourself accordingly.

CHOOSING AN ONLINE BROKER

One of the most important decisions the day trader can make is to choose the right online broker. The problem is that the investing world is saturated with online brokerage firms. There are over 80 to choose from, and the number is growing each month. How do you know which one to choose, when they all claim to provide the same services? The answer is simple: cost first, service second. I spent over $50,000 in brokerage commissions last year. I did over 5,000 trades, and I was paying less than $10 per trade. It may not seem like a big difference to the average online investor, but to the online day trader who makes a living trading, the difference between an $8 trade commission and a $14 trade commission could be the difference between making and losing money over the course of a year. On 5,000 shares, that is a $30,000 difference over 12 months. That is why price must be your primary concern.

In the course of the last two years, I have used several different online brokers. Each time I switched, it was not because of the cost. I choose the brokers in the first place because of the cheap trades. I do so many trades in a year that I need to reduce my transaction costs as much as possible. If I am deciding between a brokerage firm that charges $12 for limit orders and one that charges $10, I will most certainly choose the one that charges less. It is important to note that, when choosing a brokerage firm, you must compare the firms based on the price of limit orders, not market orders. As you will learn later, the day trader's key to profitability is using limit orders, not market orders. The reality is that at most online brokerage firms, limit orders cost a few dollars more than market orders (for reasons I will go into later). That is why your comparison must be based on the price of limit orders, not market orders.

SETTING UP TWO ACCOUNTS

Unfortunately, when you choose an online broker, there is really no way to tell how reliable the firm's service is going to be. It is always going to be a case of trial and error. That is why I am in no position to recommend online brokers. No one knows exactly what the next six months will bring. For this reason, I have always made a point of keeping accounts open at at least two different online brokerage firms as insurance. That way, if there are consistent problems, I can merely move my money from the old firm to the new one. This ensures that, if I do decide to switch accounts, I will not have to miss weeks of trading while the new account is being set up. Remember, missing a few days of trading could mean missing out on a few thousand dollars.

SYSTEM CRASHES AND THE LATE FILL

So what might prompt you to switch online brokers? Once your account is opened and you are trading actively, the focus switches from cost to service. The online brokerage industry is notorious for technology and system failures, and no one is immune to these problems. Over time it has gotten better, but it is still a common occurrence. The problem is much worse at some firms than at others. Unfortunately, you may find this out the hard way.

I think the single most annoying aspect of trading online is the *late fill.* This occurs when you buy a stock, and minutes or hours later it is still not in your account. Why the delay? Because your online broker is having technical problems. The real problem is that, even if you are certain you own the stock, you will be unable to sell it until it hits your account. The online brokers have systems in place that will cancel an order if the computer thinks you are trying to sell a stock that is not in your account (not to be confused with short selling). The consequence of this is that you may be prevented from making a profit if the stock is trading higher than where you bought it, simply because you will be unable to sell it.

Even worse than the late fill is the *system crash,* when the entire Web site is down. In this case, you will be prevented from accessing your account to get up-to-the-minute information until the system is running again. This is a very dangerous situation that can last anywhere from a few minutes to a few hours.

When you don't get an immediate fill report on a market order, whether because of a late fill or a system crash, you have no idea at what price you bought or sold your stock, or whether the order is lost—or worse. When you trade slow-moving stocks, you can usually tell by the parameters of the market whether your limit order was executed at your price. But if you use market orders, when the stocks are moving so fast, you have no idea where you might have been filled if you don't have the report back seconds after you enter the order.

This situation has happened to me numerous times, most often during those rare times when I place a market order. If I see that a stock is running, I enter a buy order at the market, unaware that the online broker is having system problems. As the stock runs higher, I keep checking my account to see at what price I was executed. As the minutes go by, the stock continues to head higher, but I still do not have a fill back. Then I begin to get worried, because I wonder if the order is delayed or lost. Has my trade already been executed at a lower price, and is the broker just late in getting the fill back? Or is the broker having system problems that mean the order has not even been executed yet? The second situation is definitely worse because, with the stock continuing to go higher, the later the order is executed, the higher the price I will pay for the stock. There is nothing more frustrating than knowing I was on the right side of a trade but lost money anyway because the online broker could not execute the order properly.

Another factor involved is that these systems can get bogged down on days when trading volume is heavy. The heaviest trading volumes of the year usually occur during market crashes, which means Internet trading will be much slower during these rare, dangerous times. These are the times when the market moves 400 or 500 points to the downside. It has happened twice in the last two years, and it always has to be in the back of your mind if you dare to trade during market sell-offs.

Many of the advertisements on television for online brokers mention that, if you prefer, you can talk to a live broker instead of placing a trade online. Many people are under the impression that when the system goes down, they can simply phone their orders in. Good luck trying to get through when the system goes crashes—every trader in the system attempts to call in at the same time, and most firms do not have enough reps to handle the calls. The consequence: You will be on hold indefinitely. There have been times when I have been on hold for over 45 minutes waiting to get an answer on a trade.

These are the dangers you will face when you trade over the Internet. They affect everyone, and are a fact of life of online trading. This technology is still in its infancy, and is prone to failure every so often. And, as you know, failures are always going to happen at the worst possible times. To calm my own nerves, I have accepted the fact that 95 percent of the time the system works well. As for that other 5 percent, that is when I give some trading profits back to the system. It is inevitable. That is the price online traders must pay for the luxury of being able to trade from home.

CUSTOMER SERVICE, BACK OFFICE PROBLEMS, AND TRADE DISCREPANCIES

There are a couple of other dimensions to the online trading experience that are not fun to deal with. Occasionally, if you trade actively, there are going to be situations that arise involving mistakes or trade discrepancies made by online brokers—for example, getting hit with a commission overcharge. Maybe the trade only cost $10, but the online broker hit your account with a $20 charge. It could even be something more serious, like an unfair execution. Or maybe you thought you were entitled to a fill on a sell order, and you never got one. Even worse, 5,000 shares of a stock you never even heard of might end up in your account by error. I have even had experiences where I was credited with buying or selling a stock two or three days after the trade occurred. These kinds of things happen every so often, and you have to deal with them appropriately.

These problems and discrepancies are a fact of life for traders. My experience has been that eventually, no matter how bad the problem, the brokerage firm resolves it fairly. But that does not mean there are not headaches and stress in the interim. Trading is stressful enough. Dealing with back office problems is a nightmare. This is why the big Wall Street firms have entire departments whose sole function is to resolve these problems. But that does not change the fact that you have to be on top of everything all the time. You cannot let anything slip by you. Remember, you are on your own. If you do not pick up on these mistakes, no one else will. It is your money on the line, and you have to protect it at all times.

THE REMEDY—KEEP GOOD TRADING RECORDS

There are a couple of precautions I like to take to ensure that I am protected in the event a mistake arises. I strongly recommend you do the same. These precautions are as follows:

1. For each individual trade, keep a separate 3×5 card or piece of paper detailing the precise time the trade was placed, the order or confirmation number, and the market in the stock at the time the order was placed.

   This ensures that you have a record of when the trade was entered, when it was filled, and the number of shares. If there is a discrepancy at a later date, this will be your only record of when the trade occurred and where the stock was trading at the time the order was placed. It is possible that even a week later you might have to go back and prove when the trade was entered. Remember, it's always your word against the broker's. That is why you want to do everything you can to keep accurate records. I usually keep this information on file for a few months just to be on the safe side. It looks similar to the illustration in Table 4.1.

Table 4.1 3 × 5 Transaction Card.

11/20   Sell 2,000   IF   4⅜
1:39 PM   Confirm #964552809
4⁵⁄₁₆–4⁷⁄₁₆   34 × 12   32,000 Volume
2,000 Shares Filled at 1:41 PM

2. Keep an accurate daily trading log (see Table 4.2) that includes an itemized list of the trades made, the number of shares, the commissions incurred, the profit and loss on each trade, and total net profit and loss for the day.

This trading log may be your only means of assessing your daily, weekly, and monthly profit and loss performance, outside of the records kept by the brokerage firm. But what if the firm's records are not accurate? If you get into the habit of logging your trading results after each

Table 4.2   Daily Trading Log—November 12.

Bought 2,500 FRT 23 Sold 2,500 FRT 23¹⁄₁₆	+156.25
Bought 3,000 BS 9¼ Sold 3,000 BS 9⁵⁄₁₆	+187.50
Bought 2,000 NHP 22¹⁄₁₆ Sold 2,000 NHP 22¹⁄₁₆	EVEN
Bought 2,000 JEQ 8¹⁄₁₆ Sold 2,000 JEQ 8¹⁄₁₈	+125
Bought 2,000 DHF 13¹⁄₁₆ Sold 2,000 DHF 13⅛	+125
Bought 3,000 CV 10⅝ Sold 3,000 CV 10⁹⁄₁₆	−187.50
Bought 3,000 ACG 9½ Sold 3,000 ACG 9⁹⁄₁₆	+187.50
Gross Profit before Commissions	+593.75
Less Commissions on 14 trades	−140
Net Profit after Commissions	+453.75

and every trading day, it will give you a good reference point to double-check the accuracy of the values the online broker assigns to your trading account. This is extremely important because without it you will be at the mercy of the brokerage firm's accounting department. If you do 400 trades in a month like I do, it is very easy to lose track of how much money you have made or lost in a given month. The brokerage firm will send you a month-end statement that is a summary of all of the transactions in your account, but you should never rely solely on the firm's record keeping ability. I make sure my records always match. That is the only way I know for sure that the broker's records are accurate.

Imagine making a $4,000 profit in a day that is not reflected in your account at month end. Where did the money go? Luckily, this has never happened to me, but it could happen. If you didn't keep your own records, you would never know, because you would have no way to detect that something was wrong. Maybe the brokerage firm was so screwed up that they didn't detect it either. This could be a real problem. The consequence? You would be out $4,000. That is my point: If this is your livelihood, you must be on top of everything. No one else is. The chance of this kind of error going undetected is slim. But I sleep much better at night knowing I have left nothing to chance.

THE HOME OFFICE AND THE VIRTUAL TRADING FLOOR

One of the most important things I have learned is that the environment you work in has a big influence on your ability to make profits. Wall Street firms spend millions designing state-of-the-art trading floors so as to bring out the optimal level of performance in their traders. You may be surprised to see this mentioned in a book on day trading, but the environment issue faces day traders as well. In trading, you have to give yourself every possible advantage. The fact of the matter is that you will be unable to trade to your highest level if you are stuck in an environment you loathe. It's that simple. That is why one of the biggest issues involved in trading full-time is making sure you have a pleasant work environment, especially if you trade out of your own home.

The home office is by far the most economical way to trade. In the world of day trading, you have to keep your overhead as low as possible because your earnings are so volatile. This may mean giving up the spacious office by the window that you might have in your current job in exchange for a far less glamorous work environment—your home. The plush office with the receptionist is not necessary in this line of work. Especially in the beginning, you don't want to have to pay rent for office space, because it will eat into your profits and put too much pressure on your trading. If you are successful after a few months, then go ahead and get an office. But I would not advise it at first.

Thankfully, today's technology allows you to create a virtual trading floor from your home. All the financial information you will ever need is right at your fingertips. All you need is a computer, cable television for financial news, a working phone line for an Internet connection, and a real-time quote system, and you are set.

TRADING EQUIPMENT

What the Day Trader Needs to Get Started Trading

1. Computer with modem: $1,500
2. Internet connection: $20 per month
3. Real-time scrolling quote system: $80 per month plus exchange fees
4. Online account at an online brokerage firm: free
5. Cable television to watch CNBC all day

A FEW WORDS ON CHOOSING A STOCK QUOTE SYSTEM

In this day and age of technology, you will need very little in the way of equipment to get started day trading. As long as you have an Internet connection, you will be ready to trade. The single most important piece of equipment you can have is the *quotron*, or stock quote system. Most quote systems are now fed directly over the Internet, which has reduced their cost substantially.

It is absolutely essential that you trade with a real-time quote system. If you are trading with delayed quotes, I guarantee you will lose money. These systems are well worth the $80 per month investment.

Undoubtedly you have seen the numerous advertisements by the online brokers stating that they will provide you with free real-time quotes when you place a trade or open an account. I cannot stress enough that you need a better quote system than the ones provided "free" by the online brokers. You will not be able to day trade profitably if you rely on such quotes. Why? Because every trader on Wall Street uses a scrolling quote screen that reflects every single change in the market the second it occurs. When you use the free real-time quotes the brokerage firms offer, the quotes will not update if you don't continuously update the screen. The consequence? If you are watching 15 stocks at once, you will not be able to keep track of the real trading activity because you will not see the split-second changes as they occur. You will be behind the information curve. This will put you at a severe disadvantage compared to the faster players in the marketplace, and it will usually result in your losing money.

THE PSYCHOLOGICAL EFFECTS OF WORKING FROM HOME

Working full-time out of your house is an entirely different experience than working in an office setting. From a psychological standpoint, the difference is like night and day; you won't realize this until you actually try it. There seems to be a prevailing belief among people unhappy in their current jobs that working from home is the answer to all of their problems. They may not get along with co-workers, they may be unhappy with the long commute they face every day, or they may simply dislike working in such close proximity to the boss. I've been working out of my house for over two years and I really enjoy the convenience it provides. I must admit there is something really great about not having to leave the house on those mornings when the weather is miserable. I can wake up at 8:30 or 9:00 A.M. and be fully ready for the markets to open at 9:30 without ever having to deal with a commute. When I worked on Wall Street, I was out the door at the crack of dawn to catch the subway and spent the better part of two hours each day getting to and from work.

Just as it takes certain personality traits to be a good trader, it definitely takes certain traits to enjoy working out of the house. Some people need the structure provided by a corporate work setting. I don't. Thankfully, the notion of working from home, whether it be at day trading or some other home-based business, is finally getting a certain degree of acceptance and respect from the general public. Of course, there are always going to be people who think that, just because you work out of the house, you are somehow not legitimately making a living. Take my advice: Ignore these people. The world is full of them, and they are generally people who work for someone else for a living. They are not entrepreneurs and they don't understand risk. Best of all, they have no idea of the kind of money successful day traders can make.

So what kind of person takes well to working out of the house? The same kind of person who takes to day trading. Day trading and working from home go hand in hand. It's the entrepreneur, the risk taker, the self-motivated person who doesn't need to be told what to do by others that excels in this environment. In corporate America, there is always a lot being said about the necessity of being a team player. Well, chances are, most of you reading this book either are not team players or are sick and tired of being team players. Day trading does not reward the team player. If you need the support of a group environment, then you might as well go back to working for someone else, because you probably will not last on your own.

THE ISOLATION FACTOR

Working from home also has its drawbacks. Every worthwhile attempt at achieving financial independence and wealth involves some personal sacrifices, and day trading is no different. Along with the independence of working for yourself, and the excitement of making quick profits, come some drawbacks. From a psychological standpoint, one of the toughest things you will have to endure is something I call the *isolation factor.*

There will be many days when you might not see or speak to anyone outside of your immediate family if you are trading from home. You will become so engrossed in the markets that you probably won't even notice this. But it can begin to take its toll on you mentally if you are not careful. I've heard horror stories about people who put their life savings into starting a home-based business, only to find, six months later, that they can't endure the isolation. After taking all that risk, they end up quitting a profitable business for reasons other than why they went into business in the first place. They don't give up working at home because of the money, but because they can't handle the isolation. These people are usually independent-minded, risk-taking individuals. At first, to this kind of personality, the isolation seems like a luxury. It's not the work that they despise, it's the boss breathing down their neck all day. So the idea of going out on their own appeals to them. But they learn the hard way that for them there is more to happiness than just being their own boss.

The only advice I can give in this regard is from my own experience. I have really enjoyed working for myself out of my home over the last two years. There is a tremendous feeling of accomplishment, and peace of mind, that comes from knowing that your success is entirely in your own hands. If this means working out of the house, and spending most of your time in isolation, then so be it. Life is short, and you may not have the chance to do everything you want to do. And you are never going to know what it is like to trade from home unless you try it. I look forward to each and every day I spend trading. If that is an indication, then I stand as evidence that you can work from home and love every minute of it.

CHAPTER 5

Considerations for Quitting Your Job and Trading for a Living

*Day traders should not attempt to trade full-time unless they have
at least $50,000 in risk capital. Part-time traders should not begin
to trade unless they have at least $5,000 in trading capital.*

What is the day trader's recipe for disaster? Cutting your winning
trades and riding your losers right into the ground. This happens when
you are trading with money you can't afford to lose. For many, day trading from home is a dream job. The temptation of quick profits is very
strong, and is often hard to resist. And most people would agree that
the combination of being your own boss, working short hours in the
comfort of your own home, and most importantly, being dependent on
absolutely no one but yourself for success is the best of all possible
worlds. After reading this far, you might feel ready to quit the 9-to-5
world and join the growing ranks of day traders. As with many other
things in life, however, the reality is not as sweet as the fantasy. Day
trading is a different kind of work, but it is work. As with any business
venture, you must plan ahead, be prepared, and proceed cautiously. If
you are considering this career path, there are several important issues
you must address.

THE ALLOCATION OF TRADING CAPITAL

As a day trader, the single most important tool you have is your trading capital. This is the lifeblood of your business. Obviously, you cannot trade without it. The problem is that the allure of day trading for a living is so strong that many people who are currently day trading are simply financially unfit to bear the risks involved. This can be a recipe for disaster. There are several considerations that must be taken into account before you can decide how much money to allocate toward day trading. The first step is to make realistic assumptions about your lifestyle and your personal finances.

Obviously, you must first determine exactly how much trading capital you can afford to set aside for trading. This has to be considered *risk capital*. When I say risk capital, I don't mean it in the sense of gambling money, or money you save up every year to spend in Las Vegas. I mean money you can afford to have tied up for extended periods of time without having to dip into it to meet living expenses. This is the same kind of money you might use to start a business, or currently may have tied up in the markets in long-term investments. The idea is that, over time, you want your trading capital to grow untouched. Think of day trading as a war, and your trading capital as your ammunition. Without enough ammo, you are dead. You do not want to be in a situation where you have to keep pulling money out of your trading capital to meet living expenses. This will severely limit your profit potential. As you get more experience and your level of skill improves, your profits will start to build up so long as the trading capital remains in your account. This increase in trading capital gives you substantial leverage to add to your gains. As you become a better trader, your profits will increase exponentially as your trading capital builds. This is what enables you to increase your profits month after month. Even the most profitable traders, if they have to draw from their accounts continuously to meet expenses, will have difficulty doing this.

I would even consider money you have invested in the stock market as risk capital. Most investors only commit money in the markets if it is money that they can live without. Considering the volatility in the markets, and the incredible run this aging bull market has produced, it would not be that far-fetched for people to consider pulling a fraction of their money out of mutual funds and other investments and putting it toward day trading. I am a firm believer that risk capital is far more secure in the hands of a good day trader than in the hands of a financial planner, in a stock mutual fund, or passively invested in the stock market. Remember, good traders can earn well over 100 percent per year on their money. Historically, the stock market, in a good year, will return about 20 percent.

In other words, risk capital must be money you can afford to lose. Under no circumstances should you take rent money, credit card debt, or money you need to live on and allocate it toward day trading. There are two reasons for this. The first is obvious; the second is more subtle, but far more destructive. For the simple reason that losses are a part of day trading, you have to make sure you can live without the money you are trading with in the event that you lose it. The markets have a strange way of destroying wealth at the worst possible times, when it is needed most. Every day trader hopes to eventually make back any money lost during a bad streak. The problem is that if this is money normally set aside to meet everyday living expenses, you are going to put yourself and your trading under a tremendous amount of pressure to turn a profit.

One of the most important lessons I have learned is never to force a trade. This is the tendency when you enter a trade because you have to make money to meet your bills, and it is the easiest way to lose money. Your judgment is impaired, and instead of waiting for a trade where the odds are in your favor, you throw money at a stock in desperation in the hopes that it goes higher. The minute you find yourself in a situation of hoping the stock moves in your favor, you are sure to lose.

There is another side to this as well. Your trading capital is your vehicle of risk. As with any business or investment decision, there is a certain degree of danger involved. One vital component of your success as a trader is your attitude toward risk. It sounds strange, but you cannot look at your trading capital in the same way you look at spending money. This is not money you buy groceries with, or go to the movies with. You have to tell yourself that this is not "money" at all, it is trading capital. Psychologically, that makes all the difference in the world, and will save you much mental pain and anguish. The reality is that you will make and lose more money in a single afternoon trading than you have ever spent in a single afternoon in your entire life. How you deal with this will make or break you. The bottom line is that you cannot get emotionally attached to the money you trade with. If you do, you will be unable to handle risk, and you will most certainly self-destruct.

We all love money. Traders, perhaps more than anyone, hate to lose money. Yet the best traders are the ones who separate themselves from their work. Even though your trading capital is real, hard-earned money, you must deal with it as if it were "play money," merely a tool used to achieve success. It is only then that you can have some degree of detachment from the inevitable profits and losses you will encounter. Imagine a heart surgeon who is madly in love with the person he or she is operating on. The surgeon's performance is bound to be affected by emotion. The same is true in trading. The further your decision making is separated from your emotions, the more profitable you will be. You will be unable to separate your emotions from your trading if you are risking money you cannot afford to lose.

Emotional attachment is a very dangerous thing. If you are trading money you cannot afford to risk, you will find it very difficult to cut your losses. It becomes impossible to cut your losses if you are married to your positions. The easiest path to self-destruction is to ride a losing position into the ground. Riding your winners and cutting your losses is one of the most important skills you can develop as a trader. The reason people hesitate to sell a losing position when they should is because they can't stomach the loss. It becomes even worse if they are losing money that was needed to pay bills. The fact that the stock has gone against them and the loss is already realized even though the stock hasn't been sold is of no significance to emotionally attached traders. The all-consuming loss will begin to take on a life of its own. I speak from experience when I say that this type of thing can easily snowball out of control. I have seen an entire week's profits erode in an hour when this happens.

The same destructive psychology can come into play during winning trades. Inexperienced day traders, in addition to letting their losses run, have a tendency to lock in profits the second they are on the right side of the trade. This is because they can't afford to leave a profit, no matter how small, on the table, especially if the money is needed to meet bills. At this point, these people too are trading out of desperation. They *must* turn a profit. They force themselves to close out the position precisely when they should not sell. This type of trading leaves large profits on the table. How is it possible to make a living trading if you sell your winners and ride your losers into the ground? You are bound to fail. You are essentially limiting your upside and exposing yourself to unlimited downside risk. You have to do the opposite. If you are right, let the stock run. If you are wrong, get out! The common denominator for all successful traders is having the self-discipline to book the loss in a losing position, and to refrain from selling a winning position if it continues to go higher. This is only possible if you are detached from the money you are trading.

One final thought on why you shouldn't trade your rent money. Day trading requires a tremendous amount of stamina. Burnout is common among people who have a hard time dealing with the pressure. You will sleep much better at night, and enjoy your weekends more, if you can separate yourself from your trading capital and your losses. Inexperienced traders, after losing $500 for the first time, will inevitably take the loss personally. Irrational thoughts are bound to cross their minds. Maybe they feel that if they hadn't made that last trade, they'd be able to afford a new television or go on a nice vacation. I know from personal experience that these kinds of thoughts will ruin you. The best traders look at their trading capital as a means to an end. Losses are an unavoidable part of trading. No one is right all the time. If you were, you'd be the richest person in the world.

The reason I've taken the time to explain this is because it plays a big role in deciding how much money to allocate toward day trading. The bottom line is that you never want to be in a position of trading that month's rent—not because you could lose it (you could, but you probably won't!), but because the urgency of having to turn a profit is going to affect your trading ability adversely. The more urgent the profit, the less likely it is to happen. Murphy's law is unfortunately alive and well in day trading.

PART-TIME VERSUS FULL-TIME

With this in mind, how much money should the beginning trader allocate toward trading? I strongly suggest that you have at least $50,000 of risk capital if you plan on trading full-time, and at least $5,000 if you plan on trading part-time. If you plan on trading full-time, I think $50,000 is about the minimum needed to give you a realistic chance of making good money. For someone trading part-time who has a primary source of income, $5,000 is the bare minimum required to attempt to turn a consistent profit. The first question most people ask is how much they can expect to make in their first year. If you are a beginner, the reality is that you cannot make any accurate predictions of how much you will earn as a trader. There is no way to tell. It is entirely based on your ability and your self-discipline.

TRADING ON MARGIN

It is very important to remember that the $50,000 minimum for full-time traders, and the $5,000 minimum for part-time traders, are based on the fact that you will be trading on *margin*. Trading on margin is essential to profitable day trading. Trading on margin simply means you are allowed to take positions up to double the amount of cash you have in your brokerage account. The brokerage firm lends you the money and charges interest. The beauty is that if you don't hold the positions overnight, you don't have to pay any interest. For the day trader, this is like free money. For example, if you deposit $50,000 with an online brokerage firm, you actually have $100,000 worth of buying power. If you buy a $100 stock, you could buy 1,000 shares. If you resell the stock in the same day, you don't pay any margin interest. If you hold the stock overnight, you are charged what amounts to about 8 percent annually, depending on the brokerage firm and interest rates. At that rate, you are charged a few dollars per night to hold $100,000 worth of stock with only $50,000 of cash. This interest will decline as the amount you borrow increases.

There is a dangerous side to trading on margin, however. You are on the hook for 100 percent of any losses you incur on the borrowed money. It is loan, and nothing more. It's the same as if your local bank loaned you money to open a business. Imagine if the business went belly-up. Not only would you lose your investment, but you would also owe the bank the balance of the loan, regardless of the profitability of the business. The same is true in trading. But the dangerous thing is that, unlike for a bank loan, there is no approval process for margin borrowing. So long as you have money in your account, the broker will let you borrow against it up to 2 to 1, no questions asked. Margin interest is a good source of revenue for brokerage firms. So what's the catch?

THE MARGIN CALL

The brokerage firms are not stupid. They are fully aware of the risk they are taking by loaning you money. That is why they have *margin calls*. If you hold positions overnight, the brokerage firm's margin department will monitor your account to make sure the money loaned to you is protected. Let's look at an example.

Imagine you open a margin account with $100,000 cash. The brokerage firm will loan you an additional $100,000 against the money in the account. So you are actually playing with $200,000 of trading capital. Assume you buy 1,000 shares of a $200 stock and you hold the position overnight. Now imagine that, to your horror, the stock loses 70 percent of its value in one day. All of a sudden, the value of your holdings is cut to less than one-third. You had invested $100,000 and borrowed $100,000 from the brokerage firm to buy a $200,000 stock position. Now that stock position is only worth $60,000. The accountants at the brokerage firm will get a little concerned that you won't be able to pay back the money they loaned you. They couldn't care less that you just lost $100,000 of your own money, which was the entire amount of your initial deposit. They just want their money back.

The margin call is when the broker forces you to deposit more money in your account as collateral against the margin loan. If you can't come up with more money, the broker will simply sell out the remainder of your holdings (whether you like it or not) and take back the money loaned to you, if possible. This is the brokerage firm's version of a bank foreclosure. This ensures that, in most instances, the firm gets its money back one way or another. This only occurs when the value of your account drops drastically.

There is another dynamic that protects the brokerage firm against losses from margin loans. Stocks under $5 are not marginable. This means you can't borrow the brokerage firm's money to buy stocks below $5. You have to pay for them entirely with your own money. This is because so many stocks trading below $5 are cheap for a reason: They might be on their way to being worthless. And the brokerage firm is not going to take that risk with its money. Therefore, if you are a day trader with less than $5,000 in trading capital, the universe of stocks you can afford to trade on margin is extremely limited. This is especially true if your strategy is to buy several thousand shares at a time, which I feel is the only way to be consistently profitable.

The reason you need at least $5,000 of trading capital to begin trading part-time is because that is about the absolute minimum amount of money that would enable you to trade 2,000 shares of a low-priced stock at a time on margin. As you will learn later in the book, the key to profitable day trading is to be able to buy a large number of shares and trade for small profits. You are not going to make consistent money by buying 100 or 50 shares of a high-priced stock and trying to make 1 full point on the trade. But you can make a living by buying 2,000 shares of a stock at 6 and reselling it at 6⅟16 for a $125 profit. This is a much easier and more profitable way to trade. However, for you to be able to buy these low-priced stocks on margin and get the most out of your trading capital, the stocks have to be priced at least at $5 per share.

If you have less than $5,000 of trading capital, you are much better off investing with a longer time horizon. The problem is that, with the commissions being fixed around $8 to $10 per trade (depending on which brokerage firm you use), the smaller the amount of money you are playing with, the larger the percentage of your profits that will go to commission charges if you are an active trader. If you are only playing with $2,000 or $3,000, and thus only buying 200 shares at a time, the profits you make on ⅟16 or ⅛ point will go entirely to the commission. Simply put, you will not be able to buy enough shares to overcome the transaction costs. Yet, ironically, it is this same small profit margin of ⅟16s and ⅛s that enables traders with more capital to make a living trading. The difference is that they are buying 2,000 shares at a time, not 200.

As Table 5.1 shows, if you have anything less than $5,000 of trading capital, you are going to severely limit your ability to buy and sell 2,000 shares of a stock at a time. As previously mentioned, any stock below $5 is not marginable, so you will have a difficult time finding stocks in your price range. The less trading capital you have, the less you will be able to pick and choose trading opportunities on their own

Table 5.1 Buying Power When Trading on Margin.

Price of Stock	Number of Shares Bought with $5,000	Number of Shares Bought with $10,000
$5	2,000	4,000
$6	1,666	3,333
$7	1,428	2,856
$8	1,250	2,500
$9	1,111	2,222
$10	1,000	2,000

$5,000 assumes $10,000 of buying power on margin; $10,000 assumes $20,000 of buying power on margin.

merits. Instead, you will be buying and selling stocks based on what you can afford. This will limit your ability to consistently turn a profit.

THE PROS AND CONS OF TRADING PART-TIME

The goal of trading part-time is twofold: to make a few hundred dollars per week in trading profits on top of the income you are making in your current job, and to do so while learning the ropes of day trading without risking large sums of money in the process.

There are several great advantages to trading part-time. As long as you have online access and a computer, you can trade right from your current office or home office. The most important thing is that trading part-time will allow you to get your feet wet in day trading without risking too much trading capital or giving up the income from your full-time job. Losses are a part of trading, but you learn from those losses. The reality is that you really won't learn a thing until your money is on the line. That is when everything will begin to make sense. In the beginning, I wouldn't suggest quitting your full-time job until you learn the ropes and see how you do for a few months with a small amount of capital. That way, your fallback is your full-time job if you find out day trading is not for you.

There are several other issues to consider if you are deciding to trade part-time while still working at your full-time job. The important thing to remember when considering whether to trade part-time is that you are in this for the money. It has to be worth your while to justify the time commitment you are going to make. Even trading part-time requires a tremendous amount of concentration and effort. And, unfortunately, I'm sure most of you happen to have your full-time jobs during market hours. Therefore, you will probably be trading from the same office or desk where you do your full-time job. The reality is that trading will distract you from your full-time job. When your money is on the line, you will find it very hard to do anything else but watch the markets. And, if you are losing money, you might snap at your co-workers. It is extremely important to remember that very few people in your office are going to know anything about what you are doing. They will not be too sympathetic when those inevitable mood swings set in. I'm sure you've heard stories of traders throwing phones at their assistants in anger. I guess that's okay on a trading floor, but in a civilized office you won't have that luxury. In fact, it might even get you fired.

The other issue to consider is that the distraction factor can work both ways. Day trading will be a distraction from your 9-to-5 job, but your job will also be a distraction from your trading. You should never be so busy in your primary job that you place a trade and then forget about it while you attend to your everyday business. This is a recipe for disaster. If you are extremely busy in your current job and you try to trade, I guarantee you will lose money. Making money in the markets requires a tremendous amount of concentration. The last place you want to be when the market is crashing is in a two-hour meeting with your boss. And remember, Murphy's law is alive and well. The day the market crashes will inevitably be the day you are away from your quote screen and tied up in something else. So, with that said, I would only suggest trading part-time if and only if your full-time job allows you to devote a sufficient amount of time during the day to trading without being distracted.

THE PROS AND CONS OF TRADING FULL-TIME

Obviously, the most important consideration for quitting your job and trading full-time is the amount of trading capital you have. If you have less than $50,000 of risk capital, I would not suggest that you start trading full-time. Remember, when trading on margin, $50,000 of cash actually gives you $100,000 of buying power—the minimum needed to give you a realistic shot at making good money. With less than $50,000 cash, it might be better to start part-time and then work your way up from there. As I said, it is very difficult to make any realistic predictions of how much money you will earn in your first year, because you don't know what the markets will do or what your own abilities are. Good traders can make in excess of 100 percent return per year on their trading capital. Some make much more than that. But there is no way to tell how well you will do. If you stick to the strategies laid out in this book, I believe you will do well. I have done very well following them. With this in mind, the more trading capital you have, the better your chances of making good money will be. It will be far easier to make a living trading when you have $300,000 of trading capital than when you have only $50,000.

SECTION III

How to Beat Wall Street at Its Own Game

Successful day traders take food out of the mouths of the Wall Street firms that trade against them. For even a single share of stock to trade, there must be a buyer for every seller. Did you ever ask yourself who is taking the other side of your trade? Does that person know something you don't?

This thought is what keeps day traders on their toes, constantly on guard, and always fearful of the markets they trade. But fear is a good thing, because it is fear alone that keeps day traders out of trouble. They must be constantly aware of the danger of their surroundings. Every profit they make comes at someone else's expense. And every loss they suffer is a profit in someone else's pocket.

Never trust the people taking the other side of your trades. They are not friends, they are enemies. Everyone is trying to trade against you. Without some degree of fear, without anxiety, you are doomed to fail. Beware, and always watch your back. Danger lurks behind every corner.

CHAPTER 6

Price Takers versus Price Makers

Internet day traders must fight for each and every profit they make. 1/16 here, 1/8 there; it sounds simple, but there is no such thing as easy money. The markets do not give away money. Day traders battle for every last penny they extract from the market. How do they do this? By exploiting the market's inefficiencies; by using every possible edge to their advantage; by beating Wall Street at its own game.

What is Wall Street's game? It's quite simple. For every buyer there is a seller, and for stock to trade, one of two things must happen: Either you agree to the prices of others, or they agree to yours. The advantage, the profit, and the edge lie in getting others to agree to your prices.

In the short term, the opportunities for quick profit are created as an imperfect marketplace brings together buyers and sellers with varying degrees of experience, trading ability, and knowledge. Against this backdrop, the day trader must realize that there are essentially two types of people in the market: price makers and price takers. The price makers make or set the prices in the stock market, and the price takers take or accept the prices the market gives them. The day trader's edge—the key to making consistent short-term profits—is to be first and foremost a price maker, allow-

*ing participation in Wall Street's age-old game of making money at
the expense of the buying and selling public.*

When people ask me to explain the nature of stock trading, I summarize
it in one phrase: For every buyer there is a seller. The markets are
nothing more than a collective difference of opinion. No matter how
cheap or expensive a stock looks, whether you buy or sell, there is
always someone taking the other side of your trade. And that person
always disagrees with you. Think about it. That is the only way the stock
can trade. When you sell, you must find a buyer. When you buy, you need
a seller. Either you are agreeing to the seller's price, or the seller is agreeing to your price. Did you ever ask yourself what motive someone might
have to take the other side of your trade? What kind of information does
that person have? Does that person know something you don't know?
Smart sellers will only sell to a buyer at a price where they feel it is in
their best interests to sell. And smart buyers will only buy at a price
where they feel they are getting a good deal at the expense of the seller.

PRICE MAKERS

Need evidence? Look no further than Wall Street. In 1998, the average
salary on Wall Street was over $170,000. That means that for every per-
son making $20,000 there is someone making well over $350,000. Where
does this extraordinary wealth come from? How do these select few
people make so much, year in and year out, regardless of whether the
stock market goes higher or lower?

Obviously, the money comes from somewhere. Wealth is not just
created out of thin air. Every dime that is earned comes out of someone's pocket. The money is being made at someone's expense, but
whose? It is made at the expense of the investing public. Wall Street is
in the business of trading against its customers. Wealth is created when
Wall Street takes the other side of your trades. When you want to buy,
Wall Street sells. When you want to sell, Wall Street buys. All the while,
traders are capturing pennies along the way. These $\frac{1}{16}$s, $\frac{1}{8}$s, and $\frac{1}{4}$s add
up to literally billions of dollars per year in trading profits. Wall Street
always wins in the end, and when Wall Street wins, the customer loses.
And usually, the customer doesn't even know it.

But how does Wall Street do this? If it is taking the other side of
your trades, what's the catch? It's actually quite simple. Wall Street

earns its money when it takes the other side of your trade by dictating or setting the price at which the stock trades. Wall Street forces the investing public into agreeing to the terms and prices it sets, ensuring that Wall Streeters never risk a dime of trading capital unless it is in their best interests to do so.

WALL STREET'S CONFLICT OF INTEREST

Anyone who has been around Wall Street long enough will come to the conclusion that the work the firms engage in is an inherent conflict of interest. These financial institutions are in the business of advising their clients on the buying and selling of securities, while simultaneously taking the other side of the trades for themselves. Think about this for a moment. When a Wall Street brokerage firm tells its largest clients to buy a stock because it is a great value, who is selling the stock to the clients? The brokerage firm itself. You have to ask yourself: If this stock is such a great deal, why is the brokerage firm selling it to someone else instead of keeping it? Why would the firm ever give away its hard-earned secrets? You have to believe that, with their teams of highly paid analysts, investment bankers, and other rocket scientists, these firms are in possession of far more information and knowledge as to the real value of the stock than their customers are.

But the customers don't see it that way. Greed has funny ways of clouding a person's perception. Investors rely on the brokerage firms for guidance, and depend on the firms' analysis and insight to steer them toward good investments and away from bad ones. Yet the banks and brokerage firms would still rather sell even the best stock pick of the year to their customers than keep it for themselves. Why? It comes down to dollars. When their customers want to buy the securities, the brokerage firms are making substantial amounts of money by taking the other side of the trades—selling the securities to their clients. How do the firms make this money? By setting the price at which they sell the securities. The key is that the brokerage firms will only agree to a selling price that is to their best advantage, usually ¹⁄₁₆, ⅛, or ¼ point higher than the price at which they can buy the stock for themselves. This is known as the *spread*. That is the essence of stock trading, and is precisely how Wall Street makes billions of dollars per year.

This is done by the entire gauntlet of Wall Street financial institutions. Big investment banks, full-service brokerage firms, NASDAQ market makers, NYSE member firms, specialists, even the discount and online brokerage firms: They all do it. They all trade against their customers for their own self-serving interests, namely profit. The more trading they can induce their customers to do, the more money they make in the process. That is why, regardless of what the market is doing, these brokerage firms always have an opinion. If the market looks bad, they advise their clients to sell. If the market looks good, they advise their clients to buy. Either way, Wall Street wins, because the firms are skimming ⅟₁₆s, ⅛s, and ¼s off the order flow, regardless of whether or not their clients make money.

These firms know that as long as customers buy the stock, at some point it will come back out of their accounts as a sell order. And when customers sell, they will immediately be putting the money to work by buying something else, thus generating even more commission revenue and trading profits for the firm that handles the trade. The only way the firms would lose would be if their customers stopped buying and selling. That is why hell would freeze over before these brokerage firms would tell their clients to stop trading, to hold cash for extended periods of time until market conditions improve.

But what about the discount brokers, who aren't in the business of advising their clients on investment decisions? Naturally, because they make all their money on trade commissions, they want their clients to trade as much as possible, regardless of whether their customers make or lose money. Their goal is make their customers feel as comfortable as possible with the trading process, even if that means giving away "free" trades at first. The more comfortable clients are with trading, the more likely they are to trade actively. The discount brokerage firms couldn't really care less how the clients ultimately fare. Their job is to provide trade executions, not to worry about making their customers money.

Every single penny a Wall Street brokerage firm makes by trading against its customers is one more penny out of the customers' pockets. And that adds up to billions of dollars per year.

That is why the discount and online brokerage firms have come under fire from their full-service brethren, who say they are doing their clients a disservice by inducing them to trade excessively. This is because studies have shown that excessive trading reduces returns for the average investor and that the investor is better off in a buy-and-hold strategy than actively trading in and out. Why? Because the returns of active traders are reduced due to the combination of commissions and the bid-ask spread eating into the traders' profits. If you do 30 trades per day, like I do, you have to make at least $300 in trading profits per day just to break even after commissions. Over the course of year, the active trader may spend $50,000 or more on brokerage commissions. That is why it is absolutely essential that you have the edge, so you can overcome the disadvantages you face.

THE EDGE

The basic premise of this book is that you should only trade when you have this edge. After you finish this section, you will know precisely what I am talking about. The edge is very subtle, but using it is the key to success as a day trader. Without the edge, you don't stand a chance. Just look at average investors. They are the ones that inevitably get the short straw, simply because they lack the knowledge and awareness that the edge even exists. To make matters worse, they don't even realize that the edge is being used against them every time they place a trade.

So what exactly is this edge Wall Street has used to its advantage for over 100 years? The edge is the ability to dictate the prices at which you agree to trade. In other words, you have the edge when you trade on your terms, not someone else's. You set the price at which you are willing to buy or sell before you agree to the trade. That is the key to making consistent short-term profits as a day trader.

THE BARGAINING PROCESS

Let's look at an analogy. Think of the process of buying a used car. Let's say you are in the market for a 1975 Corvette. You've been doing your homework, and you've come to the conclusion that one with about 100,000 miles has a fair market value of about $7,500. You arrive at this price based on your observation of the prices at which Corvettes have been changing hands this year. Imagine you are driving along and you see the exact car you are looking for on a neighbor's lawn with a For Sale sign on the window. To your delight, you find out the car has approximately 100,000 miles on it. You speak to the owner, who says the asking price is $10,000.

What steps to you take to get the best possible deal? Do you ever just accept the first price that the seller asks? I hope not! Is there better way to buy? Of course there is: by trying to negotiate a better price, bidding down, haggling, and making the seller lower the offering price. No one is stupid enough to just take the seller's first offer, unless it is a phenomenal deal. Why would you pay more money than you have to? You have to negotiate a better price for yourself. The key is that you have a good idea of what the car is worth based on what you have seen and read in the marketplace. You are not going to pay the asking price because you know it is too high. You'd love to buy the car for less than $7,500, but you know that chances are the owner won't sell it that cheaply. It would be unrealistic and a waste of time to bid anything less than $7,500.

So, you tell the seller you'll pay $7,500 for the car, and not a penny more. The seller now has essentially three choices. First, he or she could agree to your price—hit your bid—and sell you the car at $7,500. Second, he or she could refuse you outright and keep the sale price at $10,000. Or third, he or she could try to meet you halfway by coming back with a lower offering price of, say, $8,500. But you have stated that you are not going to pay any more than $7,500. Your tough stance has put the seller in a real dilemma. The seller can get $7,500 right now from you, or walk away and run the risk of never selling the car. You are smart and you say the offer is only good for 10 minutes, after which you will walk. This puts added pressure on the seller. The beauty of this strategy is that the power is in your hands. You know what the car is worth, and you know you can always shop elsewhere if you can't agree on a low price right now. The last thing you are going to do is just accept the seller's terms. In trading terms, by setting the price you bid for the car at $7,500 and no higher, you have essentially used a limit order.

What you have done by bargaining is put yourself in a no-lose situation. Either you buy the car at the price you have set, or you will shop elsewhere. Your refusal to accept the seller's terms (of buying the car at $10,000) and only buy at the price you have dictated makes you a price maker. Obviously, the seller would much prefer that you were too stupid to negotiate a better price. That way he or she could make a nice profit at your expense if you just accepted the offering price.

Imagine what it would be like if you were an active trader of cars and were unaware that you could negotiate a better price than the seller's first offer. Think of how much money you would leave on the table if you never made any effort to negotiate a better price for yourself. You wouldn't last in the business, because you would eventually be broke. No sane person would ever do business this way.

Yet, ironically, this is precisely the way most people buy and sell stocks. What the public doesn't realize is that they are doing precisely the same thing when they buy and sell stocks at the market as when they buy a car by accepting the seller's first offering price. By buying and selling at the market, these investors are agreeing to the terms of counterparty to the trade without attempting to negotiate a better price. And guess who is on the other side of the trade? A Wall Street trading firm that makes millions or billions of dollars per year by trading against the investing public. Do you think for one second that the price the firms set—and the public agrees to—is in the investors' best interests? Not a chance in hell.

So what really enables Wall Street to make so much on the public's buying and selling of stocks? It is the ignorance of the investing public, who are unaware or unsure of how they can negotiate a better price for the stock they buy and sell. The general public blindly accepts the prices Wall Street sets. Why don't they try to negotiate a better price? Because either they don't know how or they don't understand that it is even possible. I tend to think it is the latter. The investing public has for decades been brainwashed into thinking that the only way they can buy a stock is at the market, by purchasing stock where Wall Street has it for sale. They don't know that there is a better way. The concept of being able to negotiate a better price is probably foreign to most people's preconceived notions of trading. As such, the last thing Wall Street wants is for the general public to be educated in the ways of stock trading. As long as investors still subscribe to the myth that the only way to buy and sell stocks is at the market, and as long as they fail to see that they can negotiate a better price, the financial institutions will remain rich and happy. This ensures that the public remains the food and the prey of Wall Street.

Buying 1,000 shares of stock should be no different than buying a used car. Every purchase and sale, whether it is a home, a car, or a stock, should involve some degree of bargaining and negotiation. Every transaction that occurs is an agreement between buyer and seller, and a buyer should never accept a seller's first sale price without first trying to negotiate a better price. The average investor will likely spend far more money per trade on buying a stock than on buying a car. Think about it. If an investor buys 1,000 shares of a $25 stock, that is a $25,000 trade. Yet most investors put far less effort into that purchase than they would into buying a car. By buying at the market, the investing public is unknowingly getting ripped off by the firms that specialize in taking the other side of the trade. All because the trade is being done on the firms' terms, not the investors'.

THE PROCESS OF PRICE NEGOTIATION— MARKET VERSUS LIMIT ORDERS

Whether the individual investor realizes it or not, the process of buying and selling stocks is no different than the process of buying any other large-ticket item, whether a home, a car, a boat, or some other luxury item. Every purchase or sale is based on an agreement between buyer and seller as to the price and terms of the deal. And, as we said, for the trade to occur, one of three things must happen. Either you agree to someone else's price, that person agrees to your price, or the two of you arrive at something in the middle. As you know, it is far better when you get someone to agree to your price. But how do you get them to do this?

Before we can answer that, we have to look at the nature of buying and selling. For this, let's go back to the used car example. What are the two ways to buy a used car? Either you can buy the car by accepting the seller's higher price, or you can try to set your own lower price and get the seller to agree to it. The fastest way to make sure you buy the car is to lift the seller's offer. When you agree to the seller's offering price, you are guaranteed to buy the car, but chances are you are paying more for it than it is worth. This is because the seller generally knows more about the true worth of the car than you do, and is only going to sell at a price that he or she feels he is getting the best deal possible at your expense. That is the problem with accepting someone else's terms. The only advantage to doing this is that you are avoiding the risk that another potential buyer will end up with the car before you do. You are guaranteed to take the car home so long as you accept the offering price.

The second way you can attempt to buy the car is on your own price terms, by putting a limit on how much money you are willing to pay for the car. By telling the seller you will pay $7,500 and not a cent more, you are putting the decision back in the seller's hands. You have stated your intentions, and now it is up to the seller either to sell you the car or refuse your bid. The advantage is that the seller knows you will not pay more for the car than you offered originally. If the seller wants to get rid of the car badly enough, he or she will agree to your price. Who knows when the next buyer may come along? It could be months, it could be years, or it could be never. But what if the seller doesn't need to sell the car immediately? Under these circumstances, the problem with this strategy is that you run the risk of not buying the car. The seller may refuse your bid. Trying to save a few bucks always comes with a cost. This kind of strategy takes a certain amount of patience, because you must be willing to walk if the seller does not agree to your buying price. If you really want the car badly, that is the risk you must face when you try to bargain for a better price.

It is always important to remember that something is only worth what someone else is willing to pay for it. This always puts the negotiating advantage, or edge, in the hands of the buyer over the seller, if the buyer puts a limit on the buying price. By setting the price, the buyer is determining what the item is worth. It doesn't matter what the seller thinks, because without a buyer, what is an item really worth? The same is true in stocks. A stock is only worth what someone else is willing to pay for it. That is why negotiating is key. As with buying a used car, there are essentially two ways to buy stock. You can agree to the seller's price, or you can get the seller to agree to your price. This is the difference between market and limit orders.

THE MARKET ORDER

The market order is the investing public's most popular and most used means of buying and selling stocks. When investors buy and sell at the market, they are agreeing to whatever price the market will give them. There isn't any negotiating involved. What the investing public doesn't realize is that when they buy stock at the market, they are agreeing to buy the stock at the price the seller has set. The seller is not accepting the investor's price terms, the investor is accepting the seller's. And anytime the seller sets the price and the buyer agrees, the advantage goes to the seller. The seller is only going to sell the stock at a price he or she feels is sufficient.

The buying and selling public's reliance on using market orders is essentially what allows Wall Street to make so much money year in and year out at clients' expense. Wall Street can only trade against its customers when those customers agree to Wall Street's prices, when the customers agree to trade at the market. It is the *spread,* or the difference in price between where the Wall Street firms will buy and sell stock to the general public on market orders, that enables the firms to continually make billions of dollars in trading profits on ⅟₁₆s, ⅛s, and ¼s off their customers. All because the investing public does not know how to use limit orders.

Getting back to the analogy of the used car, it is important to note that that transaction really only had one side. We had a seller, and we had an interested buyer. Unlike the used car example, the curious thing about Wall Street is that the brokerage firms are on both sides of the fence. They are both buyers and sellers in the stocks they trade at the same time, regardless of whether they are bullish or bearish on the stock. The key to their profitability is that they always set both the price at which they are willing to buy stock and the price at which they are willing to sell. The key word here is *willing.* These firms are not ever going to buy or sell stock to the public at a price that is not to their best advantage. They ensure that they make or set the prices themselves. If it is not at their price, they would rather not do the trade. It's that simple.

So how do the firms set the prices themselves? What mechanism enables them to be on both sides of the market at the same time? How can they always profit on these trades? All these questions have the same answer: limit orders.

THE LIMIT ORDER

The limit order, unlike the market order, is not the preferred choice of the individual investor. But it is the method of choice for the professionals who make a living buying and selling stocks. The day trader must use limit orders to be profitable. A limit order is nothing more than an order to buy or sell stock with a price limit attached to it. If it is a buy limit order, the buyer sets the price, and is not willing to pay even a penny more than that price limit. This prevents the buyer from paying more than the preset price. It is just like the buyer of the Corvette, who is willing to pay $7,500 and not a penny more. Either the buyer gets the car at that price, or he or she doesn't. But, regardless, the buyer won't be paying more than $7,500 for the car. That is the basic premise behind the limit order.

The limit order is precisely what allows the Wall Street firms to set the prices at which they will buy and sell stock. The tricky part is that when the firms set the price at which they will buy stock, there is no guarantee they will find a seller to agree to their terms. There is never a guarantee. But the firms don't care. The key to the equation is that they only buy on their terms, or they won't buy at all. It is a no-lose situation.

The way these large trading firms make their profits is the exact same way you will make yours as a day trader: by only buying at price levels where you know you can immediately resell for a small profit. That is why you have to be a price maker, and not a price taker. By using limit orders, you are setting the price and then waiting. The trap is set. You wait patiently in the hopes that you find someone who is stupid enough to sell you stock at your price. If someone does, you will then turn right around and resell the stock higher yourself. If you can't find someone who will buy on your terms, you simply move on to another stock. Eventually, if you set enough traps, someone will walk right into one of them. How are you able to buy the stock low and sell higher? By using limit orders. But what do you see that the sellers don't? Obviously, if the sellers knew what you knew, they wouldn't be foolish enough to agree to your low price. They would try to get a higher price for themselves.

What you see is exactly the same thing the rest of Wall Street sees: that the general public is foolish because they blindly buy and sell at the market. What people fail to realize is the reality that they are leaving money on the table every time they place a trade. As price takers, the public does not watch their stocks carefully. Nor do they attempt to bargain for a better price. Even worse, they don't have anyone to negotiate on their behalf. Remember, even the brokerage firms that manage the investing public's money trade against the very customers they advise. Customers are really on their own, and most of the time they don't even know it. That is why they walk right into the trap Wall Street sets for them.

Thus, the day trader is forced to compete with all of Wall Street for the profits created when the investing public buys and sells at the market. Every single profit that Wall Street makes is a profit taken directly out of the investing public's pocket. And, ironically, every single profit the day trader makes is one less profit reserved for Wall Street. The food on the day trader's table is food taken directly out of the mouths of the Wall Street firms that trade against him or her.

SETTING THE TRAP

With this in mind, you always have to be aware of the agenda of the other players in the market, especially the Wall Street firms. Who is really taking the other side of your trade? If you are a good trader, it certainly won't be Wall Street. This is because, if you are on top of your prices, the Wall Street firms will be too smart to take the other side of your trades, and you will be too cautious to take the other side of theirs. You will each know the trap the other is trying to set. You are both price makers, and you need to find price takers. So the only other group left is the investing public. These people are Wall Street's prey, and by consequence, they are your prey as well. You are both after them for the same thing, both in it for the same reason: to trade against the investing public's ignorance, to use your negotiating skills to buy stocks and resell them for $\frac{1}{16}$-, $\frac{1}{8}$-, and $\frac{1}{4}$-point profits all day long.

This is a tremendously profitable way to make a living. Wall Street would like to keep this game, this secret, all to itself. But the cat is out of the bag. The brokerage firms certainly don't want or need the day trader to be taking food out of their mouth. This is their turf. And the day trader is an unwelcome trespasser. But what can they do? They have no choice. The day trader is here, side by side with them, whether they like it or not. And the day trader is here to stay.

PRELUDE TO THE BID-ASK SPREAD

As you can see, the key to making profits as a day trader is the use of well-placed limit orders. Because you are essentially taking food out someone else's mouth every time you make a profit, you have to be extremely careful how you use these limit orders. Danger lurks behind every corner, and if you are not cautious, you will step on a land mine. The world of trading is filled with them. Many people have gone broke by letting their guard down. You have to be constantly aware of this fact.

In this chapter we have touched briefly on the differences between market and limit orders. But we have only begun to scratch the surface. Knowing how to use limit orders, and where to place them, involves much more than just knowing the difference between trading at the market and trading with a price limit. If you are going to make a living trading, you really need to have a firm understanding of how stocks trade. And that can only come from an examination of the bid-ask spread.

It is extremely important that the day trader understand that the situations described here and in the following chapters were written within the framework of trading on the New York Stock Exchange. Under no circumstances should they be applied to NASDAQ stocks. The NASDAQ market operates under slightly different rules, which we will touch on in the later chapters on momentum trading.

Remember, if the stock has a four- or five-letter symbol, it is a NASDAQ stock. If it has a one-, two-, or three-letter symbol, it is a New York Stock Exchange or American Stock Exchange stock.

CHAPTER 7

The Day Trader's Crystal Ball

Understanding the Bid-Ask Spread

Successful day traders are able to make thousands of dollars per day by extracting tiny profits from stocks in a way that very few people understand. Many times, the stocks don't have to move for day traders to make a profit. So what do day traders see that other people don't? What is their secret? The answer lies in exploiting the bid-ask spread. That is why understanding the mechanics of the bid-ask spread is the day trader's single most important task.

Yet very few people understand how this works. The uninitiated will waste all their time combing through piles of charts, graphs, and research in the futile attempt to see something that others don't. This is wasted effort and will not lead to profits. What these people fail to grasp is that they need to look no further than the bid-ask spread for answers. Hidden under this veil lie the only real clues to predicting what a given stock will do in the next five minutes. Interpreting the bid-ask spread is the day trader's crystal ball.

The bid-ask spread is the most basic, yet misunderstood component in the trading of stocks. For a day trader, interpreting the bid-ask spread is the key to making profits. The whole premise of this book is that, in the short term, markets can be exploited for quick profits. This is because the markets are inefficient. And the markets are inefficient because of the mechanics of the bid-ask spread.

If there is one certainty in the world of day trading, it is that trading patterns and cycles constantly repeat themselves. In the course of your trading, you are going to be confronted with the same situations over and over again. A solid understanding of the nature of the bid-ask spread will enable you to predict price movements based on your experience with similar situations in the past. You may only have a few seconds to react. How you react will determine whether you make or lose money trading.

The best way to look at the bid-ask spread is as the parameters within which the buying and selling of stocks occur. The stock market is nothing more than a difference of opinion. For every buyer, there is a seller. The floor of the stock exchange is the place where the buyers and sellers meet to negotiate prices. As we mentioned in the last chapter, whether the individual investor realizes it or not, every single share of stock that changes hands does so on the basis of an agreement between buyer and seller as to the price and the number of shares. These agreements are reached by negotiation. The beauty of trading from home is that this negotiation process is nameless, faceless, and anonymous. With today's technology, you do not have to be face to face with the other buyers and sellers in your attempt to get a better or more fair price. All the tools you need to communicate and negotiate effectively are found inside the parameters of the bid-ask spread. This is why the New York Stock Exchange is the most effective and fair marketplace in the entire world.

As a day trader, you play a crucial role in this negotiating process. Through the application of certain trading techniques, you will be able to step into the marketplace when the other buyers and sellers cannot agree on price or number of shares. By using well-placed limit orders, you will attempt to bring out other buyers and sellers in the stock by offering to buy and sell at better prices than are currently available in the marketplace. That is what makes markets, and what allows you to make profits.

The trading techniques used in the negotiation process are difficult to comprehend without having a firm understanding of the mechanics the bid-ask spread. This entire chapter is devoted to understanding the bid-ask spread and answering the most basic of all trading questions: What makes a stock move up or down?

It seems like a simple question, yet 99 percent of the investing public does not have the correct answer. Most would answer that buyers move a market higher, and sellers move a market lower. Some would even go as far as saying that a stock moves down because there are more sellers than buyers, and it moves up when more buyers than sellers enter the market. This is partially correct, yet the real reason is a bit more complex. The true answer lies in the bid-ask spread.

The essence of trading is that every single share of stock that trades has both a buyer and a seller. That is why it is not 100 percent accurate to say that a stock moves higher because there are more buyers than sellers. For the stock to trade, there must be an equal amount of shares being bought and sold. The real answer is that the stock moves higher because of simple supply and demand.

All you need to do to make a stock go higher is to buy all the stock available for sale at a given price level, then buy more at the next highest level where it is for sale.

The reason for this is that for each and every stock there is only a limited number of shares for sale at each price level. Your buying and the buying of others will cause the stock to tick higher if you are willing to buy more stock than is for sale at a given price. You and the other buyers will inevitably buy all of the stock for sale at the first price level, and then the remainder of your buy order will be bought at the next highest level or levels where stock is for sale. In other words, if the stock is in demand because of good news, the buyers will simply clean out the stock at each consecutive higher price level, causing the stock to trade higher.

Let's look at an example. Suppose you want to buy 10,000 shares of IBM at the market. The stock looks like this:

5,000 shares are for sale at 101

2,000 shares are for sale at 101⅛

3,000 shares are for sale at 101¼

What happens when you want to buy 10,000 shares at the market? The problem is that there are only 5,000 shares for sale at the current price. So, you will buy those 5,000 shares at 101 (the current asking price) and then buy the remaining 5,000 shares at the next highest price level or levels at which stock is for sale. You will keep causing the stock to tick higher until you have bought all the stock on your order, in this case all 10,000 shares.

In order to get you filled on 10,000 shares, the sellers will sell you:

5,000 shares at 101, then

2,000 shares at 101⅛, and finally,

3,000 shares at 101¼

Your buying alone made the stock move up ¼ point from 101 to 101¼ as you cleaned out all the available stock at each price level. Assuming the stock opened the day at 101, if you checked the quote after your order was complete, it would read:

IBM   Last Trade *101¼* + ¼

As you can see, IBM did not trade up ¼ because there were more buyers than sellers. It went up because the buyers bought stock from sellers at higher levels, because at the moment that was the cheapest price at which there was stock for sale.

Another way to look at this is that if you are willing to buy stock, you are always going to be able to find a seller at some price. It's just a matter of at what price the seller is willing to sell you stock. If sellers were willing to sell IBM for $95 a share yesterday, and today, because of good news on the company, they are only willing to sell at $101, the stock will inevitably go up. As you can see, it didn't go up because there were more buyers than sellers. It went up because the potential buyers were forced to pay higher prices to accumulate the stock. The higher price level is the only place where the buyers and sellers could agree to exchange stock. Stock that was for sale at lower prices earlier has already been taken, and the buyers now have to "pay up" to entice sellers to sell them stock. This whole negotiation process plays itself out in the mechanics of the bid-ask spread. This may seem a bit confusing now, but it will become clearer as we examine the components of the bid-ask spread.

EXAMPLE 1: THE QUOTE

This first case study demonstrates a typical market scenario on the New York Stock Exchange. We are not going to make any trading decisions yet; this is only to show what the quote reveals. This is the most basic step in understanding the mechanics of price movement.

Let's say you are interested in trading in a stock called Zeta Inc., a stock that happens to be listed on the New York Stock Exchange under the symbol ZZZ. You pull the stock up on your real-time quote screen, and the basic quote reads as follows:

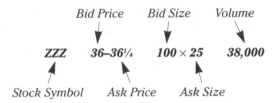

What does this say about ZZZ?

There is a wealth of information about ZZZ to be found in this simple quote. Basically, this is the blueprint of the intentions of buyers and sellers in this stock at this point in the trading day. The breakdown is as follows:

Buyer is willing to pay $36 and no higher (limit order)

Buyer is willing to buy 10,000 shares at $36

ZZZ   36–36¼   100 × 25   38,000

Seller is willing to sell at $36.25 (36¼) and no lower (limit order)

Seller is willing to sell 2,500 shares at 36¼

The Bid

The bid is 36, or $36 per share. This is the highest price at which stock is currently willing to be bought. This is the absolute highest price a potential buyer is willing to pay for stock at this time. Of all of the potential buyers of ZZZ in the entire world at this time, $36 is the best bid. However, this buyer, by putting a limit on the price, is stating that he or she is not willing to pay even a penny more than $36 for stock. This is a limit order, and as such, there is no guarantee the buyer will get the stock at $36. The buyer will first need a seller at the market to agree to the price before the stock can trade.

The Ask

The ask is 36¼, or $36.25 per share. This is the lowest price at which stock is currently willing to be sold—the absolute lowest price at which a potential seller is willing to sell stock at this moment. Of all of the people willing to sell ZZZ in the entire world at this time, 36¼ is the best offer. In other words, this seller is willing to sell stock with a price limit of 36¼, and is not willing to sell for even a penny less than $36¼. This is also a limit order, so here there is also no guarantee the seller will sell the stock at $36¼. The seller will first need a buyer to agree to the price before the stock can trade.

It is important to note that the only way you can bid or offer stock is through the use of limit orders, in which you put a price limit on how much you are willing to buy or sell for.

As you can see, the bid and the ask are the two primary components of the market. If someone ever asks, "What is the market in a stock?", you now know that it is the highest bid and the lowest offer, in this case 36 to 36¼. The market is always going to reflect the highest price a buyer is willing to pay for stock (the bid) and the lowest price a seller is willing to sell stock for (the ask). This is what dictates the price at which stock trades.

In plain English, we have a buyer who thinks the stock is worth no more than $36, and a seller who believes that the stock worth no less than 36¼. In other words, the seller wants ¼ point, or 25 cents, per share more than the buyer is willing to pay. You are seeing the negotiating process in progress. The seller and the buyer simply cannot agree on a price, which is exactly why their buy and sell orders sit on the floor of the exchange and remain unexecuted. Both the buyer and the seller are holding out. The seller wants more money, the buyer wants to pay less. Each is refusing the other's proposition. If there were buyers willing to pay more than $36 per share, or sellers willing to sell for less than $36.25, the bid-ask parameters of the market would be updated to reflect that.

Although we know for a fact from the quote that there are not any buyers willing to pay more than $36, nor are there any sellers willing to accept less than $36.25 (if there were, the market would not be 36 to 36¼), it is important to note that in ZZZ, as in all other stocks, there could be hundreds of buy orders in the stock at prices below $36, and hundreds of sell orders at prices above $36.25. But we will never see those limit orders reflected in the quote unless they are the highest bid and lowest ask, respectively, because they are considered away from the market.

This is no different than the real estate market or the car market. If Porche 911s are changing hands for $50,000 in the current environment, there are always going to be people who would love to buy those same Porsche 911s for $20,000 and people who would like to sell Porsche 911s for $100,000, even though both are away from the market. The same is true with stocks. If ZZZ is trading around $36 per share, there are inevitably going to be numerous buyers below the market and numerous sellers above the market. There might even be a buyer of 10 million shares of ZZZ at $20, but that person will never buy the stock that low because the stock is changing hands at $36. As such, because that buyer is so far away from the market, that buy order is insignificant to the trading in the stock. A real buyer would not be waiting for the stock to get to $20 before purchasing it.

Bid Size

The bid size is the number of shares the buyer is willing to buy. In our example, the bid size is 100. This means there are 10,000 shares of ZZZ willing to be bought at 36. It is important to note that this means a *total* of 10,000 shares willing to bought at 36 at this time. This could be only 1 buyer, or 20 different buyers willing to buy different amounts that total 10,000 shares. There is no way to tell the difference.

Ask Size

The ask size is the number of shares the seller is willing to sell. In our example, the ask size is 25. This means there are 2,500 shares willing to be sold at 36¼. As with the bid size, this could be one potential seller of 2,500 shares, or a combination of sellers totaling 2,500 shares.

One of the basic principles of stock trading is that the differences in the amount of the bid size and ask size reveal that there are rarely equal numbers of shares willing to be bought and sold in a stock at the same time. The supply and demand in the stock is in a constant state of flux. In this case, there are 10,000 shares willing to be bought (at 36), but only 2,500 shares willing to be sold (at 36¼). Most of the time, due to fluctuating market conditions, there will be large differences like this in the amount of stock willing to be bought and the amount of stock willing to be sold. This is known as a *lopsided market*. This is extremely important because it is one of the first indications of a short-term supply-demand imbalance, one that may precipitate a rally or a sell-off in the stock.

It is important to note that most quote systems refer to the bid size and the ask size in abbreviated format, leaving off the last two zeros. Therefore, 100 means 10,000 shares, 10 means 1000 shares, and so on.

Volume

This is the last component of the quote. The volume is the number of shares traded that day since the opening bell. Volume is very important in gauging the activity in the stock. Not a single share can change hands without it being reflected in the volume. In this case, 38,000 shares have changed hands so far in the trading day.

Thus the market is made. The highest bid (36) and lowest offer (36¼) set the parameters. In trading lingo, we would say that the market in ZZZ is 36 bid, offered at 36¼, 10,000 by 2,500. The market of 36 to 36¼ is known as the bid-ask spread.

As you can see, the bid-ask spread indicates the intentions of the buyers and sellers who are using limit orders. Limit orders are what dictate the parameters of the spread. This process ensures that the best prices will always be posted in the market, namely the highest buyer and the lowest seller. By looking at the stock quote in real time, by seeing the market parameters change, we are witnessing the negotiating process firsthand. In the preceding example, the buyer and the seller could not agree to each other's terms. Both are considered price makers, because they are only willing to trade if it is on their terms and at their price. The buyer will only buy at 36, and the seller will only sell at 36¼. Both are stubborn, and would rather wait and take their chances than agree to the other's price. And, as we said in the last chapter, the key word is *willing*. Neither the buyer at 36, nor the seller at 36¼, is guaranteed to get the order executed. But both are willing to take that risk in the hopes of finding someone who will take the other side of the trade.

EXAMPLE 2: THE MARKET ORDER TO SELL— HITTING THE BID

In Example 1, we learned the basics of how a stock is quoted. We will now look at the stock in further detail and see what happens when stock trades. We now know that the bid-ask spread ensures that buyers will always buy stock from the seller who is offering stock for sale at the lowest price at any given moment. Conversely, if there is a seller, his or her stock will always be sold to the buyer willing to pay the highest price for the stock. This ensures that both parties to the trade receive the fairest execution and the best possible price at all times.

Going back to the last example, the market in ZZZ was:

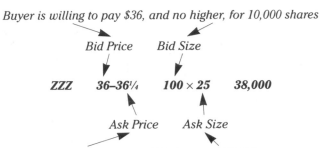

Buyer is willing to pay $36, and no higher, for 10,000 shares

Bid Price   Bid Size

ZZZ   36–36¼   100 × 25   38,000

Ask Price   Ask Size

Seller is willing to sell 2,500 shares at $36.25

Now, assume an investor wishes to sell 100 shares. What happens next?

The investor essentially has two choices: either to negotiate a price or to sell at the market. What occurs next depends on the intentions of the seller. For simplicity, we will assume the investor wishes to get an immediate execution. In this case, the investor has no choice but to sell at the price at which a buyer has stated intentions to buy stock. So, to get an instant fill, the investor decides to sell the stock at the market. Known as a *market order,* this order will be executed immediately. This stock will trade at the highest price a buyer is willing to pay the seller for the stock. No matter where a stock is trading, there is always a price at which a market order will be executed. A market order will usually only take a few seconds to get filled.

The market order is the investing public's method of choice for buying and selling stock. The advantage of a market order is that, under all market conditions and circumstances, an immediate execution is guaranteed. The danger is that investors don't know what price they will get, because the market maker must go out and find someone who is willing to take the other side of the trade. In both fast- and slow-moving markets, the market order can be very dangerous for this reason.

So, in our example, where will the order get executed if it is entered at the market? To answer that question, we have to ask: At what price is there a buyer willing to buy stock? We know from the bid-ask spread that there is a buyer willing to pay 36 for up to 10,000 shares. So, as long as the market parameters do not change before the order is entered, the stock will trade at 36, the bid.

The investor enters the order over the Internet:

Sell   100   ZZZ   Market

The order is now sent down to the floor of the exchange for execution. When the specialist, or market maker, receives the order, he or she will immediately match the sell order with a buyer and the order will be filled. If you have real-time quotes, you can watch the stock trade. Here's how it will look:

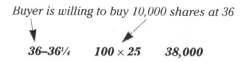

Buyer is willing to buy 10,000 shares at 36

36–36¼   100 × 25   38,000

changes to:

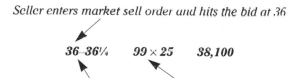

Seller enters market sell order and hits the bid at 36

36–36¼   99 × 25   38,100

Buyer buys 100 shares from the seller at 36, and now has 9,900 shares left to buy

100 shares of ZZZ trade at 36

Remember, we had a buyer willing to buy 10,000 shares at 36 and no higher. The seller, by placing a market order, agrees to sell the stock to whoever is willing to pay the best price for it. There will be no negotiating in this trade, because it is at the market. In this case, the highest bidder was at 36. Therefore, 100 shares trade at 36. It is important to notice how the market in ZZZ has changed. Two components of the snap quote have changed: the volume and the bid size.

Volume

First, the volume has changed to reflect the 100-share trade. Before the trade was entered, 38,000 shares had changed hands. Now, with this 100-share trade, a total of 38,100 shares have traded since the opening bell.

Bid Size

Second, and more important, the bid size has changed. Before the seller entered the order, the bidder was willing to buy 10,000 shares at 36. As we mentioned before, there is no way to tell if it is just one bidder who wants 10,000 shares, or a combination of several bidders each wanting different amounts at 36 that together total 10,000 shares. Either way, 100 shares were just bought, and there are now 9,900 left on the order. That is why the bid size changed from 100 to 99. In market terms, the bid was hit on 100 shares.

EXAMPLE 3: THE MARKET ORDER TO BUY— LIFTING THE OFFER

The market in ZZZ when we last looked was:

Buyer will pay $36 and no higher (the bid) for 9,900 shares (the bid size)

$$36–36\tfrac{1}{4} \qquad 99 \times 25 \qquad 38{,}100$$

Seller will sell 2,500 shares (the ask size) at 36¼ and no lower (the ask)

Let's review what we have learned. So far, we know that the market parameters are determined by the highest price a buyer is willing to pay for stock (the bid) and the lowest price at which the seller is willing to sell the stock (the ask). The highest bid and lowest offer are known as the bid-ask spread. From the snap quote, we know that there is a buyer for 9,900 shares at 36 (the bid) and a seller of 2,500 shares at 36¼ (the ask or offer), and that 38,100 shares have traded so far today.

At this point, let's assume there is a buyer looking for 1,000 shares of ZZZ. This buyer is a long-term investor who believes that the stock is cheap and is poised for an explosive move upward. Because of this, the buyer has no interest in haggling to save an extra ⅛ or ¹⁄₁₆ point by trying to buy the stock cheaper than where it is for sale, which is 36¼ (the offer).

As with any investor or trader who is ever buying or selling stock, there is a certain element of greed involved. This buyer would like to have the stock in his or her account immediately, and is not willing to run the risk of missing the stock in the event it begins to run higher. This could happen if the buyer tried to negotiate a better price through a limit order. Therefore, the buyer is willing to take the price the market is willing to give in exchange for getting an immediate execution. Thus, the buyer enters a market order to buy:

Buy 1000 ZZZ Market

When the order reaches the specialist on the floor of the exchange, 1,000 shares are immediately filled at 36¼. Remember, the lowest price at which a seller is willing to sell stock is the price at which the buyer will buy stock on a market order. Here's how the market in ZZZ changes:

Seller is willing to sell 2,500 shares at 36¼ and no lower

36–36¼   99 × 25   38,100

changes to:

Buyer enters buy of 1,000 shares at the market and lifts the offer at 36¼

36–36¼   99 × 15   39,100

Seller sells 1,000 shares to the buyer at 36¼ and now has 1,500 shares left to sell

Notice which components have changed: the volume and the ask size.

Volume

The volume changes from 38,100 shares to 39,100 as 1,000 shares trade.

Ask Size

The ask size changes from 25 to 15. We had a potential seller willing to sell 2,500 shares at 36¼. Now that the seller has sold 1,000 shares to this investor, there are 1,500 shares remaining on the seller's order. That is why the ask size changed from 25 to 15. In trading lingo, the offer was lifted on 1,500 shares.

EXAMPLE 4: THE LIMIT ORDER TO BUY— BIDDING FOR STOCK

When we last looked at ZZZ, the snap quote read:

36–36¼   99 × 15   39,100

The last trade in the stock was 1,000 shares at 36¼. Now assume another potential buyer comes in looking to buy 2,000 shares. This time the buyer is a trader who was drawn to the stock after seeing the stock trade 1,000 shares on the offer at 36¼. Typically, unless convinced that the stock is running higher, most good short-term traders will attempt to purchase the stock at a cheaper price than where it is for sale. This is where the negotiation process begins.

How is this done? Quite simply, by entering a limit order. By doing so, the trader is putting a limit on the price he or she will pay for the stock. In plain English, the trader is saying the stock is worth a certain amount, and not a penny more. So, the trader is willing to buy the stock at the price he or she sets, but is not willing to pay a higher price. The problem and risk of using limit orders is that there is no guarantee of an execution. As we learned in the last example, using a market order ensures an immediate execution. What is not so sure is the price at which the order gets filled. The exact opposite is true of limit orders. The price is certain, but not whether we will buy the stock. Limit orders carry with them the risk that if we try to save ¹⁄₁₆ point by using a limit order instead of a market order, the stock may run higher before our order gets filled. Then, if we really want the stock, we will be forced to pay a much higher price. Thus, using a limit order means that the attempt to buy the stock cheaper than where the market has stock for sale comes with the risk of missing the market.

Let's see exactly how a limit order works. In this example, we have a trader who wants to buy 2,000 shares of ZZZ. The trader is aware that the stock is for sale at 36¼, and that 1,000 shares just traded at that price, but feels that there is a good chance to buy it cheaper if he or she is patient.

If this person is a true short-term trader, his or her intention might be to buy the stock and then try to immediately resell it to make a quick ⅛ or ¹⁄₁₆ point. With that in mind, the trader decides that 36⅛ is the absolute highest price he or she will pay for the stock at this time. Like any other trader or investor, this person would love to buy the stock even cheaper than 36⅛, but knows that the chances of getting filled any cheaper than that are slim based on where the stock has been trading.

So here is the situation: The trader does not want to pay more than 36⅛. Yet the stock is not for sale at 36⅛, it is for sale at 36¼. And, to add to the difficulty, even up at 36¼ there is not enough stock for sale. There are only 1,500 shares for sale, and the trader wants to buy 2,000. Based on the supply and demand in the stock, if the trader is lucky enough to buy the stock at 36⅛, he or she has bought a real bargain.

Over the Internet, the trader enters the order:

Buy 2000 ZZZ 36¹⁄₈ LIMIT Day

It is important to note that there are two different types of limit orders: day and good until canceled (GTC). Day orders will be automatically canceled at the end of the day if not executed, and GTC orders will remain on the books until the trader or investor cancels them. To protect the investor, most brokerage firms will usually cancel GTC orders if they go unexecuted for 30 days. This ensures that an investor doesn't forget about an order and unknowingly buy the stock months or years later when he or she is no longer following it.

This order states that the buyer is willing to buy 2,000 shares of ZZZ at $36.125 or less, good until the end of the day (unless the buyer cancels the order before the end of the day). How will the snap quote change?

Remember, the bid-ask spread is set by the highest price a buyer is willing to pay for stock (the bid), and the lowest price at which a seller is willing to sell stock (the ask). The current quote (see Example 4) says we have a buyer willing to pay 36 (and no higher) for 9,900 shares only. Once this new order is entered, we have a buyer willing to pay more than $36 per share for stock. When the order is received by the specialist, we have 2,000 shares willing to be bought at $36.125, or 36⅛—⅛ point, or 12½ cents per share, higher than the previous highest bid of $36. Therefore, the market changes from 36 bid to 36⅛ bid to reflect the intentions of this new, higher bid.

There is a buyer who will pay $36 and no higher for 9,900 shares

36–36¼   99 × 15   39,100

changes to:

New buyer enters the market who is willing to pay higher than 36 for stock

36⅛–36¼   20 × 15   39,100

New buyer is willing to pay 36⅛ for 2,000 shares, raising the bid ⅛ point to 36⅛

It is absolutely essential to understand what has happened here. First of all, notice that the volume has not changed, but the bid and the bid size have.

The Bid

Even though we now have a buyer willing to buy stock at 36⅛, it is not for sale at that price. By posting the bid (36⅛), the potential buyer hopes to bring out sellers who are willing to sell stock at that price. In a sense, by being the best bid, the trader is advertising to the entire financial world that he or she is willing to buy 2,000 shares of ZZZ at 36⅛. This is important because, although no stock has traded, the bid-ask spread itself has changed.

The Bid Size

Because we now have a new, higher bid (36⅛), we also have a different amount of stock willing to be bought. We now have 2,000 shares willing to be bought at 36⅛, which is why the bid size change to 20. But why hasn't any stock traded?

As we mentioned earlier, the most important lesson to be learned from entering limit orders is that, by attempting to get a better price for your stock, you run the risk of not getting your trade executed. In our example, the stock was offered for sale at 36¼, not 36⅛. It is still for sale at that price. Therefore, in the event the stock begins to run higher, the buyer may miss the stock and never purchase it again at 36⅛. There is even the chance that the stock may never trade below 36¼ ever again.

This is a great example of the negotiating process in action. This new buyer at 36⅛ knows the stock is for sale at 36¼, but refuses to agree to those terms. The buyer is stating that he or she will pay 36⅛ and not a penny more. If the buyer gets the stock at his or her price, that's great. But if not, it's no big deal. If the buyer can't get the price he or she wants, he or she would rather not buy the stock. This is a no-lose situation.

The great thing about this example is that, although no stock has traded, the bid-ask spread has just given us a clue, a glimpse into the future. If we were watching our real-time quote screen carefully, we saw something most people probably missed, a subtle change in the parameters of the bid-ask spread. This is a firm indication of possible future movement in the stock. As a day trader, some of your most profitable trades will come from limit orders. You will come to understand that the first clues to reading the future direction of a stock come not from where a stock has traded, but from changes in the bid-ask spread itself. As an alert day trader, you will immediately see that there is now a higher degree of buying demand in ZZZ even though no stock has traded. This is because there is now a buyer (at 36⅛) who thinks the stock is worth more than 36 per share. The first signs of a potential move upward have been revealed. One of the earliest indications of future movement in a stock comes not from seeing where the stock is trading, but from reading up or down movements in the parameters of the bid-ask spread.

In this case, although no stock has traded, the fact that the bid is now ⅛ point higher than it was is a clear sign that there is now more buying demand in the market. Perhaps a serious buyer has entered the market. This may be the only clue the stock reveals before it moves higher. It is our job to form a conclusion and react to this information. And, as we know, we may only get a few seconds to react.

EXAMPLE 5: THE LIMIT ORDER TO SELL— OFFERING STOCK

The market in ZZZ when we last checked was:

36⅛–36¼   20 × 15   39,100

As we saw in Example 4, there is a buyer at 36⅛ sitting on the bid waiting for someone to sell the stock at that price. Since the buyer had entered a limit order to buy 2,000 shares at 36⅛, a price level cheaper than where stock is for sale, there is no guarantee that any stock will trade at that price limit.

Now we will see what happens when a seller of 1,300 shares enters the market. If the seller wants an immediate execution, he or she can be sure that the buyer will get 36⅛ per share for the stock. That is the best price at which there is currently a buyer in the stock. But this seller, like the trader who is bidding for stock at 36⅛, believes that he or she can do better than what the current market is offering. The seller is unwilling to hit the bid by selling 1,300 shares at the market at 36⅛. Essentially, the seller would rather hold out for more money, fully aware that he or she is passing up a guaranteed fill at 36⅛ to try to get a higher price and is running the risk that the stock may trade lower before he or she is able to sell. As you know, using a limit order comes with a risk. Missing the market is the risk that comes with trying to negotiate a better price than the market is willing to give. If you are successful, the reward is to get more money on the sale of your stock than you would have by selling at the market.

We know from the quote that the lowest price at which stock is for sale is at 36¼. Since our seller refuses to sell at the market at 36⅛, he or she essentially has three choices when placing a limit sell order:

1. Enter an order to sell above the current market—above 36¼; this could be 36⁵⁄₁₆, 36⅜, or even higher.
2. Join the offer at 36¼ with the other seller.
3. Underoffer the seller at 36¼ by offering the stock for sale at 36³⁄₁₆.

It should be noted that none of these options are guaranteed executions. The only price at which there is an immediate fill is at 36⅛, where there is a buyer advertising intentions to purchase stock (2,000 shares). There is nothing to say that the stock can't trade lower. Imagine how this seller would feel if, while he or she tries to squeeze an extra ⅟₁₆ or ⅛ point above the 36⅛ bid, the stock drops 2 points. Instead of saving a few bucks, the seller might lose a few thousand. That's the risk of entering a limit order instead of a market order.

One of the most important decisions the trader can make is the price at which to enter the limit order to sell. For simplicity, the trader decides that 36³⁄₁₆ is a good price at which to attempt to sell stock. Therefore, the order is entered:

Sell 1300 ZZZ 36³⁄₁₆ LIMIT Day

When the order reaches the specialist, the market changes from:

Stock was for sale at 36¼

36⅛–36¼   20 × 15   39,100

Stock is still for sale at 36¼,
but now there is stock for sale at a cheaper price, 36³⁄₁₆

to:

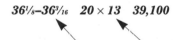

36⅛–36³⁄₁₆   20 × 13   39,100

New seller has underoffered the other seller by ¼₆ at 36³⁄₁₆

Notice how the market has changed. The only thing that has changed is the ask.

The Ask

This seller of 1,300 shares has underoffered the asking price by ¹⁄₁₆ point. Before, we had a seller willing to sell 1,500 shares at 36¼ (the ask). That seller hasn't gone anywhere. We now have a seller willing to sell stock cheaper than 36¼, at 36³⁄₁₆. The volume has not changed, because no stock has traded. Only the parameters of the bid-ask spread have changed.

As we know, the parameters of the market—the bid-ask spread—are entirely a negotiated market, set by limit orders. Pure supply and demand is at play. Here we have a situation where buyers and sellers are haggling over a mere ¹⁄₁₆ or ⅛ point. This ¹⁄₁₆, or 6.25 cents a share, does not seem like much to the average investor, but to the active trader it means everything. When trading at high volume, over the course of the year, it may mean the difference between making a small fortune and losing money. Even in this case, if the stock trades at 36³⁄₁₆, the seller saves 6.25 cents on 1,300 shares, amounting to an extra $81.25 over selling at the market.

With the New York Stock Exchange being essentially an auction market, it is inefficient in the short term as traders and investors negotiate over prices. This is why the opportunities for quick profits are boundless. This fact enables talented traders to make substantial amounts of money in very short periods of time. The job of the day trader is to exploit these inefficiencies by taking part in the negotiating process. With this in mind, one of the most important skills a day trader can possess is knowing when to use limit orders and when to use market orders.

One of the most important facts about trading is that the individual is never forced to buy and sell at the market. Most of the investing public is under the false assumption that there is no room for negotiation, that they must accept the price the market gives them. They think that when they sell, they get the bid; that when they buy, they get the ask; and that there is no room for price improvement. The limit order does not seem to be a viable alternative in the mind of the investing public. Ironically, the public's misled tendency to use market orders, and ignorance on how to use limit orders, is what enables both Wall Street and the day trader to make profits at the public's expense.

EXAMPLE 6: MOVING THE STOCK HIGHER

Now that we have some idea of the mechanics of the bid-ask spread, we will demonstrate the mechanism that makes a stock trade higher. Perhaps we customarily watch financial television or read the financial section of the local paper, and we see that our favorite stock is trading up ¼ point from the previous day's close. Have you ever wondered what physically makes the stock trade higher? The answer lies in the bid-ask spread. Very few people understand how this phenomenon actually works. As we said earlier, there is only a limited amount of stock for sale at each given price level. All we need to do to move a stock higher is to buy all the available stock at a given price and then buy more at higher levels. Our buying alone will cause the stock to tick higher. Let's see how it looks on paper.

Let's go back to our old example. The market in ZZZ is now:

36¹/₈–36³/₁₆ *20 × 13* *39,100*

Now assume a buyer comes forward who wants to buy 5,000 shares of stock at the market. This is an investor who heard a bullish rumor that the company's business prospects were improving. This investor thinks the stock is going to fly, and is afraid to miss the market by trying to buy the stock cheaper than where it is for sale. This investor believes the stock could easily be at 45 by the end of the week.

Therefore the investor wants an immediate execution at the best available price, and is not willing to bargain for a better price.

By entering a buy of 5,000 shares at the market, the investor is agreeing to buy the stock at whatever price the market has stock for sale. In exchange for a guaranteed execution that will take only a few seconds to fill, the investor forfeits the ability to negotiate a better price for the stock. Looking at the bid-ask spread, the investor knows that there are 1,300 shares for sale at 36⅜₁₆, but is uncertain at what price or prices the remaining 3,700 shares of the order will get executed.

So, the investor enters:

Buy 5000 ZZZ Market

When the order reaches the floor of the stock exchange, the specialist immediately trades 1,300 shares at 36⅜₁₆, the lowest price where stock is currently for sale.

1,300 shares are for sale at 36³⁄₁₆

$36^{1}/_{8}$–$36^{3}/_{16}$ 20×13 $39,100$

changes to:

Buyer of 5,000 shares at the market lifts all of the stock at 36³⁄₁₆

$36^{1}/_{8}$–$36^{1}/_{4}$ 20×15 $40,400$

Once the stock at 36³⁄₁₆ is taken, next best price at which stock is for sale is at 36¼

as 1,300 shares trade at 36³⁄₁₆.

What happened to the 36³⁄₁₆ stock? Simply put, the offer was lifted. This buyer took 1,300 shares at 36³⁄₁₆. Now the market reflects the next lowest offer, at 36¼. So far, only 1,300 shares of the 5,000-share order have been filled.

But the order is not done. We have 3,700 shares remaining. It is very important here to see how the market has changed. Remember from Example 5 that there were 1,500 shares for sale at 36¼. Then a trader came along who was willing to sell 1,300 shares at 36³⁄₁₆, underoffering the investor at 36¼. This seller at 36¼ did not cancel the order just because he or she got underoffered. The order still remains on the books.

So, there are now 3,700 shares left to buy on the order. As the bid-ask spread shows, the next price at which there is stock for sale is at 36¼. There are 1,500 shares for sale at that price. So, 1,500 shares immediately trade at 36¼.

There are 1,500 shares for sale at 36¼

36⅛–36¼   20 × 15   40,400

changes to:

Buyer of 3,700 shares buys all available stock for sale at 36¼

36⅛–36⁵⁄₁₆   20 × 42   41,900

Seller at 36¼ is cleaned out by the buyer

The next cheapest price at which stock is available for sale is at 36⁵⁄₁₆, as 1,500 shares trade at 36¼.

As we can see, the 1,500 shares were lifted at 36¼. So far, the buyer has bought 1,300 shares at 36³⁄₁₆ and 1,500 shares at 36¼. The order has been filled on a total of 2,800 shares. But the order is still not done. The buyer now has 2,200 shares remaining, which will get executed at the next lowest offer. Notice that the next lowest offer after 36¼ is 36⁵⁄₁₆, ¹⁄₁₆ point higher than the last print.

Now, with 4,200 shares for sale at 36⁵⁄₁₆, the specialist trades 2,200 shares at that price.

Buyer completes the order by buying 2,200 shares at 36⁵⁄₁₆

36⅛–36⁵⁄₁₆   20 × 42   41,900

changes to:

Seller at 36⁵⁄₁₆ had 4,200 shares for sale—now has only 2,200 left

36⅛–36⁵⁄₁₆   20 × 20   44,100

as 2,200 shares trade at 36⁵⁄₁₆ to complete the order.

Therefore, it took three different price levels to get a 5,000-share buy order filled. The buyer bought 1,300 shares at 36³⁄₁₆, 1,500 shares at 36¼, and 2,200 shares at 36⁵⁄₁₆. In the process, the stock ticked up ⅛ from 36³⁄₁₆ to 36⁵⁄₁₆ in a matter of only a few seconds. The stock was at 36³⁄₁₆ before this buy order reached the floor. Now, as we can see, the last trade was at 36⁵⁄₁₆, up ⅛. This is exactly what makes stocks move higher.

As this example demonstrates, the easiest way for a stock to move higher is if a buyer is willing to buy more stock than is for sale at a given price level. The buyer then lifts each consecutive higher offer until the order is complete.

As we can see, there is tremendous room for negotiation within the parameters of the bid-ask spread. We never want to trade at the market unless we absolutely have to. Using limit orders, we are able to buy and sell stock at better prices than by trading at the market. This is the difference between making money and losing money. Remember, the day trader is nothing more than a middleman in the buying and selling of stocks. The beauty is that the playing field is not level. We are in possession of trading techniques that give us a huge advantage over the buying and selling public. What we just saw in this chapter is information that 99 percent of the investing world does not understand. Their ignorance is the day trader's opportunity. We will gladly take the other side of their trades. This is the way Wall Street operates. It is the continual $\frac{1}{16}$s and $\frac{1}{16}$s that add up to thousands of dollars per month, if we trade enough. But it is not an easy job. These small profits must be fought for and earned at the bargaining table. The limit order is our bargaining tool. Use it wisely.

Unfortunately, we are not the only middlemen in the business of buying and selling stocks. On the New York Stock Exchange, there is someone much faster, better equipped, and more knowledgeable than the day trader—the specialist. The specialist is the one who controls the bid-ask spread, and is the best negotiator of all. And the specialist certainly doesn't like or need the day trader. The only way to make quick profits is to first deal with the specialist. That is why the next chapter is devoted entirely to understanding how the specialist operates.

Day traders must ask themselves one simple question: How does Wall Street make its money? The answer may surprise some people. Wall Street firms do not make billions of dollars per year by hitting home runs. They are not in the business of risking everything to make huge one-time gains. Instead, they make their money by hitting singles—small, consistent, high-percentage profits. These singles come in the form of $\frac{1}{16}$s, $\frac{1}{8}$s, and $\frac{1}{4}$s. It doesn't matter if the market goes higher, goes lower, or stays flat. The day trader should take note of this: 2,000, 3,000, 4,000 shares at a time, $\frac{1}{16}$ is $\frac{1}{16}$ any way you look at it. If you can make $\frac{1}{16}$ on every trade, and you trade enough volume, you are going to be rich in a very short time.

CHAPTER 8

The Role of the Specialist on the New York Stock Exchange

When day traders trade low-volatility NYSE Stocks, their profits come directly out of the specialists' pockets. The bid-ask spread allows the specialists to earn their profits at the expense of the investing public; and, ironically, by exploiting the bid-ask spread, the day traders earn theirs at the expense of the specialists. A good day trader is one who takes food out of the specialist's mouth. However, the day traders are not trading against the specialists, but rather with the specialists, by reading and copying the specialists' every move and then stepping in front of them on their trades. The specialists are the best negotiators and traders in the market. Where specialists buy, so should the day traders. That is why it is absolutely essential that day traders understand how specialists trade and the specialists' role in maintaining an orderly market.

Knowing the mechanics of price movement and the bid-ask spread is essential to being able to read the markets. But that is only half the challenge. Although the New York Stock Exchange brings together traders and investors with varying degrees of ability and knowledge, the reality is that in this market there are bigger and better players than you. There are mutual funds, hedge funds, banks, brokerage firms, and day traders all competing against each other and conspiring to outsmart the market. The competition among these groups is fierce, which is exactly why most opportunities for quick profit last only one to two seconds before someone capitalizes on them.

Of all the players in the market, the biggest threat to the day trader is not posed by the hedge funds, banks, or brokerage firms. It is posed by the person who sets the odds in the stock, namely the specialist. We have touched on the role of the specialist briefly in the earlier chapters. The role of the specialist is to maintain an orderly market. On the New York Stock Exchange, there is one specialist assigned to oversee all transactions in a particular stock. Each and every transaction that occurs on the floor of the exchange in that stock has to go through the specialist. A similar procedure is followed on the American Stock Exchange.

In the previous chapter, we used examples of various market and limit orders to show how the bid-ask spread moves to reflect changes in the intentions of buyers and sellers. As new buyers and sellers come into the market, and as stock trades at different prices, the bid, ask, bid size, ask size, and volume will change. It is the specialists' job to set and update the bid-ask spread and to ensure that the current market parameters are accurate. This can be a very difficult job in fast-moving and volatile markets, as the specialists' stocks get bombarded with limit and market orders at all different prices and sizes that must be reflected in the market.

In addition to ensuring that the general public's buy and sell orders are reflected in the market, specialists also take positions for their own accounts. Specialists are the best day traders of all. They will risk their own capital to take the other side of customer orders if the buy orders cannot be matched with sell orders. This ensures that stocks can trade freely and that liquidity doesn't dry up. The specialists' presence goes a long way in preserving stability and confidence in the market. Buyers and sellers know that under all circumstances there will always be someone who will take the other side of their trades at some price. In addition, they know their best interests are being protected in that they will always receive the best possible execution on their stock.

If a customer enters a buy or sell order at the market, the specialist in that stock is required to give an immediate execution regardless of market conditions. If the specialist cannot find buyers to match the sellers, he or she will take the stock into position, risking his or her own capital to ensure that the customer gets a fair execution.

Let's look at an example. If you pull up Hawaii Electric (HE), an electric utility, on your real-time quote system, the market might look as follows:

Specialist is willing to buy 500 shares from the public at 40¾

HE   40¾–41   5 × 5   18,900

Specialist is also willing to sell 500 shares to the public at 41

This quote tells you that there are 500 shares willing to be bought at 40¾, and 500 shares for sale at 41. Chances are, this is the specialist on both the bid and the offer. As an investor, if you want to sell 500 shares at the market, the specialist is usually the one who takes the other side of the trade by buying your stock from you. By bidding 40¾, the specialist is indicating to the investing public that he or she is willing to buy stock at 40¾. If you sold your stock at the market, you would be immediately filled by the specialist at 40¾. You would be the seller, the specialist would be the buyer.

Why would the specialist want to buy your stock? Two reasons. First, because he or she has to maintain an orderly market; but more importantly, because he or she hopes to be able to turn around and resell the stock to someone else at a higher price. He or she is indicating the intention to do so by the offer to sell 500 shares at 41. The next person to enter a buy at the market will pay $41 per share. Who will sell the stock to this person? The specialist, because he or she just bought the stock at 40¾ seconds ago from you. The specialist can make ¼ point, or $250, for every 1,000 shares he or she trades this way all day long, even if the stock doesn't move.

The specialist has a specific job to do, and gets compensated very handsomely for the work. In the preceding example, the specialist ensured that buyers and sellers both received a fair execution for their stock. And, the specialist got to skim a little off the top. But this job is not easy. The key to understanding the nature of the specialist is to be aware that he or she is forced to act in the best interests of the buying and selling public. Specialists will always ensure that you receive a fair execution because that is their job. They have to answer to the regulatory bodies if a customer complains of receiving an unfair execution. Therefore, specialists will always give priority to your buy or sell order over their own. This creates a tremendous opportunity for day traders, because they can essentially use the specialist to their own advantage in their trading. This seems relatively simple, but in reality it is far from easy.

As we said earlier, specialists are first and foremost day traders themselves. They are out to make as much money as they can by trading. They risk their own capital in order to earn a living in this process of maintaining an orderly market. So how is it possible for specialists to make money for themselves while also looking out for the best interests of the investing public?

Specialists are able to make money for themselves through the bid-ask spread, by taking the other side of your trades. At all times and under all circumstances, they are willing to be both buyers and sellers in the stock they trade. Like any good day trader, the specialist attempts to grind out ⅟₁₆s, ⅛s, and ¼s all day long. In other words, the specialist makes money by trading against the investing public.

So what makes specialists willing to put themselves at risk to buy and sell stock at all times, no matter what the circumstances? They are motivated by profit. As the last chapter demonstrated, there is always a price difference, or spread, between where potential buyers and sellers are willing to transact trades. If the market in Bethlehem Steel (BS) is 8 to 8⅛, there are buyers willing to pay $8 per share (the bid) and sellers willing to sell at $8.125 (the ask). The specialist will often be on both sides of the spread. This means that, if the stock doesn't move, the specialist buys from customers at 8 and sells to customers at 8⅛, making ⅛ point, or $125, for every 1,000 shares that trade evenly. Imagine a stock that trades 1 million shares in a day this way. The specialist would net a trading profit of over $125,000 in a stock that didn't move! Not bad for one day's work.

Specialist is willing to buy 1,000 shares from the public at 8

BS   8–8⅛   10 × 10   515,000

Specialist is willing to sell 1,000 shares to the public at 8⅛

It is important to note that even though the specialist is profiting handsomely on the trade, he or she is ensuring that the customer gets a fair execution. Imagine if the specialist were not in the stock. Stock would only trade at prices where buyers and sellers would agree. With no one willing to take the other side of any order, stocks would have wild intraday swings. Inevitably, the stock would trade in a choppy and erratic fashion, thus undermining the orderly nature of the New York Stock Exchange.

Let's look again at the preceding example in Bethlehem Steel. Assume, for the sake of argument, that the specialist is bidding for 1,000 shares at 8 and offering 1,000 shares at 8⅛. So long as the stock trades back and forth evenly, the specialist will be skimming ⅛ point for each position he or she can buy and sell. But what would happen if there weren't a specialist monitoring the stock? The bid-ask spread would widen substantially, because absent the specialist, traders would have to find price levels where true natural buyers and sellers were willing to pay for stock. The bid at 8 would disappear, as would the offer at 8⅛. What if the only other buyer in the stock wasn't willing to pay more than 7½ for stock? 7½ would be the new bid. And what if there weren't any sellers willing to sell stock for less than 8½? 8½ would be the new offer. The market would look like this:

Absent the specialist, the highest price a customer is willing to pay is 7½

BS   *7½–8½*   *10 × 10*   *515,000*

Absent the specialist, the lowest price at which a customer is willing to sell is 8½

A market that was 8 to 8⅛ now becomes 7½ to 8½. The bid-ask spread has widened from ⅛ point to 1 full point. Who loses when the spread widens? The investing public. Without the specialist someone who wanted to sell 1,000 shares at the market, would get filled at 7½ instead of 8, a full ½ point less than if the specialist was in the stock maintaining an orderly market. Conversely, a buyer of 1,000 shares at the market would have to pay 8½ for stock instead of 8⅛, because that is the only price at which stock is for sale. This is ½ point higher than if the specialist was in the stock. This wide spread essentially cost both of these customers $500 in lost profits. The price makers in this example made out like bandits by putting the screws to the general public, because the specialist wasn't there risking his or her capital. If the specialist had been present, he or she would not have allowed this to happen.

As you can see, the profit specialists make is their compensation for risking their capital to keep the market orderly. But their job isn't that easy. There are times when specialists are called on to be the buyer or seller of last resort. The most extreme example of this is when there is a huge sell-off in a stock. What happens if the news is so bad that there are very few potential buyers for the stock, but there are 2 million shares to be sold by the general public? Who is going to take the stock off these people's hands? If these sell orders are entered at the market, the specialist is obligated to give them an execution at some price. In a huge sell imbalance, the specialist will be unable to find buyers to match the sell orders. As a result, to ensure an orderly market in the stock, the specialist will be forced to buy a large piece of the 2-million-share position. But there is a catch. Specialists are able to set the price at which they buy the stock. Remember, they are risking their own capital to maintain an orderly market, and they are not stupid. Like good day traders, they will only buy at a price where they believe they can make a profit. Though exposing themselves to a substantial amount of risk by taking on such large positions, specialists will most likely make huge profits over the course of the day this way. They will buy the piece in one large 2-million-share share block, or *print,* then gradually feed the stock out to the investing public, hopefully making $\frac{1}{16}$s, $\frac{1}{8}$s, and $\frac{1}{4}$s along the way at prices higher than where the stock was bought.

The question may arise as to how fair it is that specialists are able to make such large sums of money at the expense of the public in an example like the preceding one. First of all, in this case the specialist was taking on a huge risk by buying 2 million shares from the public. In a sense, the specialist was looking out for sellers' best interests by stepping up to the plate as the buyer of last resort. No one else was willing to buy the stock, and for good reason. What if, after the specialist opened the stock for trading, there were a second investor stampede out of the stock? The specialist could stand to lose literally millions of dollars if the situation in the stock worsened, because he or she would still be forced to buy no matter how grim the circumstances became. Imagine what this situation would be like without the specialist. A stock like this could very easily lose 15 points if it were inundated with sell orders without any matching buy orders. So, as much as the specialist traded against the customers, he or she also acted in their best interests by guaranteeing them a fill on such a large sell order. That is why any profit the specialist makes in such a case is justified.

Part of the inherent advantage specialists have over the investing public lies in their ability to see the order flow. One of the prerequisites for being able to properly maintain an orderly market is having access to information the investing public is not privy to. It is often said that specialists have a license to steal, because they can act on priveleged information for their own benefit and profit, so long as it is within the parameters of the market. This essentially means that they are aware of buyers and sellers at price levels other than the current market, because they are holding these orders on their books. The general public will only see the highest bids and lowest offers posted, and will never have access to lower bids or higher offers. These orders are on the specialist's book, and may have an impact on the supply and demand, and thus the future price, of a stock.

Table 8.1 shows an example of a specialist's book in Hawaii Electric, using the same market as before:

HE   40¾–41   5 × 5   18,900

What the quote doesn't reveal to the day trader is how many other buyers and sellers there are in HE away from the market. The only one with access to this information is the specialist, who keeps it in his or her book.

Table 8.1   Specialist's book.

Buyers			
Shares	Price	Type	Firm
1,200	40½	Day	Prudential
2,500	40⅜	GTC	Olde
900	40	Day	Citigroup
100,000	39⅞	GTC	Goldman, Sachs
1,400	39¾	Day	Morgan Stanley Dean Witter

Sellers			
Shares	Price	Type	Firm
400	41¼	Day	Spear Leads
100	42	GTC	Waterhouse
200	42⅛	Day	Olde

As you can see, having this secret information is vital to knowing the true supply and demand in the stock. And the investing public is not privy to any of it. This gives specialists a huge advantage in determining at what price levels they want to buy and sell stock for their own accounts. In this case, what does the specialist see that you can't? Remember, the only information you have on HE is what your quote reveals: highest bid and lowest offer. That's it. You have no idea if there are big blocks of stock willing to be bought or sold at prices lower than the highest bid or higher than the lowest offer. In other words, is there stock in demand at prices lower than 40¾? Yes, there is. What the general public doesn't see about Hawaii Electric through the bid-ask spread is that a huge buyer lurks in the shadows. Look at the buyer at 39⅞. Goldman, Sachs is willing to buy 100,000 shares at 39⅞. If the stock never trades that low, you won't know that this order even exists, because you won't see it in your quote. It would have to get to a 39⅞ bid before you would see 100,000 reflected in the bid size. But the specialist knows. And, if anything, the specialist now knows, because of this large buy order, that there is a very good chance the stock won't trade lower than 39⅞ today. For the stock to trade lower, it will first have to trade through 100,000 shares at 39⅞, provided Goldman, Sachs doesn't cancel the order first.

This fact alone will make specialists more confident in taking the other side of customer sell orders by buying. They can be aggressive buyers because they know there is decent buying support at lower levels, which means the stock is not going to go lower. In this case, the specialist is probably even thinking that Goldman, Sachs might even raise their bid to a higher price if they get impatient. This buying alone could move the stock higher. Either way, at this point in the day, there is definitely an upward bias in the stock that you don't see. This fact magnifies the disadvantage you as a day trader face against the specialist. You are essentially trading with only half of the information.

Using this same example, imagine if the roles were reversed and there was a huge seller sitting ⅛ point above where Hawaii Electric was trading. If this is the case, the specialist will be less inclined to take stock into position, for fear that this seller has so much stock for sale that the stock will be unable to move higher. If this seller decides to unload, any buyer stepping into this stock, including the specialist, will feel like he or she has just unknowingly stepped in front of a freight train. Again, there is no way for you to tell. The stock is sure to go lower, but the bid-ask spread gives no indication. The only potential seller in HE that the public sees is the offer to sell 500 shares at 41.

BEING ON BOTH SIDES OF THE MARKET

The key to the specialist's trading profits is being on both sides of the market at the same time.

The best way to understand how the specialist makes profits is to show specific trading examples. Let's say you pull up the quote for Niagara Mohawk, an electric utility. The symbol is NMK, and the quote is as follows:

14⅝–15⅛   12 × 15   93,000

You know by now what the snap quote tells you. The bid is 14⅝ and the ask is 15⅛. The size of the market is 1,200 by 1,500 and the volume is 93,000. There is a buyer willing to buy 1,200 shares at 14⅝ (and no higher) and a seller willing to sell 1,500 shares at 15⅛ (and no lower). At this point in the day, 93,000 shares have changed hands.

The snap quote paints a surprising picture of the market in NMK. Look at the difference between the bid and the ask—a full ½ point. This spread seems unfairly wide for a stock that has traded 93,000 shares for the day. A spread of ½ point on a New York Stock Exchange–listed utility stock is not normal. There is a reason for this.

As already stated, the specialist is required to maintain an orderly market. In the case of Niagara Mohawk, at this point in the day assume the market is quiet. The active buyers and sellers in the stock, for whatever reason, have stepped away. In plain English, the buyers are not willing to step up, and the sellers are not willing to come down. The liquidity in the stock has dried up.

This is when specialists really earn their paychecks. With a bid-ask spread this wide, you would be at a severe and unfair disadvantage if you decided to buy or sell at the market. In fact, if you were to buy 1,000 shares at the market, and then immediately resell those 1,000 shares at the market, you would lose ½ point, or $500, on the trade. You would buy the stock at 15⅛ (where it is for sale) and then sell it at 14⅝ (the nearest buyer).

This is an extremely unfair market environment. With bid-ask spreads so wide, you would not be receiving fair market value for your stock. This is precisely when the specialist is needed most. The specialist will step into this market and narrow the spread. Chances are, the specialist would never allow the bid-ask spread to get this wide in the first place without first trying to close the gap.

The specialist would take a market that was:

14⅝–15⅛   12 × 15   93,000

and narrow the spread, updating the market to:

Specialist is both a buyer at 14⅞ and a seller at 15

14⅞–15   5 × 5   93,000

How did the specialist do this? By being on both sides of the market at the same time. The specialist is now both the highest bid and the lowest offer. Remember, there were no buyers willing to pay more than 14⅝ for stock, and there were no sellers willing to sell for less than 15⅛. The specialist, by bidding 14⅞, is now the highest bid, and is willing to pay ¼ more for stock than the bidder at 14⅝. In addition, by offering stock at 15, the specialist is now the lowest offer as well, and is willing to sell stock ⅛ point cheaper than the seller at 15⅛. The specialist has aggressively stepped up to the plate when no one else was willing to. As a result, the bid-ask spread has narrowed from ½ point to only ⅛ point. Anyone who buys or sells at the market will now benefit greatly from the narrowed spread. A seller would now get 14⅞ instead of 14⅝ for each share of stock, and a buyer would now only have to pay 15 instead of 15⅛. The benefit to the investing public is money saved. This benefit is due to the specialist.

What would prompt specialists to do this? In a sense, it is their job. They are required to maintain a fair and orderly market in the stock. A ½-point spread in a $15 electric utility is certainly not an orderly and liquid market. You would only expect a spread that wide in an extremely volatile stock, such as a technology stock. Wide spreads typically occur when the specialist is unsure of the future direction of the stock and therefore doesn't want to aggressively bid or offer stock for fear of getting picked off. But a low-volatility stock such as Niagara Mohawk, like most electric utilities, generally trades in a predictable fashion. A wide spread is unacceptable in a situation like this. If the stock is not volatile, the wide spread will hurt individual investors who trade at the market by forcing them to pay above-market prices for stock when they buy and to accept below-market prices when they sell. In this case, some investors might complain that they received an unfair execution. The New York Stock Exchange, as the champion of the individual investor's rights, has a reputation to preserve and would frown on this. That is why the specialists will acknowledge their job and responsibility to step forward, risking their own capital to ensure that both buyers and sellers receive fair market value for their stock.

But that is not the only motivation. Specialists are primarily motivated by profit. Remember, they are first and foremost day traders. By narrowing the spread, specialists put their trading capital at risk. And they will only put themselves at risk if they think they can profit in the process. By bidding 14⅞, and offering stock at 15, this specialist is advertising to the world that he or she is a buyer of NMK at 14⅞ and a seller at 15. Think about that. If the specialist can buy stock at 14⅞ and sell stock at 15, he or she will make ⅛ point even if the stock doesn't move. That would be $125 for every 1,000 shares that trade evenly. If there is enough trading volume in the stock, the specialist could make a small fortune in just a few hours this way.

As you can see, specialists can make a lot of money by trading actively in a stock when it doesn't move. They do this merely by taking the other side of the random buy and sell orders throughout the day. Day traders must attempt to do the same, making ⅟₁₆s and ⅛s on the market orders of the investing public.

That is the real reason the specialist steps in. At all times, this specialist will make sure there is an active and liquid market in Niagara Mohawk. This means he or she must be the buyer and the seller if no one else is willing to do so. If this case, there were buyers and sellers already in the stock, but at unrealistic price levels. The buyer was only willing to buy stock too low, and the seller was only willing to sell too high. If someone agreed to these prices, it would only be because that person didn't know any better: 14⅝ is far too cheap a price for someone to get stuck selling stock, and 15⅛ is too expensive for someone to have to buy. Usually, it would be the unknowing, unsophisticated individual investor who would get the short end of the stick in this kind of market. Those are the people who trust that the market is fair, which is why they enter market orders in the first place. The specialist will not betray their trust and allow that to happen. In this example, preventing that from happening means the specialist must raise the parameters of the market by keeping a two-sided market. The narrow spread ensures that buyers and sellers will receive fair market value on the executions.

HANDLING A LARGE SELL ORDER

The previous example demonstrated how a specialist could make quick trading profits by risking his or her own capital. By being on both sides of the market, specialists narrow the bid-ask spread to the point where they are involved in every trade that goes through the stock, regardless of whether they are buying or selling. At first glance, it seems like the specialists have an easy job, being able to make $\frac{1}{8}$s and $\frac{1}{16}$s all day long on the customer order flow even if the stock doesn't move. It is important to remember that anytime specialists keep a two-sided market, by being both the bid and the ask, they are at risk. There are no guarantees that the stock will trade in an orderly manner. Let's look at an example.

Here is the market in Niagara Mohawk:

14⅞–15   5 × 5   93,000

As the previous example showed, the specialist is both the bid and the ask. He or she is a buyer of 500 shares at 14⅞, and a seller of 500 shares at 15. Let's see what happens when a seller comes into the market and tries to pick off the specialist.

Let's say this seller knows bad news is going to come out about the stock at the end of the trading day. He or she wants to unload 5,000 shares at the market. This seller wants out of the stock immediately and doesn't care at what price. He or she is trusting that the specialist, unaware of this bad news, will provide a fair execution. So the order is entered and reaches the specialist's booth on the floor of the New York Stock Exchange:

Sell 5000 NMK Market

This presents a real dilemma for the specialist. It is his or her job to maintain an orderly and liquid market in the stock. The specialist is obligated to give this seller an immediate execution, because this is a market order. With the sell order in hand, the specialist now has to find buyers in the stock who will take these 5,000 shares. But where are the buyers? The previous example indicates that there is a buyer of 500 shares at 14⅞. This buyer is the specialist. But what about buyers other than the specialist? The preceding example also shows that there is a buyer of 1,200 shares at 14⅝. Aside from that, there isn't anyone else willing to buy the stock.

So this is a real problem. There is a seller who has decided to sell 5,000 shares at the market, agreeing to whatever price the market gives. The problem is that there seems to be no fair price at which there are enough buyers to match this sell order. There is a buyer of

500 shares at 14⅞ (the specialist) and a buyer of 1,200 at 14⅝. But that only takes care of 1,700 shares of the 5,000-share order. Other than that, there are no buyers anywhere. Regardless, the seller is guaranteed an execution at some price in the next few seconds.

This is where the specialist steps up to the plate. As the buyer and seller of last resort, the specialist is called on to take the other side of this 5,000-share sell order. Risking his or her own trading capital, the specialist will buy 5,000 shares from this seller. But at what price?

The price at which this stock will trade is entirely at the discretion of the specialist. Because there aren't enough natural buyers to buy the stock from this seller, the specialist can buy the stock at any price. He or she is fully aware of the responsibility to give the seller a fair market price for the stock. Naturally, the specialist is only going to buy the stock at a low enough fair market price to guarantee a profit. The specialist is not going to run a risk unless he or she can make money on the trade.

Most likely, the print will be at some price below 14⅞, possibly 14⅝. In that case the seller will receive 14⅝ for the entire 5,000-share order. The specialist will match the seller at the highest price at which a buyer can be found for the block of stock. The specialist picks the level where the old buyer is: at 14⅝. That buyer wants 1,200 shares. So the specialist matches the 1,200-share buyer with the seller. But that only takes care of 1,200 shares of the 5,000-share order. What about the remaining 3,800 shares, which must get executed? The specialist buys those 3,800 shares. The whole 5,000-share print occurs at 14⅝. Notice how this print occurs below the market, even though there was a bid at 14⅞. Is this a fair price? And why didn't some stock trade at 14⅞, where the highest bid was?

This is unquestionably a fair price. Other than the specialist, there were no buyers anywhere near where the stock was trading. Everyone wins in this kind of trade. The seller receives a fair execution, and the specialist buys at a level where he or she feels confident of making a small profit on the trade. The specialist hopes to be able to feed the stock out for ⅟₁₆s, ⅛s, and ¼s in the next few hours. This is his or her compensation for being the buyer of last resort. Remember, without the specialist, this seller might have driven the stock down a full point, because 14 or 13½ might have been the only price level where enough buyers could be found for this 5,000-share sell order.

This also raises another interesting question. How was it possible for the stock to trade at 14⅝ if there was a bid for 500 shares at 14⅞? Isn't the seller entitled to 14⅞ for the first 500 shares of the order? The answer is that because there was more stock for sale than there were buyers at the highest price level (14⅝), the whole piece could trade at a lower price. If this seller complained to the New York Stock Exchange that this was an unfair execution, the specialist would only have to point out that there weren't enough buyers anywhere, and 14⅝ is more than fair under these circumstances.

By buying the majority of this 5,000-share piece, the specialist is now exposed to a substantial amount of market risk. There really isn't anywhere to sell the stock right now if necessary. Therefore, the specialist is well aware that he or she will have to hold the stock in position for a while before becoming able to unload it. And there is no guarantee that the specialist will be able to sell the stock for more than he or she paid for it. This undoubtedly factors into the equation when determining the price. In addition, what would happen if this seller decided to sell another 5,000 shares at the market? Again, the specialist would inevitably have to buy the whole piece, as the buyer of last resort. The specialist could get buried by all the selling pressure. And there is no way to tell how much more stock might come out for sale before the end of the day. This is the risk the specialist must take. But this risk is in the best interest of all customers and traders involved in the stock—if, and only if, they are buying and selling at the market.

THE REAL INTENTIONS OF THE SPECIALISTS

The day trader must not be fooled into thinking that the specialists are only looking out for everybody's best interests. Within the parameters of market, specialists will use every possible advantage to trade against the day trader for their own profit. This is what the majority of the investing world does not understand. Specialists are obligated by certain rules to watch out for the individual investor. And, in the grand scheme of things, the individual investor's welfare is far better off with the specialists than without, because of the individual's reliance on buying and selling at the market. By taking the other side of these customer market orders, the specialists give the individual a fair execution while still watching out for their own best interests.

THE DAY TRADER AS SHADOW SPECIALIST

Thus, it can be said that the specialist ensures that market orders get executed fairly. But what happens if you are not trading at the market?

What if you want to enter a limit order? Does the specialist still look out for your best interests? In most instances, no. This is the fine line you must walk as a day trader. When you enter a limit order, the specialist is usually not the one who takes the other side of your trade. Therefore, the specialist looks at you as an adversary, as competition in the business of making money from the investing public. Specialists do not like day traders, and they will try to trade against you.

In fact, you don't want the specialist to take the other side of your trade because it usually means the stock will move against you and you are off your market. The specialist always has a stronger hand and more knowledge than you do. Always beware when, on a limit order, the specialist is willing to fill your order from his or her own account. Basically, when this occurs, the specialist is accepting your negotiating terms. This is very dangerous, because the specialist is the best negotiator of all and will only accept your terms when it is in his or her best interest. Whom do you want to take the other side of your trade? Someone who is smarter, better equipped, and more knowledgeable than you? Or someone with less information and less trading ability? Which of these two will lead to profits? You be the judge.

Anyone interested in day trading would conclude that being a specialist is the greatest of all jobs. Specialists have a huge advantage in the stock they trade, and as such, will usually make large sums of money over the course of the year by exploiting that advantage. Wouldn't it be great to be a specialist? The beauty of day trading New York Stock Exchange stocks is that day traders, by using well-placed limit orders, can serve the same function as specialists. Day traders can buy and sell at the same exact prices, before specialists are able to buy even one share. Limit orders allow day traders to step in front of specialists to get their orders executed. And the specialists cannot do anything about it. They are forced by the rules to give priority to customer orders over their own. This allows day traders to make high-percentage profits, normally reserved for the specialists, off the market orders of the buying and selling public. In a sense, by trading this way, day traders are taking food out of the specialists' mouths.

If you, as a day trader, are taking food out of the specialists' mouths and the specialists really can't do anything about it, what is their defense? The only thing they can do is try to trade against you. Specialists have far more information about the stock they trade than you do. They are better equipped, more knowledgeable, and better able to react to market moving information. When they can't profit off you, they will trade against you. Always beware when a specialist is trading against you, because you will inevitably lose money this way.

How exactly do specialists trade against you? Primarily in two ways. First of all, as mentioned earlier, specialists trade against you by taking the other side of your orders at the market. Anytime you enter a market order, you are fair game for specialists, because they are inevitably on the other side of your trade, only giving you a price that is in their best interests. Second, and more important for the day trader, specialists will attempt to trade against you when you use limit orders.

Using well-placed limit orders is the day trader's key to making consistent profits. It is also the key to the specialist's profits. Remember, specialists, by using limit orders, can make ⅛s and ₁/₁₆s all day even if the stock doesn't move. It is the random market orders of the investing public that occur throughout the day that allow this to happen, providing the specialists with the order flow from which they trade. Without orders, there is nothing for specialists to take the other side of. That is why they love an active market.

But what happens when the day trader also enters limit orders alongside the specialist? If the day trader is on top of the market and only bidding for stock at prices where he or she thinks a profit can be made, the specialist will be unwilling to take the other side of the trade. Why? Because it is not to the specialist's advantage to fill the order if it is at a low enough price, especially if it is at the same price where the specialist's limit order is. In other words, if the specialist is willing to buy at 14⅞, and the day trader is also willing to buy at 14⅞, the specialist is not going to take the other side of the day trader's order by selling. Why would the specialist sell stock to you at 14⅞ if he or she is willing to buy stock at 14⅞? The specialist will simply let the order go. He or she has no choice. When specialists can't profit off you, they will do everything in their power to trade against you, because they feel you are now invading their turf. And, in reality, you are.

By copying the exact moves of specialists, you serve the same function in the market as the specialists. How? By bidding for stock where the specialists are bidding, and offering stock where the specialists are offering. Obviously, the specialists don't like the fact that you are there with them. They probably look at you as a "parasite" that they can't get rid of. By what can they do? Nothing, really. The New York Stock Exchange has rules in place that always give priority to customer orders over the intentions of the specialist. This essentially means that if a customer (or day trader) is willing to buy stock at the same price where the specialist is willing to buy stock, the customer gets priority.

There is a reason the customer's order gets priority over that of the specialist. The New York Stock Exchange enacted these rules to keep the market fair for the individual investor. Think how unfair it would be if it were up to the specialist to choose whether the day trader or the specialist would get the stock first, assuming both were trying to buy at the same price at the same time. What would inevitably happen is that the specialist would allocate the stock to the customer's account when the stock was headed lower, and if the stock traded higher, the specialist would keep the stock and profit off it. That is why the New York Stock Exchange put these rules in place: to level the playing field so that individual investors were not unknowingly getting dumped on by specialists. All day traders do is exploit that rule to their advantage.

On the New York Stock Exchange, if a customer (or day trader) is willing to buy stock at the same price as the specialist, and stock trades at that price, the customer is entitled to the stock over the specialist. While the day trader may step in front of the specialist, under no circumstances can the specialist jump in front of, or front-run, the day trader. Exploiting this rule is the day trader's key to making consistent short-term profits.

This is an extremely important concept to grasp. Perhaps an analogy would shed some light on this. Think of the largest used car dealership you know of. How do they make their profits? By buying cars from the general public at low prices and reselling to the general public at higher prices. The owner of the dealership profits from the spread between where the cars are bought and where they are sold. The general public, unfortunately, is at the mercy of this spread. The owner of the dealership is entitled to the profit because of the risk he or she takes. The dealer might not be able to resell a car after taking it into inventory. In addition, there is overhead and salaries to pay. The profit the dealer makes on the spread is his or her livelihood.

How do you think the owner of the used car dealership would feel if you went into the office and demanded to buy and sell the same cars at the same price as the dealer? Even worse, if you demanded first dibs on any car that came to the dealership to be sold? Suppose the dealer was prepared to bid $5,000 for a used car, and you were too. And you said that, because you were a customer, you were entitled to the car over the dealer if you were both bidding the same price. This would never happen in a million years. The owner of the dealership would not appreciate your attempt to take food out of his or her mouth. Chances are, the owner of the used car dealership would kindly ask you to leave before he or she called the cops.

As crazy as it sounds, when the day trader bids at the same prices as the specialist, this is exactly what is happening. Look at the specialist as the owner of a used stock dealership. The specialist earns a livelihood by buying and reselling stocks, just as the used car dealer buys and resells cars. The rules that give priority to a customer over the specialist at the same price create a situation exactly like being able to step in front of the owner of a used car dealership and have first crack at the car, at the exact same price the dealer is willing to pay. Think of the amazing possibilities for profit that this rule would allow.

If this could happen, and enough people knew about it, eventually the car dealership would go out of business. The customers would be taking food right out of the owner's mouth by intercepting his or her profits. The customers, not the dealership owner, would now be the middlemen in the buying and selling of cars. Although this rule doesn't exist in the world of used car dealerships, it does exist in stock trading. So how is the specialist able to stay in business? Don't most people try to exploit this rule for their own profit? The answer is no. The specialist is able to stay in business because so few people understand how this rule works and that it even exists. That is why the day trader who knows how to exploit this rule can make a small fortune.

But just like the used car dealer, the specialists are not going to be happy when a customer or day trader attempts to take food out of their mouths. In fact, specialists will do everything possible within the rules to make it difficult for you to make money trading this way. Can you blame them?

As long as you are on top of your market, there is really no way the specialists can do anything. It is only when you are off your market that they get the opportunity to pick you off and trade against you. So how can you be assured of being on top of your market? The only way is to buy at the exact levels where the specialists are buying, and to sell exactly where they are selling.

The only way for day traders to ensure they won't get picked off by specialists when using limit orders is to bid for stock at the exact same price as the specialists. The specialists know the stock they trade better than anyone else, and as such, they know what are good price levels and what aren't. Day traders must realize that the specialists are only going to buy stock at levels where they feel they can make a profit, so copying them by picking the same price level to buy at is the easiest way to make profits day trading.

For an example of how this strategy works, let's use the original example of Niagara Mohawk. The market when we looked last was:

The specialist is a buyer at 14⅞ and a seller at 15

14⅞–15   5 × 5   98,000

As a good day trader, you will absolutely love a bid-ask spread like this. There is ample opportunity for profit in this example. The trading strategy is clear: You will bid alongside the specialist at 14⅞. How do you know the specialist is bidding 14⅞? That comes later in the chapter. For now, just realize that if the specialist is willing to buy 500 shares at 14⅞, it must be a safe level for you to buy as well. The beauty of this strategy is that you do not have to do any homework on the stock before entering the trade. You are aware that the specialist knows the stock better than anyone else in the world. Specialists will not buy at a level where they think they will lose money. That fact alone is reason enough for you to join in.

Bidding alongside the specialist is the day trader's short-term equivalent of an investor buying the same stock that Warren Buffett is buying. Billionaire Warren Buffett of Omaha is considered the greatest investor of all time. Many of the best investors in the world will throw caution to the wind and buy the same stock he is buying, even if they have not done any homework on the stock. They only need to know that Buffett is buying. They justify this by saying that if Buffett likes the stock, he must see something that other people don't see. Many investors have a made a fortune investing with Warren Buffett this way over the last 30 years.

So, with this in mind, you will attempt to buy NMK at the same price where the specialist is attempting to buy, 14⅞. Over the Internet, you enter the order:

Buy 2000 NMK 14⅞ DAY

Now, notice what happens when the order reaches the floor of the New York Stock Exchange. Because the specialist is bidding 14⅞, he or she must let your buy order go in front. Therefore, the market will change from:

Specialist is willing to buy 500 shares at 14⅞

14⅞–15   5 × 5   98,000

Day trader wants to pick off specialist and also buy stock at 14⅞

14⅞–15   20 × 5   98,000

Specialist is obligated to give first priority to day trader's buy order at 14⅞
Specialist is forced to cancel own buy order at 14⅞ as day trader steps in front

As you can see, the specialist lets your 2,000-share order go in front of his own. If the 500-share bid were a customer order and not the specialist, the bid size would change to 25, not 20, and you would be in line behind the 500 shares that were there first. However, because it was the specialist bidding for 500, your stock gets first priority at 14⅞. This means that the next 2,000 shares that trade at 14⅞ go to you before the specialist buys even a single share of stock.

If you are fortunate enough to buy the stock at 14⅞, there is a very good chance you will be able to make $\frac{1}{16}$ on the trade. The strategy is to resell the stock at 14¹⁵⁄₁₆, making $125 on the trade. The great thing about this trade is that there is very little downside risk. You know that, with the specialist also bidding 14⅞, this is a great entry point in the stock. This is an example of a trade where the odds of success are greatly in your favor as a day trader. And remember, the stock doesn't have to move for you to make $\frac{1}{16}$ this way.

So, with the odds in your favor, how is it possible for the specialist to trade against you in this example? Fortunately, there is only one way: smoke and mirrors. The specialist can try to scare you away from the trade by making it appear that the stock is heading lower when in fact it is not. The specialist will do this by manipulating the ask price or ask size, or both, in the attempt to give the appearance that there is a big seller looming. If it looks like the stock is going lower, you might be tempted into canceling your order. Remember, specialists will do all they can to trade against you within the parameters of the market. This kind of strategy is fair game for them because it does not violate any rules.

As a day trader, you will find that specialists generally will not bother you unless you repeatedly trade in and out of their stock. If you are an active trader in the same stocks, their specialists will probably get to know your trading strategy because they see every order you enter. For instance, after a while, the specialists will know that you are not an investor but a day trader who will resell the stock for a $\frac{1}{16}$-point profit as soon as you buy it. If you are trading in and out of the same stocks frequently, their specialists will probably get annoyed by your presence, because your trading is taking profits away from the specialists. Remember, the 1/16-point profit you make by exploiting the bid-ask spread is one less 1/16 the specialist will make that day.

This is why I prefer to move around and trade different stocks. If you are only in a stock once, and you are trying to buy at the same price where the specialist is buying, the specialist will be more inclined to leave you alone than if you trade in and out of the stock frequently. If the specialist is unfamiliar with you, the environment will be far more favorable for a quick 1/16 than if he or she is familiar with your strategy. It's just like a poker match. You never want to reveal your hand to anyone, particularly not the specialist. The last thing you want is for the specialist to know when you are attempting to buy stock that the stock is going to be coming right back seconds later in the form of a sell.

HOW CAN YOU DETERMINE WHERE THE SPECIALIST LURKS IN THE STOCK?

The key to making money day trading NYSE stocks is to pick the same buy and sell levels as the specialist. It sounds easy enough, but before you can pick the same buy levels, you have to identify exactly where the specialist is in the stock. You certainly don't want to pick a buy level because you mistakenly think the specialist is bidding there, only to find out it is another day trader or customer like yourself. If that happens, you will be setting yourself up to get picked off. Making this distinction is one of the most important skills you can develop as a trader. Remember, when you look at the quote in the stock, you only see prices and size; you can't see who the players are. For instance, if the market is 14⅞ bid, offered at 15, 10 × 10, you won't know who is bidding for stock and who is offering stock. The only thing you know for sure is the number of shares willing to be bought or sold and the price. However, that does not tell the whole story. Is the specialist trying to accumulate stock, or is it one of the big brokerage firms? Does someone have an ax to grind in the stock? Being able to answer these questions is vital to predicting short-term movement in the stock.

The problem is that there is really no way to know with absolute certainty who is bidding or offering stock at any given time. Only the specialist and other traders on the floor of the exchange have access to that information. As a day trader trading from home, the only thing you can go on is the clues the market gives you. In trading, there are no certainties. At all times, you are basing your actions on your instinct, your best guess of what the situation is. That is all you can do.

So you will have to do some detective work. Study the stock. Examine the prints. Look where the trades have been. Are they little trades or big ones? Are they 100-share trades, or 5,000-share trades? Have they all been at the same price? Is stock trading on the bid or the offer? These clues will help you formulate your conclusion. But the first and best clue is revealed by the bid size and the ask size. The rule of thumb I use is that if the size of the bid (or ask) is a round number like 500 or 1,000 shares, there is a good chance it is the specialist and not a customer bid. If it is an odd number, like 2,700 or 5,500, you can be almost certain it is a customer bid and not the specialist.

Why do specialists normally bid in 500- or 1,000-share lots instead of larger amounts? Because they don't ever want to get blindsided by a large sell order they can't see coming. By only bidding for 500 shares, they are assured that a seller can only sell a maximum of 500 shares at most to them at the current price. The specialist will be able to buy anything more than 500 shares at a lower price. Because of the specialists' responsibility to be buyer and seller of last resort, they never want to accumulate large pieces of stock unless they are forced to. This helps keep their position light when the market is quiet. This way, if a large seller comes into the market, the specialists are able to buy the stock at lower prices at their discretion. Specialists bidding for 5,000 shares instead of 500 might run into trouble because, if that is the market they are advertising, they will be forced to buy 5,000 shares at that price if a seller comes out. Under no circumstances are specialists allowed to back away from a trade, unless they cancel their bid before the seller arrives. So, by only bidding for small amounts, the specialists' exposure to risk is somewhat protected.

Let's look at an example of how to tell the difference between a specialist bid and a customer bid in Equity Residential Properties (EQR), a real estate investment trust.

Look at the size of the sell order at 41⅛—it is for 10,900 shares

EQR   41–41⅛   34 × 109   98,500

This market is clearly a customer offer to sell

A specialist who really wanted to unload 10,900 shares would not reveal his or her hand to the investing public by advertising an intention to sell.

Notice the evenly matched bid size and ask size here:

EQR   41–41⅛   5 × 5   98,500

This is clearly the specialist bidding and offering stock, and not customers

Remember, you only want to attempt to buy at prices where the specialist is buying. You don't want to mistakenly buy at levels where other customers, and not the specialist, are buying. The odds of turning a profit on the trade are much better when you are trading with the specialist.

JOCKEYING FOR POSITION

You want to know where the specialist is in a stock so that you can mirror his or her moves. But it is extremely important to identify where the specialist lurks for another reason as well. When you are trading low-volatility stocks, position is everything. The New York Stock Exchange is a first come, first serve market. This means that, when you are bidding, you always want to be first in line at the price level at which you are trying to buy stock. Otherwise, if your order does not arrive first, you will have to get in line behind any orders that arrived ahead of yours. The only way you can be assured of being first in line is when your bid replaces the specialist's bid. Where you are in line can determine whether you make money or lose money on the trade.

Remember, these are not market orders. They are limit orders, and as such they require a wholly different approach, because with a limit order there is never a guarantee that you will buy your stock. For example, let's say you have been watching a group of electric utilities all morning. Niagara Mohawk has caught your eye today because of the wide bid-ask spread in the stock. You are confident that, if you can buy it on the bid, you will be able to flip it out for a quick ⅟₁₆ based on its trading range this morning. The bid was 15, but the stock has just ticked ⅛ lower, and now the bid is 14⅞ for only 500 shares. This is the opportunity you have been waiting for all day.

You immediately enter a buy of 2,000 shares on a 14⅞ price limit. The market changes as follows:

Specialist is willing to buy 500 shares at 14⅞

14⅞–15   5 × 5   98,000

changes to

Customer order to buy 2,900 at 14⅞ takes priority over the specialist

14⅞–15   29 × 5   98,000

Specialist cancels own buy order as customer steps in front

changes to

14⅞–15   49 × 5   98,000

Second customer order reaches the floor for 2,000 shares at 14⅞, but must get in line behind customer order for 2,900 shares that arrived first

What has happened here?

You are a bit taken back as you see the market change. In the span of two seconds, the bid at 14⅞ went from 500 shares to 2,900 shares to 4,900 shares. You thought you were the only person watching the stock. Obviously, you weren't. Someone else is bidding alongside you at 14⅞! You only wanted 2,000 shares, but now there are 4,900 shares willing to be bought at 14⅞. Now you are not alone. Someone else wants 2,900 shares at 14⅞.

This is a very important point about day trading. You are not the only one who is watching these stocks. Every opportunity that looks good to you usually looks good to other people as well. That is why it is imperative that you enter your orders as quickly as possible when you see the chance to make a quick profit. I cannot tell you how many times I have missed out on profits because I was a second too slow.

HOW DO YOU KNOW WHERE YOU STAND IN LINE?

The first question you must answer is where you stand in line. There are a total of 4,900 shares willing to be bought at 14⅞. And 2,000 shares are yours. This is all you know for sure. There is no way to tell where your 2,000 shares are in line, unless you examine how the market has changed. You must attempt to find out, because this could mean the difference between buying the stock and making a $\frac{1}{16}$-point profit, or not being able to buy the stock at all. Remember, there might be only 2,000 shares that trade at the magic price of 14⅞ all day, and you want to make sure you are first in line so that you are entitled to the stock if someone is stupid enough to sell it to you there. If you find out you are last in line, you might think about canceling and moving on to another stock where you will have a better opportunity to buy at your price level.

There are two ways to can find out where you stand. The way most Wall Street traders do it is by sending one of their firm's floor brokers out to talk to the specialist directly. The specialist will usually give this information out to friends and colleagues on the floor, who then relay the information upstairs to the trader. In this example, if the information came back that there were 2,900 shares ahead, it would mean you were not first in line. There would be 2,900 shares ahead of your order at 14⅞. Unless this other order canceled, you would will have to wait until at least 2,900 shares traded at 14⅞ before you would be able to buy a single share. The reality is that, because this other trader got in line before you, that person might be able to have the stock bought and sold for a $\frac{1}{16}$-point profit before you even got your order filled. All because that order reached the specialist's booth a few seconds before yours did. Those few seconds were the difference between making $125 and not making anything at all.

Unfortunately, when trading from home over the Internet, you don't have the luxury of being able to send someone down to the floor to talk to the specialist. That kind of service costs money. The online brokers are generally not going to take the time to find out this kind of information for you. But that doesn't mean you can't find out. There is an easier way to determine the position of this order. All you have to do is look at changes in the bid size. In this case, if you are watching the quote carefully, you will see how the specialist updates the market. The bid size goes from:

14⅞–15   5 × 5   98,000

to:

14⅞–15   29 × 5   98,000

to:

14⅞–15   49 × 5   98,000

Notice how the bid size has changed. It went from 5 to 29 to 49—in other words, from 500 shares to 2,900 shares to 4,900 shares—in a matter of a few seconds. That alone gives you enough information to go on. Your order was the last one to get down to the floor. The other trader, who wanted 2,900 shares, got there before you. There is no question about this. The bid went from 5 to 29, or from 500 shares to 2,900 shares. The specialist was bidding for 500, then gave priority to the 2,900-share order when it arrived. Then, about two seconds later, your order for 2,000 reached the specialist, who put you behind the 2,900 shares for a total bid size of 4,900 shares. As you can see, you have to be alert and watch the quote as your order is entered. If your quote system has *Time and Sales,* you will be able to pull up the recorded changes in the market. *Time and Sales* is usually only available on the more expensive quote systems: Therefore, if you don't have it, you have to be extra careful not to miss the changes in the market. If you do, you will be left guessing as to where your order stands.

The alert reader might be confused by why the bid size is 4,900 shares and not 5,400 shares. There were 500 shares bid for at 14⅞, the customer order for 2,900 shares, and then the order for 2,000. So that makes a total of 5,400 shares and not 4,900 shares willing to be bought at 14⅞. Therefore, the bid size at 14⅞ should be 54, not 49, right? Wrong! The first 500 shares was the specialist. Therefore, the specialist simply cancels his or her bid for 500 shares and lets the customer orders for a total of 4,900 shares go instead. In essence, both traders have stepped in front of the specialist, and there is not a thing the specialist can do about it.

In these slower-moving markets, there will only be a limited number of shares that trade at a given price level where it may be easy to make a quick ⅟₁₆-point profit. The game of day trading requires that you be patient enough to wait to accumulate your stock at your price, if an unknowing seller is foolish enough to sell it to you there. It is very easy to buy stock at higher price levels where you won't be able to make a quick ⅟₁₆, because you will always be able to find someone to sell it to you there. You alone could buy 10 million shares of this stock if you had enough capital. But it certainly wouldn't be at a price where you could make a quick profit. Remember, the market does not give money away. You are going to have to fight for every precious share you buy at levels you deem cheap, and the last thing you want is for someone else to get to the stock before you. "Cheap" is always that level where you will be able to sell immediately for a quick profit, no matter what price that is. That is why it is absolutely imperative that you attempt to get your hands on as many cheap shares as possible when the opportunities arise. That is why position is everything. In some of the less active stocks that have daily volumes of less than 50,000 shares, you may only see 2,000 shares trade at your price level throughout the whole day. If there are two people both trying to bid for 2,000 shares at the same price, the difference between getting an execution and not getting an execution might be your place in line. And that place in line is determined by who gets there first.

If the specialist is the only one bidding for the stock, and you decide to bid along, he or she will let you go in front and you will be first in line. This means that you will be entitled to the next stock that trades at your price, even if the specialist was there before you. The rule is different if another day trader or customer has gotten there first. If another customer is already bidding in the stock, you will have to get in line behind him or her; you will only be entitled to stock after the entire first order has been filled.

THE IGNORANCE OF THE INVESTING PUBLIC

In this chapter I have outlined the basic principles behind exploiting the bid-ask spread. As you can see, by trading with the specialist, you tip the odds of success in your favor because you are only buying at levels that are deemed cheap. You should not care if the stock is cheap in the absolute sense of the word. It is only considered cheap at the price where the specialist is willing to buy it. That is all you need to know. Respect the judgment of the specialists. They didn't get where they are by being bad traders or making foolish decisions. They are the best day traders in the world, and they are only going to buy at levels where their instincts tell them stock is cheap.

It seems as though 99 percent of the investing world is unaware of the rule that specialists must give priority to customer orders over their own. The idea that you can buy stock at the same price where the specialist is willing to buy it seems strange to most people. The general public has for decades been brainwashed into thinking that the only way they can buy a stock is at the market, by purchasing it where the specialist or market maker has it for sale. The concept of being able to negotiate a better price, to buy on the bid and sell on the ask, is probably foreign to most people's preconceived notions of trading. Most think they have no choice but to buy at the ask and sell at the bid, because the market maker is entitled to the spread. Well, this book shows otherwise. You have to look at things inversely from the way you previously understood them. This is not an easy thing to do. Taken a step further, the fact that you can make a small fortune in a stock that doesn't move by day trading is probably the hardest thing to fathom, because it seems to go against common sense. You'd be surprised to know how many people, even those working on Wall Street, have no idea this can even be done.

The irony of this fact is that the general public's ignorance is exactly what allows you to make profits. Remember, for a limit order to be executed, there has to be a market order to take the other side of the trade. But who are the people buying and selling at the market? Don't they know they can save money by trying to negotiate a better price? Well, it certainly isn't the specialists taking the other side of these limit orders. Of all people, they are the absolute last ones to buy and sell at the market. It's the investing public that buys and sells at the market. Their actions are what makes Wall Street go around. As such, the last thing Wall Street wants is for the general public to be educated in the ways of stock trading. As long as investors still subscribe to the myth that the only way to buy and sell stocks is at the market, the specialists, market makers, and brokerage firms will be happy. This ensures that the public remains the food and the prey of Wall Street. And, in the process, the public helps put food on the day traders' tables.

BEWARE OF THE SPECIALIST

Now that you know a little bit about how the specialist maintains an orderly market, and how to exploit the specialist's two-sided market for your own profit, a word of caution is appropriate. As you know, the reality of exploiting the bid-ask spread is that the day trader is taking food out of the specialist's mouth. This is a very dangerous thing to do, but it is the only realistic way for you to make consistent money if you subscribe to the belief of only trading when the odds are in your favor. Remember, the specialists do not like day traders. They do not want or need customers like you. As such, specialists are fully aware of your presence. You are not going to be able to hide from them. The only way you can protect yourself is to be very selective as far as what prices you put your limit orders in. Specialists will exploit any weakness you have in the attempt to drive you away from their markets. This means they will trade against you every chance they get. But the only chance you give them to do this is when your bid or ask is off the market. When this happens, the specialists will take the other side of your order, usually resulting in your losing money.

That is why it is absolutely essential that you only use this strategy on stocks that don't move. Low-volatility stocks, such as closed-end funds, utilities, and real estate investment trusts are ideal markets for this kind of trading. The larger stocks, however, are not. If you try to get in the specialists' way on the bigger, more volatile stocks, you will get crushed. I guarantee you will lose money if you attempt to exploit the bid-ask spread in Dow stocks or other fast-moving issues. These markets simply move too fast for the day trader to react, and the specialists' advantage is too great. That is why other strategies are needed in those markets. We will deal with these in later chapters.

SECTION IV

Trading for Teenies

Taking Food out of the Specialist's Mouth

As a day trader, you must leave no stone unturned in your quest for profits. But the New York Stock Exchange has over 3,000 issues. Where do you even begin? Where do you look for your first trade? Surprisingly, the best opportunities are often found in areas overlooked by the rest of the investing community. In the New York Stock Exchange's other markets, including closed-end funds, electric utilities, and real estate investment trusts, lies a gold mine for the day trader who knows what to look for.

Does a stock have to move for you to make money in it? No, it does not. What the investing world doesn't understand is that you can make just as much money, or in some cases even more money, day trading a stock that doesn't move instead of one that moves.

But if the stock doesn't move, where are the trading profits coming from? Right out of the specialist's pocket. How do you do it? By exploiting the bid-ask spread, grinding out $\frac{1}{16}$s, or teenies, one trade at a time, all day long.

CHAPTER 9

The Day Trader's Secret Weapon

Exploiting the Bid-Ask Spread

The reality of online trading is simple: the second day traders enter a trade over the Internet, they enter a dangerous playing field where they are outgunned, outmatched, and outclassed by the faster players in the market. To survive, they must be risk averse, cautious, and alert. And they must never forget one simple fact: when you have a slow execution, volatility is not your friend, it is your enemy.

Smart day traders will do all they can to eliminate this inherent disadvantage caused by the Internet's slow execution. Their livelihood depends on it. How can they achieve this? Sometimes by leaving the glamor stocks to someone else, and sticking with "boring" low-volatility stocks instead. Others can have Yahoo!, Dell, and Compaq: The intelligent day trader will realize that these stocks are not the only game in town. Remember, day traders do not need movement to make money. Nor do they need to take on a high degree of risk to turn a profit.

So what is the key? The answer lies in $\frac{1}{16}$s. The trade for the teenie in a slow-moving stock, if done correctly, is probably the safest on the face of the earth. Why pick slow-moving stocks? Because 99 percent of the trading world doesn't bother with them. These stocks tend to fall through the cracks because they are not hot, exciting, or "sexy." But this lack of interest by the trading com-

munity is the day trader's secret weapon. And the weapon allows day traders to do one thing: grind out ¹⁄₁₆s all day long without the rest of the world even noticing.

Contrary to popular belief, stock trading does not have to be like playing the slot machines, craps, or roulette. If your strategy is to make every trade relying on instinct, on gut, and on chance, your fate is sealed. Over the long term, you will not win. In fact, you probably will not last more than a few weeks. Unfortunately, this is the way many people approach trading. They begin by trading volatile stocks like Microsoft, Dell, Yahoo!, and IBM. And they usually find out the hard way that they can't compete. These stocks simply move too fast to get in and get out. It seems there is always someone faster beating the online day trader to the punch. But there is a better way. Day trading can be more cerebral, more like a chess match, as long as you stick to the right stocks.

I have spent the first sections of the book trying to give you an idea of the dangerous environment you will enter when you make your first trade. But there comes a certain time when you have to take the leap of faith, stop leaning on the advice of others, and start relying on your own ability and skill. Right now that time has arrived. It is time to get down to the task at hand: trading. All the preparation in the world means nothing when your money is on the line. So you have to proceed very cautiously and make sure you have every base covered before you risk even a single penny of your trading capital. We will start by addressing the most basic questions.

HOW CAN YOU POSSIBLY MAKE ANY MONEY TRADING STOCKS THAT DON'T MOVE?

Think of the last time you glanced in your local paper to see how your favorite stocks had done the day before. Remember all the stocks that were unchanged, up ⅛, or down ⅛ on the day? On any given day, there are literally hundreds of stocks that fall into this category. The investing public's first impression is that because there was no action in these stocks, there was no way to make any money in them. But did anyone make any money in these stocks? Was it a lost cause? No, it was not. I guarantee that in each and every one of these stocks, someone made a small fortune. And the way they did it would surprise most people. Thousands of dollars were made, and all the while no one even noticed. But how did this happen?

Let's look at an example. Say you have been keeping your eyes on Bethlehem Steel (BS). It had a nice run earlier in the week, but for the last two days it has hovered around $10. In fact, in yesterday's paper, the quote reads:

BS *Last* **10** *Unchanged High* **10⅛** *Low* **10**

Most investors would agree that no money was made or lost in the stock on this day. The stock didn't even fluctuate higher than ⅛ point from its high to its low all day long. This belief that no money was made is based on the fact that long-term investors saw that the stock remained unchanged on the day. For them, this means that, regardless of the price at which they bought the stock, their account's value remained unchanged if the stock didn't move. In other words, the 1,000 shares they own are worth no more today than yesterday.

The important thing to remember is that these people are investors, not traders. They have a much longer time horizon, and they tend to look at things in a different way. But traders see things differently. They don't look at Bethlehem Steel as a lost cause, as a stock that was unchanged on the day. Smart traders see a potential gold mine in the stock.

THE ROLE OF THE SCALPER

The first thing the day trader would look at is the trading volume. Bethlehem Steel traded over 300,000 shares yesterday. For the 300,000 shares that traded, someone took the other side of every single trade. What does this mean? It means there is a very good chance that short-term speculators were active in the stock. Who are these speculators? The primary speculator is undoubtedly the specialist, the one who oversees all trading in the stock. Is there anyone else? Yes, a type of day trader called a *scalper.* Scalpers are so named because they exist by scalping razor-thin profits in stocks that aren't moving. I consider myself a scalper, and I hope that by the end of this book you will consider yourself one as well.

What does the scalper see that other people don't? Volume. When the scalper sees volume, he or she sees the chance to make ¹/₁₆s, or teenies, all day long on the order flow. Remember, the stock does not need to move in any one direction for ¹/₁₆s and ⅛s to be made. The important thing to keep in mind is that anytime a stock trades a few hundred thousand shares in a day, there is ample opportunity for short-term profit. On 300,000 shares of volume, someone made out like a bandit.

*BS Last **10** Unchanged High **10⅛** Low **10***

What the general public sees is a stock that remained unchanged from the day before. What the quote doesn't reveal is the real action in the stock. What was the specialist doing? What were the day traders doing? Both were scalping small profits in the stock all day long.

Table 9.1 is a copy of a scalper's activity in the stock. As you can see, this day trader, or scalper, traded in and out of Bethlehem Steel eight times in one day, netting $420 in the process. Think about that. The scalper made $420 day trading in a stock that didn't fluctuate more than ⅛ point all day. What is the secret? There is none. The key is that the scalper is trading 2,000 to 3,000 shares at a time. When a scalper trades size, he or she only needs to make ¹⁄₁₆s, or teenies, to make a very substantial profit. The teenies begin to add up by the end of the day. If you do this enough, you may find that you have a made a few thousand dollars in a day trading this way.

Your easiest and most profitable trade as a day trader is for ¹⁄₁₆s, or teenies. But you must trade at least 2,000 shares at a time, so that each trade nets at least a profit of $125 before commissions (see Table 9.2). The chances of profit are much better when you try to make ¹⁄₁₆ on 2,000

Table 9.1   Scalper's daily trading log.

Bought	3,000	10	
Sold	3,000	10¹⁄₁₆	+187.50
Bought	3,000	10	
Sold	3,000	10¹⁄₁₆	+187.50
Bought	2,000	10¹⁄₁₆	
Sold	2,000	10⅛	+125
Bought	2,500	10	
Sold	2,500	10	EVEN
Total for the Day		+500	On 8 Trades (Less $80 in Commissions)
Net Profit after Commissions +420			

Table 9.2   **Profit margins when trading for teenies.**

⅟₁₆ on 1,000 shares	+ 62.50
⅟₁₆ on 2,000 shares	+125.00
⅟₁₆ on 3,000 shares	+187.50
⅟₁₆ on 4,000 shares	+250.00
⅟₁₆ on 5,000 shares	+312.50

shares than when you try to make ½ point on 200 shares of a more volatile stock.

HIT SINGLES, NOT HOME RUNS

It is important to note a theme mentioned earlier in the book. Look at Wall Street. What do the brokerage firms do differently than the investing public when they trade? It is very simple. They are not in it for the long term, nor are they trying to make big gains on each trade. This is what I mean when I say that they are not trying to hit home runs. That is not why these firms pay their traders multimillion-dollar salaries. Remember, every time a trade is made, someone's money is on the line. And Wall Street firms are extremely careful how and where their trading capital is put at risk. Every trade they make is a well-calculated, precise move. In addition, they are very content with taking small profits and not getting greedy. All because they know that, year in and year out, these small profits are exactly what keep trading firms in business.

That is the point I am trying to drive home: The teenie is your best trade. You can literally make a living on teenies, as I have done for over two years. Why does going for singles work so well? Because it is done in an environment where the rest of the world is trying to hit home runs. Think about it. Why do investors buy a stock in the first place? Most are not in the game for ⅟₁₆, ⅛, or ¼ point. They are in it for the long haul—to buy a stock at 10, hold it a few years, and hopefully sell a few points higher. When these investors buy their stock, they buy at the market. They are not picky about the price they pay. And someone is always taking the other side of the trade. But who is selling stock to the investors? Chances are it is either the specialist or a day trader. And the trade is always done on the specialist's or day trader's terms, so long as it is done at the market.

Think about the specialist for a moment. If the day trader in the Bethlehem Steel example was able to grind out a net profit of $420 on eight trades, think how much money the specialist made in the same stock. Remember, Bethlehem Steel traded over 300,000 shares. There is a good chance the specialist was probably in on the majority of those trades, buying when there were no buyers and selling when there were no sellers. There is a very good chance the specialist made a few thousand dollars, or more, with very little risk. And guess what—no one even noticed, because the stock didn't move. It was all done with $\frac{1}{16}$s and $\frac{1}{8}$s.

As Table 9.3 shows, the key to trading for $\frac{1}{16}$s is to trade enough volume. If you can make $\frac{1}{16}$ on 2,000 shares four times in a day, you will have made $500 before commissions. This is the same as buying 1,000 shares of a stock and making $\frac{1}{2}$ point on it. However, the odds of making $\frac{1}{2}$ point on 1,000 shares are far worse than those of making $\frac{1}{16}$. Not to mention that you would need to make your $\frac{1}{2}$ on much more volatile stock than the stocks that made the teenies. That is why this strategy is a gold mine.

THE BACKDROP FOR SELECTING WHICH STOCKS TO TRADE FOR TEENIES

In the grand scheme of things, the Bethlehem Steel day trader netted $420 without exposure to a high degree of risk. Look at the trades. Where did the trader buy and sell the stock? Within a very tight range. Stock was bought at 10 and 10$\frac{1}{16}$, and sold at 10$\frac{1}{16}$ and 10$\frac{1}{8}$.

There is an old cliché that says hindsight is 20-20. By the end of the day, it was very easy to see the level of risk that this trader faced. These eight trades were riskless trades. The stock didn't trade any lower than 10, and it didn't trade any higher than 10$\frac{1}{8}$. The day trader who bought stock at 10 and sold at 10$\frac{1}{8}$ must have felt like a genius.

Table 9.3   The teenies add up.

$\frac{1}{16}$ on 2,000 shares once in a day	+$125
$\frac{1}{16}$ on 2,000 twice in a day	+$250
$\frac{1}{16}$ on 2,000 shares 3 times in a day	+$375
$\frac{1}{16}$ on 2,000 shares 4 times in a day	+$500

That person had hit the sweet spot, doing what every day trader dreams of: making a profit by buying on the day's low and selling on the day's high.

But these trades only appeared riskless after the fact. The trader didn't know going in what the stock had in store. The reason the day trader was able to make a profit was because his or her money was at risk. Remember, the markets are based on fear and greed. How was the trader able to buy the stock at 10? Only because someone agreed to sell it there. And why would that person sell on the low of the day? Obviously, that person was fearful the stock was going lower, not higher.

My point in all of this is that you never know what the stock is going to do after you buy it. Regardless of how the trade turns out, you are always at risk the instant you buy the stock. Anything can happen. The stock could drop ½ point, or it could rise ½ point, or it could stay the same. Not even the experts know for sure what the stock is going to do. That's the nature of trading. The only control you have over this is in the stocks and segments of the market you choose to trade, because some are more volatile than others.

The question you must ask yourself is: When trading for a teenie, how much risk to do you want to expose yourself to? If your plan is to only make ⅟₁₆ on the trade, why would you ever risk losing more than that? In other words, if your upside on the trade is ⅟₁₆, you do not want your downside to be ¼, ½, or more. If it is, you will eventually give back all of your profits. Why? Because you will be making ⅟₁₆s and losing ½s. This is a recipe for failure. In the end, no matter how many teenies you make, you will be at a net loss at the end of the day if you are giving back your profits in large chunks. What can you do? The answer is simple. If you are trading for teenies, you must avoid volatile stocks at all cost.

AVOID THE GLAMOR STOCKS

The reality is that the glamor stocks, the high flyers, like Intel, Dell, Cisco, Microsoft, and Yahoo!, are simply too volatile for this kind of trading strategy. These stocks could move 10 points or more in a single day. Remember, to the online day trader, volatility is an enemy, not a friend, because the day trader's execution is so slow. The bigger players in the market love volatility, because they have the resources and the means to take advantage of it. You and I do not. That is the price we pay for being able to place trades that cost less than $10.

I have learned the hard way that trading volatile stocks for ¹⁄₁₆s doesn't work. Inevitably, in the beginning, it will seem very easy to get in and get out for a small profit. In a stable market, the high flyers are so liquid that it may seem like making teenies in them is easier than taking candy from a baby. In fact, you might be able to do this all day long. Do not be fooled, however. These stocks rarely stay calm for long. Eventually, you will get clipped. The stock will drop a point or two in the blink of an eye, at the worst possible time—when you are long 2,000 shares. You will give back a week's or a month's worth of profits in a few minutes. And when that happens, you will never want to trade these stocks again.

If you are taking on a high degree of risk, a teenie is not going to cut it. You need to make ¼s, ⅜s, and ½s. If you are going to trade volatile stocks that can move several points in a few minutes, you have to change your strategy. There are certain times when volatile stocks are a good trade, but that is for later in the book. For now, you want to make sure your risk is limited. And that means sticking with stocks that don't move.

HIGHER-YIELDING STOCKS—THE IDEAL MARKETS FOR THE "TEENIE" TRADE

The single most important decision you can make as a trader is determining which stocks to trade (see Table 9.4). As you can see, if you are trading for ¹⁄₁₆s, you want stable stocks that aren't going to move drastically in any one direction. Where can you find these stocks? The best place is in the areas of the New York Stock Exchange that do not get the same attention as the more volatile areas. You do not want high-profile stocks. Remember, headlines create volatility. You want stocks that are not in the news.

There are a couple of areas I like to focus on. Most of these stocks have one thing in common: They pay high dividends. Any stock that is said have a high yield is usually a safe stock to trade. This is because the high yield serves as a cushion against volatility. What is a high yield? It is the stock's return based on the dividend it pays to shareholders. If you buy a $10 stock that pays a 50-cent-per-year dividend, the stock is said to yield 5 percent. In other words, you are going to make 5 percent on your money for holding the stock regardless of what happens.

The reason I like to trade higher-yielding stocks is the stable market environment they trade in. Most yield-hungry buyers are not buying these stocks for the same reasons they buy Intel, Microsoft, and

---

Table 9.4   Cutsheet for trading for ¹⁄₁₆s—the best stocks to trade.

Type to trade:	Trade for ¹⁄₁₆s by exploiting the bid-ask spread
How many shares per trade:	At least 2,000 shares
What type of stocks:	New York and American Stock Exchange stocks only—this strategy will not work on NASDAQ stocks
What market segments:	The higher-yielding, less volatile areas
What stocks:	Closed-end bond funds
	Closed-end stock funds
	Utilities (only those below $25 per share)
	Real estate investment trusts (only those below $25 per share)
	Other listed issues trading below $10 that appear stable
Trading method:	Limit orders only
	Do not use market orders
	Do not use all-or-none orders
Trading strategy:	Buy on the bid, sell on the ask

Dell. They are not buying them for growth or to double their money. These investors are buying these stocks as conservative investments, as a safe place to park their money and get maybe a 5 percent, 6 percent, or 7 percent return on the dividends.

As a day trader, you do not have to concern yourself with studying loads of charts and research to find the highest-yielding stocks. You have to look no further than three areas that are among the highest-yielding segments of the market: closed-end bond funds, utilities, and real estate investment trusts. These stable markets are ideal for our trading strategy. Remember, if the stock is stable and slow-moving, we do not have to worry about getting in and getting out at lightning speed. Trading these markets is much more like a chess match, more of a one-on-one, head-to-head battle. And guess who the battle is against? You guessed it: the specialist.

MAKING THE SPREAD: BUYING ON THE BID, SELLING ON THE ASK

There may be one question in the back of your mind: Why limit yourself to only a ¹⁄₁₆-point profit when you can try to make more? Why not go for

¼s, ½s, or even higher? Obviously, it is extremely difficult to make any-thing more than a ¹⁄₁₆-point profit if your execution is slow. Remember, you are trading over the Internet. Inevitably, you are going to be the last one in, and the last one out, if and when the stock moves. That is why volatility is an enemy, not a friend.

But that answer only applies when trading volatile stocks. It still does not answer the question. Remember, the stocks you will pick will not be moving. There is a more complex reason it is difficult to make more than ¹⁄₁₆ on a trade. The answer has to do with the way in which stocks trade, and way in which the teenie is made. Remember, the trad-ing strategy is to exploit the bid-ask spread. You cannot make more than ¹⁄₁₆ on this strategy on most trades simply because the bid-ask spread is not wider than ¹⁄₁₆.

When a day trader makes a teenie, it is made entirely on the spread. How does the day trader make the spread? By buying on the bid and selling on the ask. This strategy will not produce more than a ¹⁄₁₆-point profit, simply because most stocks do not trade in bid-ask spreads wider than ¹⁄₁₆ point.

The investing public's first impression is that you make ¹⁄₁₆ by buy-ing at the market and selling at the market: in other words, buying Beth-lehem Steel at 10 on a market order, and then selling it at 10¹⁄₁₆ on a market order. This could not be further from the truth. Remember, mar-ket orders leave a substantial amount of money on the table. The real-ity is that you made ¹⁄₁₆ because the bid was 10 and the ask was 10¹⁄₁₆, and you bought on the bid and sold on the ask.

The way you make that ¹⁄₁₆ is by exploiting the bid-ask spread. Let's check the newspaper quote for Bethlehem Steel once again. Here's how it looked:

BS *Last* **10** *Unchanged High* **10⅛** *Low* **10**

EXPLOITING THE BID-ASK SPREAD

Remember the eight trades: buys at 10 and 10¹⁄₁₆ and sells at 10¹⁄₁₆ and 10⅛. The trader netted $420 after commissions on these trades, making a profit on three transactions and breaking even on one. Do think the trader was using market orders? Not a chance in hell. So what was going on? The trader was exploiting the bid-ask spread by buying on the bid and selling on the ask.

The newspaper does not give a good indication of the true situation in BS on that day. You have to look at the bid-ask spread. Examining of the bid-ask spread, this is what you will see:

10–10¹/₁₆   **20 × 10**   ***48,000*** at 11:00 A.M.

10–10¹/₁₆   **5 × 5**   ***168,000*** at 1:00 P.M.

10–10¹/₈   **50 × 23**   ***259,000*** at 3:30 P.M.

For the majority of the day, the bid was 10 and the ask was 10¹/₁₆. So how do you exploit this spread? It's quite simple: Join the buyers at 10, and if you can buy the stock, offer it out for sale at 10¹/₁₆. In other words, when you see a market that is 10 to 10¹/₁₆, you enter a limit order to buy 2,000 shares at 10. Depending on where you are in line, you will buy your stock when someone enters a sell at the market. The stock will trade at 10 and you will be the buyer.

The same split second you buy the stock at 10, you immediately put in a limit order to sell the stock at 10¹/₁₆. Hopefully, if the bid-ask spread remains unchanged (10 to 10¹/₁₆) it will now be your offer at 10¹/₁₆. If the bid-ask spread has changed to 10 to 10¹/₈, you will have under-offered the seller at 10¹/₈ by ¹/₁₆ at 10¹/₁₆. This makes the bid-ask spread 10 to 10¹/₁₆, with your stock for sale at 10¹/₁₆. So what do you do next? You wait. The next buyer who enters the order at the market will buy your stock from you. When that happens, you will have made ¹/₁₆ on 2,000 shares, or $125. And all the while, the stock did not move.

I hope you are now beginning to see the value in this kind of trade. As long as the stock doesn't move, you are virtually guaranteed to make a ¹/₁₆-point profit if you are patient. This will enable you to keep going into the same stock over and over again. On each trade, you are only making ¹/₁₆; but, if you can do that several times per day in each stock, you will have made yourself a few thousand dollars. And the rest of the investing world will have no idea how or where it was done.

NEVER TRY TO OUTSMART THE MARKET

One of the most difficult things to do in trading is to outsmart the market. This is the practice of trying to pick tops and bottoms on stocks. The financial markets, though inefficient and imperfect, represent the collective wisdom of the entire world. Usually a stock is at a certain price for a reason. When you buy a stock at 10 and resell it at 11, you have in essence outsmarted the market. Over the long term, this is a difficult thing to do consistently. Only the best of the best money managers in the world are able to do it. That is why most mutual funds underperform the market averages.

The beauty of exploiting the bid-ask spread is that you are not outsmarting the market. You are not trying to pick tops and bottoms on stocks. Leave that to the analysts. This kind of strategy is merely picking a stock and trading it as is. You buy it on the bid, and you sell it on the ask. You do not concern yourself with whether the stock is overvalued or undervalued. You do not care because making a judgment like that will not put money in your pocket. How do you make your money? Off the order flow. You make it by taking the other side of customer buy and sell orders. When a customer wants to sell stock, you are there to buy it at 10. When a customer wants to buy stock, you are there to sell it at 10¹⁄₁₆. In a sense, like the specialist, you are nothing more than a middleman in the buying and selling of stocks.

THE SPECIALIST, THE DAY TRADER, AND THE INVESTING PUBLIC—A GAME OF CAT AND MOUSE

Let's look at another example of how the day trader can make ¹⁄₁₆ in a stock that isn't moving. The stock of choice is an electric utility, Niagara Mohawk (NMK). As you now know, the specialist makes each and every ¹⁄₁₆ at the expense of the investing public. In a sense, the day trader also makes money at the investing public's expense. In reality, however, the day trader makes each and every ¹⁄₁₆ by stealing it from the specialist. How is this done? By stepping in front of the specialist to take the other side of customer orders entered at the market. What prompts the investing public to always enter market orders? Either they don't know they can do better with limit orders, or they are long-term investors and they don't care about haggling to save ¹⁄₁₆. Regardless, the investing public has a far different perception of the stock than the specialist and the day trader. Let's look at this in detail.

15–15¹⁄₁₆ *10 × 10* *596,000*

The Quote: The bid-ask spread is ¹⁄₁₆ point wide, 15 bid, offered at 15¹⁄₁₆.

What the Investing Public Thinks: "The so-called market makers control the stock, and there is nothing I can do about it. If I want to buy, I must pay 15⅟₁₆. If I want to sell, I will only get 15. I've been taught that when I buy, I get the offer. When I sell, I get the bid. There is no way I can do better."

What the Specialist Thinks: "I look at this spread in the exact opposite fashion as the investor. My strategy is laid out, and my trap is set. And I hope customers will walk right into it. If I can buy at 15 and sell at 15⅟₁₆ all day long, I'll be rich. I will keep a bid at 15, and I will offer stock at 15⅟₁₆ for as long as I can. I will be able to make teenies as long as there are customers who blindly buy and sell at the market, and as long as the volatility in the stock is low. I'm the one who takes the other side of the public's trade. And I only do it on my terms and at my price. If I am lucky, I will be able to make several thousand dollars today trading this way."

What the Day Trader Thinks: "All I have to do is to copy the specialist. If the specialist is buying at 15 and selling at 15⅟₁₆, that is what I will do as well. If I can make teenies all day, I too will be rich. Every ⅟₁₆ I make is one less ⅟₁₆ for the specialist. In a sense, I am taking food out of the specialist's mouth every time I trade."

The Investing Public: "I am not a trader, I am a long-term investor and I have a long-term perspective. As such, the market's ups and downs do not bother me, because I'm not in this for the quick trade. Whenever I buy or sell stock, I use market orders. I am not comfortable with using limit orders, because no one ever told me how to use them. Regardless, I'm really not interested in trying to save an extra ⅟₁₆ or ⅛. I trust that the specialist will give me a fair execution."

The Specialist: "I am certainly not in this for the long term. If I can sell stock a few seconds after I buy it for a profit, everything will go as planned. My hope is that the stock stays right where it is. I want volume; I don't need movement. ⅟₁₆ after ⅟₁₆ after ⅟₁₆: That is how I put food on my table."

The Day Trader: "Like the specialist, I'm not in this for the long term. I want to get in, make my profit, and get out, as quickly as possible. When I see that the specialist wants to buy at 15 and sell at 15⅟₁₆, I should be trying to do the same. But to overcome my commission costs, I like to buy at least 2,000 shares at a time. That gives me a $125 profit every time I make a teenie. And I try to make ⅟₁₆s all day long."

The Day Trader: "I am competing with the specialist. I know the specialist doesn't like me, and is going to trade against me at every opportunity. But I have a trump card. Specialists have to let my order go in front of theirs. If the specialist wants to buy at 15, and I want to buy at 15, I'm entitled to any stock that trades at that price. This is set by the rules of the exchange. This is what allows me to make a living as a day trader."

The Day Trader's Action: "By the size of the market, I know that the specialist is bidding for stock at 15 and offering stock for sale at $15\frac{1}{16}$. If the specialist is willing to buy stock at 15, it must be a safe level to buy. I know specialists will never risk their own trading capital unless a trade seems good. That is all I need to know. I will attempt to exploit the bid-ask spread by copying the specialist. I will enter a buy of 2,000 shares at 15."

15–15$\frac{1}{16}$ 10 × 10   596,000

The day trader enters a buy of 2,000 NMK at 15, and the specialist receives the order.

The Specialist: "Another order to buy 2,000 at 15. I have seen this person here before. This is a day trader. I hate day traders. All they do is try to pick me off all day. I think 15 is a great price to buy stock. And now this day trader wants to buy at 15. I have to let this order go in front of my own. I won't be able to buy any more stock for myself at 15 until this entire order is filled or canceled. I don't have a choice."

15–15$\frac{1}{16}$ 20 × 10   596,000

The Day Trader: "It is now my bid at 15. The specialist allowed me to step in front. The specialist was bidding for 1,000 at 15, but now I'm bidding for 2,000 at 15. There is nothing the specialist can do about it but step aside. Now my trap is set. I will wait patiently for a seller. I will wait here all day if I have to, because I know that eventually someone will hit my bid. There is no doubt in my mind that I can make $\frac{1}{16}$ on the trade, if only I can find someone stupid enough to sell me stock at 15."

The Investing Public: "I've been sitting on these 2,000 shares of Niagara Mohawk for over two years. Time to sell. I will call my broker and put in an order to sell 2,000 shares at the market.

The investor enters a sell of 2,000 shares of NMK at the market. The order reaches the specialist, and the stock trades at 15.

15–15$\frac{1}{16}$ 10 × 10   598,000

The Day Trader: "I just saw 2,000 shares trade at 15. Look at the market. My bid for 2,000 is not longer there. There is only 1,000 there now. I think I bought my stock. Let me check my account. Excellent! I knew someone would be stupid enough to sell me stock at 15. That was the hard part. But the drama is not over yet. The only thing separating me from a quick profit is the sale. I'm not going to get greedy. I'm only looking for $\frac{1}{16}$. All I have to do now is sell the stock at $15\frac{1}{16}$."

The Specialist: "The trader just bought 2,000 shares at 15. Finally that hurdle is out of my way. Now I can bid for stock at 15 again."

The Day Trader: "I know if I try to sell the stock at $15\frac{1}{8}$, it may not trade. If I sell at $15\frac{1}{16}$, there is a good chance it will trade quickly. There is a seller at $15\frac{1}{16}$ already. But I know from the size of market that the specialist is the seller. Once my sell order reaches the floor of the exchange, the specialist again will have to give my order priority over his or her own. First it was on the buy, now it's on the sell."

The day trader enters an order to sell 2,000 NMK on a $15\frac{1}{16}$ limit. The order reaches the floor of the exchange, and the market changes.

$15–15\frac{1}{16}$ 10×20 $598,000$

The Specialist: "Not again! That day trader is back, selling this time. I was trying to sell stock at $15\frac{1}{16}$, and now this trader wants to do the same. I have no choice. I don't like it, but I have to give the day trader's order priority."

The Day Trader: "Just like when I bought the stock at 15, I will now wait patiently to try to sell the stock at $15\frac{1}{16}$. Before, it was my bid at 15, and my bid was hit. Now it is my offer at $15\frac{1}{16}$. I will wait here all day if I have to. All I need is for someone to enter a buy order at the market. This will clean out my offer. The second part of my trap is set."

The Investing Public: "Niagara Mohawk looks like a good investment. I think I'll buy 2,000 at the market."

An order to buy 2,000 shares reaches the floor of the exchange. The offer is lifted. 2,000 shares trade at $15\frac{1}{16}$.

$15–15\frac{1}{16}$ 10×10 $600,000$

The Day Trader: "I just saw 2,000 shares print at $15\frac{1}{16}$. And look at the offer. Now there are only 1,000 shares for sale at $15\frac{1}{16}$. It must be the specialist again. My order was filled; 2,000 shares sold at 15⅟₁₆. Mission accomplished! I made a $125 profit in only a few minutes."

The Day Trader's Next Move: "The market in NMK has not changed. There is no reason to look at any other stock. If the strategy works, try it again. Same stock. Same strategy. Same price. I will bid for another 2,000 shares at 15."

THE STOCK DIDN'T MOVE

I hope this example paints a good picture of how the day trader exploits the bid-ask spread. Notice the spread in the stock. It remained 15 to 15⅟₁₆ the entire time. It didn't move even ⅟₁₆, yet the day trader was able to extract a $125 profit from the market. What you saw here is the classic example of how a scalper can make razor-thin profits in a stock that isn't moving. Remember, the profit margin is only 6.25 cents. But on 2,000 shares, that adds up to a $125 profit.

EXPLOITING A WIDER SPREAD

The previous example shows how a teenie can be made in a spread only ⅟₁₆ point wide. Now we will demonstrate how you can make the same profit just as easily in a spread that is slightly wider.

Increments of Teenies

$$\frac{1}{16} = 0.0625$$
$$\frac{1}{8} = 0.125$$
$$\frac{3}{16} = 0.1875$$
$$\frac{1}{4} = 0.25$$
$$\frac{5}{16} = 0.3125$$
$$\frac{3}{8} = 0.375$$
$$\frac{7}{16} = 0.4375$$
$$\frac{1}{2} = 0.5$$
$$\frac{9}{16} = 0.5625$$
$$\frac{5}{8} = 0.625$$
$$\frac{11}{16} = 0.6875$$
$$\frac{3}{4} = 0.75$$
$$\frac{13}{16} = 0.8125$$
$$\frac{7}{8} = 0.875$$
$$\frac{15}{16} = 0.9375$$

Let's look at ACM Managed Income Fund, a closed-end bond fund, which trades under the symbol ADF. You pull up ADF and the market looks like this:

9–9¼   28 × 92   23,800

This market is 9 bid, offered at 9¼, 2,800 shares by 9,200 shares, 23,800 volume. You will learn to absolutely love a wide spread like this. There is ample opportunity to make profits in this kind of market. The first step is to plan out your strategy for the stock. You never want to enter a trade without having a specific plan of action and an appropriate exit strategy if your plan goes against you. You have to ask yourself several questions. What do you expect to accomplish by trading the stock? Are you going to try to make ¹⁄₁₆, ⅛, or even more?

Obviously, your goal is to buy ADF at the cheapest price possible. But you don't want to enter a lowball bid and not get it executed. It's just like trying to buy a house. You want to buy it at a good price, but you don't want your bid to be so low that no one is willing to sell it to you.

So, you want to have a high enough bid that someone agrees to sell you the stock, but not so high you can't resell the stock for a ¹⁄₁₆-point profit after you buy it. Over the Internet, you enter a limit order:

Buy 2000 ADF 9¹⁄₁₆ DAY

It is also important to remember that at the price where you want to buy stock, there is none for sale. You are bidding for the stock in the hopes of bringing out a seller. Your bid for 2,000 shares will be reflected in the market because it is now the highest bid; the next best bid is at 9 for 2,800 shares.

So, the market of:

9 to 9¼   28 × 92

changes to:

9¹⁄₁₆ to 9¼   20 × 92

Your bid is now on the floor of the New York Stock Exchange. There is no guarantee you will be able to buy the stock at 9¹⁄₁₆. However, you do know that if you are lucky enough to buy the stock, you should be able to make ¹⁄₁₆ by selling at 9⅛. So, in this case, buying the stock is the hardest part of the equation.

HOW WILL YOU BUY 2,000 SHARES OF ADF?

If someone enters a sell at the market, you will be the buyer and the stock will trade at 9¹⁄₁₆. In other words, you are hoping and praying someone is stupid enough to agree to your price and sell you stock. If you are patient, there is a good chance you will buy the stock.

So you watch your real-time quote screen for any prints in ADF at 9¹⁄₁₆. You wait 10 minutes, and still nothing has traded. Then, before your very eyes, you see 2,000 shares trade at 9¹⁄₁₆.

You look at your real-time quote screen, and ADF reads as follows:

9 to 9¹⁄₄   28 × 92   25,800

So what happened to your 9¹⁄₁₆ bid for 2,000 shares? It is no longer there. Someone hit your bid. You bought 2,000 shares.

You check your positions screen and see that you now have 2,000 shares of ADF in your account. You have bought the stock. Your money is now at risk. Now the fun begins.

Because you bought the stock at 9¹⁄₁₆, you should be perfectly content with trying to make ¹⁄₁₆ on the trade and offering the stock out at 9⅛.

The great thing about the bid-ask spread in ADF right now is that there isn't any stock for sale until 9¼. Your strategy is to try to make ¹⁄₁₆. You could get greedy and try to make ⅛, but it is much easier to make ¹⁄₁₆ than ⅛. So you enter a limit order to sell 2,000 at 9⅛.

The order is entered, and the specialist updates the market to reflect your offer. The market is now:

9 to 9⅛   28 × 20   25,800

As a trader, you feel very good about your chances for making a ¹⁄₁₆ in the stock right now. All you are waiting for is a buy order at the market. This buyer would buy stock from you, because you have the stock for sale at the cheapest price, 9⅛. Your hope is that your offer to sell stock will bring out buyers.

You wait about three minutes and see a print at 9⅛. The market looks like this:

9 to 9¼   28 × 92   27,800

There is now stock for sale at 9¼. What happened to your stock, which was for sale at 9⅛? It traded! Someone took the offer. You were lifted: 2,000 shares traded at 9⅛.

You double-check your account positions and see that you no longer have a position in ADF. It only took a few minutes, but your objective was accomplished. You bought 2,000 shares at 9¹⁄₁₆ and sold 2,000 shares at 9⅛. It really wasn't that hard. All you did was position yourself ahead of the random buy and sell orders that occur in the stock. By using well-placed limit orders, you were able to exploit the bid-ask spread and make $125 in profit in the process. The beauty of the trade is that you made $125 in a stock that hasn't moved. The market is the same as it was before, yet you were able to grind out a small profit. This is how I trade for a living. I will follow almost 200 stocks and I do this strategy all day long.

Okay, you've made $125 so far today. The next thing to do is to put that money to work again, in the same stock. After a successful trade like this, which only took a few minutes to complete, there is no reason to look elsewhere. Go right back into the same stock, and try to repeat the trade again.

To summarize: You have just made $125 in ADF by exploiting the bid-ask spread. You bought 2,000 shares at 9¹⁄₁₆ and sold 2,000 at 9⅛. In summary, here's what the trade looked like.

The market before the trade was:

9–9¼   28 × 92

With a ¼-point-wide bid-ask spread, you saw the opportunity to exploit the spread and make a quick profit. You decided to outbid the buyer at 9 by bidding 9¹⁄₁₆ for 2,000 shares. The market updated to:

9¹⁄₁₆–9¼   20 × 92

It was now your bid for 2,000 shares at 9¹⁄₁₆. All you needed was for a random seller to come into the market. If a seller entered a sell at the market, the stock would trade at 9¹⁄₁₆. And you would be the buyer.

That's exactly what happened. A seller entered a sell of 2,000 at the market. The seller hit your bid at 9¹⁄₁₆. You bought 2,000 shares as the market changed to:

9–9¼ 28 × 92

Now that you were long 2,000 shares, you had to decide where to sell the stock. You were only looking to make ¹⁄₁₆, so you offered your 2,000 shares at 9⅛. The market changed to:

9–9⅛ 28 × 20

Having offered stock at 9⅛, you now needed someone to enter a buy at the market. You would be the seller at 9⅛ if that happened. It did. A buyer came in and cleaned out the offer at 9⅛. You sold 2,000 shares at 9⅛. The market changed to:

9–9¼ 28 × 92

The mission was accomplished and the trade was complete. You made $125 by buying 2,000 shares at 9¹⁄₁₆ and selling 2,000 at 9⅛. And the market in the stock is the same now as when you first found it: 9 bid, offered at 9¼. By exploiting the spread, you were able to extract a profit in the stock. That is how you make money in stock that doesn't move.

Now that your trading capital is freed up because you sold your 2,000-share position, you should generally go right back into this stock. If the bid-ask spread is the same, go right back in and try to buy another 2,000 shares at 9¹⁄₁₆.

The reason I love this strategy is because it takes all the guess-work out of trading. When you exploit the bid-ask spread, you are not buying a stock because you think it is undervalued. You are not specu-lating on future developments in the stock. Leave that to the rest of Wall Street. As a trader, the last thing you ever want to do is attempt to outsmart the market. You do not have to do that to make a living. You pick your buying price based on where the bid is. You buy where the specialist is buying. You bid the bid, and you offer the offer. It's that simple.

Over the last two years, I have made literally tens of thousands of dollars per month using this strategy. But it only works if you pick the right stocks. If you do, you will find that the teenies are very easy to come by. In the next few chapters, I will demonstrate exactly which stocks to trade, how to trade them, and when. Be patient, keep an open mind, and follow my example. We are now getting to the heart of what it means to make a living as a day trader.

Day traders are looking at the same stocks as the investing public. But what do they see differently than the public does? What enables them to make a living off the buying and selling of others, right under their noses, without even being noticed? It is because day traders see the glass as half full, when the rest of the investing world sees it as half empty.

What does this mean? Look at a typical stock spread. When the public thinks it should buy on the ask, and sell on the bid, day traders see the exact opposite. Instead, they see the opportunity to buy on the bid and sell on the ask. The consequence? Day traders are making $1/16$s while the investing public is losing them.

Imagine a stock that is 13 to $13\frac{1}{16}$. While the general public is blindly buying at $13\frac{1}{16}$ and selling at 13 on market orders, day traders are buying at 13 and selling at $13\frac{1}{16}$ on limit orders. Market orders leave the customer's money on the table. Limit orders put that money in the day trader's pocket.

CHAPTER 10

Prospecting for Gold in the Land of ¹⁄₁₆s

To make a living as an online day trader, you must be absolutely certain the odds are in your favor before you enter a trade. What does this mean? It means looking at 20 stocks and picking just 1. Regardless, you should not put a dime of your money at risk unless the conditions are absolutely perfect. This is not gambling, this is trading. This is your livelihood. Timing is everything. And patience is the key. Watch, wait, and stay alert. And then, when the time is right, go for the jugular.

I think I have spent enough time *telling* you about how to trade. Now I am going to *show* you how. Figure 10.1 shows an actual screen shot of a random sampling of several low-volatility New York Stock Exchange stocks (and one American Stock Exchange stock), including some closed-end funds, electric utilities, and real estate investment trusts. This is how the market actually appeared in real time on the afternoon of November 12, 1998. My intention here is to show you exactly what you need to look for when you go prospecting for your first trade.

Figure 10.1 provides all the information you need to know about the stocks to make a trading decision. Remember, you are not in this for the long term. You are not an investor. It is not your job to guess

Figure 10.1 Screen shot of selected low-volatility stocks on the afternoon of November 12, 1998.

	Symbol	Last	Change	Volume	Bid	Ask	Bid Size × Ask Size
1	ADF	10⅜	+⅛	47,600	10⅜	10 7/16	11 × 120
2	EE	9	+⅛	52,100	9	9 1/16	4 × 9
3	NMK	14⅞	−3/16	301,400	14 13/16	15	50 × 100
4	BS	9¼	−3/16	470,500	9 3/16	9¼	409 × 220
5	JEQ	8⅛	−3/16	62,000	8 1/16	8¼	10 × 100
6	DHF	13⅛	+⅛	203,900	13	13 3/16	145 × 70
7	ACG	9 9/16	+⅛	38,700	9 7/16	9 9/16	116 × 79
8	GCH	7¼	−⅛	57,100	7 3/16	7¼	10 × 36
9	WEC	30 13/16	−3/16	204,400	30⅝	30 13/16	200 × 10
10	CV	10⅝	0	11,100	10 9/16	10⅞	22 × 5
11	NHP	22⅛	+⅛	32,100	22 1/16	22 3/16	10 × 16
12	TCO	13 5/16	+1/16	11,800	13¼	13⅜	100 × 50
13	UDR	11⅜	−1/16	171,400	11⅜	11½	11 × 45
14	WRE	17 13/16	+1/16	20,500	17¾	17⅞	10 × 5
15	GRT	16 13/16	−1/16	43,800	16¾	16 15/16	29 × 5
16	FRT	23⅛	+¼	48,500	23	23¼	10 × 14

Real-time data courtesy of Paragon Software, Inc. (InterQuote), 1-800-311-1516, www.interquote.com.

which of these 16 stocks will be higher next week, next month, or next year. It is not your job to know the name of the CEO of a particular company issuing stock, what the company does, or what its earnings expectations are. Nor do you care about price-to-earnings ratios or growth prospects. You care about only one thing: the next five minutes. You want to pick a stock, get in, make your money, and get out. The faster you do this, the better. You will be patient, and you will not get greedy. You are only looking for a tiny profit of 1/16 point—6.25 cents per share. It is that simple.

These random 16 stocks have the potential to make substantial profits for you over the course of the trading day if you pick and choose carefully. As you know, this is not about trying to outsmart the market. You do not need charts, research, or analysis. You do not need to comb the news wires in search of headlines. Nor do you need to know the opinion of your broker, or what Wall Street thinks about these stocks. None of these things will give you the edge. The bid-ask spread alone provides everything you need to know. Remember, you are not looking for movement—none of these 16 stocks has to move for you to make money. You are only looking to get between the spread. You are a middleman in the buying and selling of stocks, and nothing more. And it is time to get down to business.

TAKING THE FIRST STEPS

Now that you are looking at these 16 random stocks in real time, what do you look for when deciding which to trade and at what price? And what signals tell you to stay away from a given stock? There is a formula that I have followed for over two years that has been very successful. I will share it with you now.

Method 1: Immediately Eliminate Any Stocks That Are Up or Down ¼ Point or More on the Day

As you know by now, trading for ¹⁄₁₆s only works well with stocks that have low volatilities. The reality of this trade is that your upside is limited to ¹⁄₁₆ point. Therefore, if you are only going to make ¹⁄₁₆ on the trade, why risk losing more than that? The best way to ensure that this doesn't happen is to trade only safe stocks, which means eliminating ones that are in motion. Even within the low-volatility area we are discussing, on any given day there could be a certain degree of movement in a given stock. With volatility comes the risk of loss. Maybe there is a news story on the stock, or maybe a big mutual is dumping shares. Regardless, you do not want any part of this volatility, nor do you need it to make money. Remember, when you are trading for teenies, volatility is not your friend, it is your enemy. There are simply too many other stocks to trade that are more stable.

    The list of 16 stocks in Figure 10.2 is actually a good sampling of stable stocks because of the low volatilities. Look at these issues. Up ⅛, down ⅛, up ³⁄₁₆, down ¹⁄₁₆: These are exactly the kinds of stocks that fit your trading strategy. The only stock that can be eliminated immediately is #16, Federal Realty Investment Trust (FRT). The stock is up ¼ point on the day at 23⅛. In the grand scheme of things, ¼ point is minimal movement. But, when you are trading at least 2,000 shares at a time, you have to be extremely careful. Remember, trading is your livelihood. You do not want to leave anything to chance. You only want

Figure 10.2   Limiting risk by eliminating stocks with the slightest hint of volatility.

	Symbol	Last	Change	Volume	Bid	Ask	Bid Size × Ask Size
1	ADF	10⅜	+⅛	47,600	10⅜	10⁷⁄₁₆	11 × 120
2	EE	9	+⅛	52,100	9	9¹⁄₁₆	4 × 9
3	NMK	14⅞	−³⁄₁₆	301,400	14¹³⁄₁₆	15	50 × 100
4	BS	9¼	−³⁄₁₆	470,500	9³⁄₁₆	9¼	409 × 220
5	JEQ	8⅛	−³⁄₁₆	62,000	8¹⁄₁₆	8¼	10 × 100
6	DHF	13⅛	+⅛	203,900	13	13³⁄₁₆	145 × 70
7	ACG	9⁹⁄₁₆	+⅛	38,700	9⁷⁄₁₆	9⁹⁄₁₆	116 × 79
8	GCH	7¼	−⅛	57,100	7³⁄₁₆	7¼	10 × 36
9	WEC	30¹³⁄₁₆	−³⁄₁₆	204,400	30⅝	30¹³⁄₁₆	200 × 10
10	CV	10⁹⁄₁₆	0	11,100	10⁹⁄₁₆	10⅞	22 × 5
11	NHP	22⅛	+⅛	32,100	22¹⁄₁₆	22³⁄₁₆	10 × 16
12	TCO	13³⁄₁₆	+¹⁄₁₆	11,800	13¼	13⅜	100 × 50
13	UDR	11⅜	−¹⁄₁₆	171,400	11⅜	11½	11 × 45
14	WRE	17¹³⁄₁₆	+¹⁄₁₆	20,500	17¾	17⅞	10 × 5
15	GRT	16¹³⁄₁₆	−¹⁄₁₆	43,800	16¾	16¹³⁄₁₆	29 × 5
16	FRT	23⅛	+¼	48,500	23	23¼	10 × 14

Real-time data courtesy of Paragon Software, Inc. (InterQuote), 1-800-311-1516, www .interquote.com.

to trade when the odds are in your favor. The odds are not in your favor if the stock fluctuates ¼ point or more. That is simply too much movement, too much risk, too much action, for your conservative strategy.

Method 2: Look for a Wide Bid-Ask Spread and Enter the Middle Ground

The very first thing to look for is a wide bid-ask spread. What does this mean? It means the difference in price between where buyers and sellers are willing to trade is large. Why? Because the potential buyers and sellers cannot agree on prices. As you know, stock trading is a negotiating process. When others cannot agree on prices, it is time for the middleman to step forward. And that middleman is the day trader.

Wide Bid-Ask Spreads Will Not Last.   In stable, low-volatility stocks like the ones pictured here, any bid-ask spread wider than ⅛ point is ripe for you to trade. You are only trying to get between the spread, so the wider the spread, the better your chances for profit. Please note that wide spreads are typical for volatile stocks in which future movement cannot be predicted easily. Anytime there is a wide bid-ask spread in a low-volatility stock, however, it is an aberration and eventually the gap will close. In other words, the specialist or another scalper will see the opportunity for profit, step in, and bid for stock. By bidding for stock, the speculator will narrow the spread. As middleman, that is your main function.

Perhaps more explanation is needed. Imagine a low-volatility stock that has a $\frac{3}{16}$-point spread, the market being 10 to 10$\frac{3}{16}$. Imagine the specialist is the only speculator in the stock, because no one else is following the issue at this time. With a spread this wide, the specialist will be buying shares at 10 and reselling them at 10$\frac{3}{16}$ all day long. In this instance, the specialist will be pocketing $187.50, or $\frac{3}{16}$, for every 1,000 shares he or she trades, with very little risk.

Remember, these are not volatile stocks. The risk the specialist faces when taking them into position is not that they are going to drop drastically in price, but that, because of the lower trading volume, it may take some time to sell stock once it is bought. There are generally fewer buyers and sellers in these stocks than in their more volatile counterparts. Any speculator who happened to notice what the specialist was doing would be drawn to the stock. If the speculator watched the specialist long enough and noticed that the stock didn't fluctuate in price any lower than 10, or any higher than 10$\frac{3}{16}$, he or she would come to the realization that this type of trading is easy money. What could be better than making $\frac{3}{16}$s on every trade all day long? The speculator would then get a buy order ready. The rationale would be simple: If it is that easy for the specialist to make $\frac{3}{16}$s on a low-risk trade, it must be a trade worth making.

This day trader would then enter the market with the strategy of stepping in front of the specialist on both the buy side and the sell side. In other words, the day trader would be getting between the spread. If the specialist was buying at 10 and selling at 10$\frac{3}{16}$, the day trader could either attempt to do the same, or trade even tighter, perhaps buying at 10$\frac{1}{16}$ and selling at 10$\frac{1}{8}$. There is no reason to get greedy: A $\frac{1}{16}$-point profit is fine. As you can see, the profit the day trader makes would come directly from undercutting the specialist. In other words, the profit would come right out of the specialist's pocket.

My point in all of this is that eventually the wide spread will narrow. Specialists will keep the bid-ask spread as wide as possible if there are no other traders in the stock to keep them honest. Obviously, the wider the spread, the more money the specialist makes. But, at some point, it is inevitable that other traders will see what is going on. And when other traders step in, the bid-ask spread will narrow. That is why, when you see a wide spread, you must act quickly and seize the opportunity: Because it will not last.

Bid-ask spreads are easiest to exploit when they are wide. That is why wide bid-ask spreads in low-volatility stocks offer the best odds for a profitable trade.

So which of the pictured stocks have wide spreads? If you look right down the line, #3, Niagara Mohawk (NMK), should grab your attention (Figure 10.3). The bid-ask spread is as follows:

$$NMK \quad 14^{13}/_{16}\text{--}15 \quad 50 \times 100 \quad 301,400$$

This is a great opportunity for a trade. The bid-ask spread, at $14^{13}/_{16}$ to 15, is $\frac{3}{16}$ wide. In other words, the buyer cannot agree with the seller.

Figure 10.3   Isolating wide bid-ask spreads.

	Symbol	Last	Change	Volume	Bid	Ask	Bid Size × Ask Size
1	ADF	$10\frac{3}{8}$	$+\frac{1}{8}$	47,600	$10\frac{3}{8}$	$10\frac{7}{16}$	11×120
2	EE	9	$+\frac{1}{8}$	52,100	9	$9\frac{1}{10}$	4×9
3	NMK	$14\frac{7}{8}$	$-\frac{3}{16}$	301,400	$14^{13}/_{16}$	15	50×100
4	BS	$9\frac{1}{4}$	$-\frac{3}{16}$	470,500	$9\frac{3}{16}$	$9\frac{1}{4}$	409×220
5	JEQ	$8\frac{1}{8}$	$-\frac{3}{16}$	62,000	$8\frac{1}{16}$	$8\frac{1}{4}$	10×100
6	DHF	$13\frac{1}{8}$	$+\frac{1}{8}$	203,900	13	$13\frac{3}{16}$	145×70
7	ACG	$9\frac{9}{16}$	$+\frac{1}{8}$	38,700	$9\frac{7}{16}$	$9\frac{9}{16}$	116×79
8	GCH	$7\frac{1}{4}$	$-\frac{1}{8}$	57,100	$7\frac{3}{16}$	$7\frac{1}{4}$	10×36
9	WEC	$30^{13}/_{16}$	$-\frac{3}{16}$	204,400	$30\frac{5}{8}$	$30^{13}/_{16}$	200×10
10	CV	$10\frac{5}{8}$	0	11,100	$10\frac{9}{16}$	$10\frac{7}{8}$	22×5
11	NHP	$22\frac{1}{8}$	$+\frac{1}{8}$	32,100	$22\frac{1}{16}$	$22\frac{3}{16}$	10×16
12	TCO	$13\frac{5}{16}$	$+\frac{1}{16}$	11,800	$13\frac{1}{4}$	$13\frac{3}{8}$	100×50
13	UDR	$11\frac{3}{8}$	$-\frac{1}{16}$	171,400	$11\frac{3}{8}$	$11\frac{1}{2}$	11×45
14	WRE	$17^{13}/_{16}$	$+\frac{1}{16}$	20,500	$17\frac{3}{4}$	$17\frac{7}{8}$	10×5
15	GRT	$16^{13}/_{16}$	$-\frac{1}{16}$	43,800	$16\frac{3}{4}$	$16^{15}/_{16}$	29×5
16	FRT	$23\frac{1}{8}$	$+\frac{1}{4}$	48,500	23	$23\frac{1}{4}$	10×14

Real-time data courtesy of Paragon Software, Inc. (InterQuote), 1-800-311-1516, www.interquote.com.

The buyer will pay 14¹³⁄₁₆, and the seller will only sell at 15. This spread will not stay ³⁄₁₆ wide forever. A speculator will eventually see this market, feel that there is a chance for a quick teenie, and step forward. It is time for you to step in and make your first trade. At what price do you buy? When you see a wide spread, you immediately enter a buy order for 2,000 shares ¹⁄₁₆ point higher than the bid. In this case, you should enter an order to buy 2,000 shares at 14⅞.

Your intention here is to attempt to buy 2,000 shares at 14⅞ and then resell the stock at 14¹⁵⁄₁₆. This is the perfect example of a trade where the odds of success are in your favor. Judging from the spread, it appears that any stock that has been bid or offered between 14¹³⁄₁₆ and 15 has traded. In other words, stock at 14⅞ and 14¹⁵⁄₁₆ has had no trouble matching buyers with sellers. Any stock that has entered this fertile ground has traded away. That leads you to believe that if you enter this fertile ground, you should have no trouble buying stock at 14⅞ and selling stock at 14¹⁵⁄₁₆. Right now, that price range is the stock's sweet spot.

Think of the downside of this trade. You want to buy 2,000 shares at 14⅞. What happens if the trade does not go as planned? Your downside is ¹⁄₁₆ point. Your insurance is that there is a buyer willing to buy stock at 14¹³⁄₁₆. If you buy your stock at 14⅞, and conditions change and the trade goes against you, you are relatively sure that your exit could be 14¹³⁄₁₆. Thus, a ¹⁄₁₆-point loss is your worst-case scenario. How can you be sure of this? Look no further than the bid size: 5,000 shares at 14¹³⁄₁₆ are willing to be bought.

Why is the spread so wide? There are two possible reasons.

1. *The Spread Is Wide Because the Specialist Is Greedy.* As mentioned previously, specialists will keep the spread as wide as possible to maximize their profits. The wider the spread, the more the specialist makes on customer market orders.

2. *The Specialist May Be Temporarily Stepping Away from the Stock.* There is the chance the specialist may be absent from the stock. There could be several reasons why specialists step away. Maybe they have a large long position and don't want to buy any more stock. Or maybe they have a large short and don't want to sell any more stock. In addition, maybe they have customer buy and sell limit orders that are sitting on the books, and they are not willing to step in front of those orders to bid or offer better prices.

If you can refrain from trading until you have a situation like this one, where your worst-case scenario is a ¹⁄₁₆ loss and the odds of making ¹⁄₁₆ are high, you will be a successful trader. When you bid for 2,000 shares at 14⅞, the outcome is uncertain, but the odds are in your favor. Remember, you are using a limit order. There is no guarantee you will buy your stock at 14⅞, but if you do, the odds are very good that you can sell it at 14¹⁵⁄₁₆ for a $125 profit.

Setting the Trap.   Now that it is your bid at 14⅞, you will wait patiently until a seller agrees to your price. Because you are the highest bid, anyone who enters a sell order at the market is agreeing to your price, whether they realize it or not. How are you able to buy a stock and then turn right around and sell it for a profit? Only because someone is stupid enough to sell you stock at the price you have set. But that is the nature of the markets. Not everyone is watching these stocks the way you are, and not everyone understands how stocks trade. Market orders leave money on the table. Limit orders put money in your pocket. That is why you have the edge, and that is how you can make a living as a day trader.

With your bid at 14⅞, the market will look like this:

14⅞–15   20 × 100   301,400

Now the trap is set. The next market order to sell hits your bid. Now let's say you get up and get a cup of coffee. When you come back, the market in NMK looks as follows:

14¹³⁄₁₆–15   50 × 100   303,400

What happened to your 14⅞ bid for 2,000 shares? It is gone. The bid was hit. Two thousand shares traded at 14⅞ while you were away. You bought your stock. You are now long 2,000 shares. So what do you do next?

Selling the Stock.   You now do on the sell side exactly what you did when you bought the stock: Get between the spread. Currently, there are 10,000 shares for sale at 15. You are not interested in selling stock at 15. If you could, you would love to make ⅛ on the stock by selling at 15, but this is not likely. Why? Look at the size of the offer. With 10,000 shares for sale at 15, you would have to get in line behind those 10,000 shares. In other words, for you to sell even a single share at 15, a full 10,000 shares would have to trade at 15 first. Remember, you are only looking to make a teenie. It is much easier to make $\frac{1}{16}$ than it is to make $\frac{1}{8}$. So, you decide to sell your 2,000 shares at $14^{15}/_{16}$. This ensures that you are first in line, because there is no one currently willing to sell at that price.

So you enter a sell of 2,000 shares of NMK at $14^{15}/_{16}$. The market changes to:

$$14^{13}/_{16}-14^{15}/_{16} \quad 50 \times 20 \quad 303{,}400$$

The second part of the trap is set. It is now your offer at $14^{15}/_{16}$. The next 2,000 shares that trade on a market order will be yours. All you need is a random buyer to enter an order at the market.

About five minutes later, the market changes to:

$$14^{13}/_{16}-15 \quad 50 \times 100 \quad 305{,}400$$

What happened? Look at the offer to sell at 15. Where is your offer to sell 2,000 at $14^{15}/_{16}$? It is no longer there because it was lifted. You are out. You sold 2,000 shares at $14^{15}/_{16}$. You made $125 profit and the stock didn't move. The bid-ask spread is the same now as it was before you entered your first trade. Yet you made a quick, low-risk profit in the meantime. This is exactly the kind of trade you should be looking for. And, as we said before, if the trade works and the market hasn't changed, there is no reason to look elsewhere. You should immediately put your trading capital back to work: same stock, same price, same strategy. Enter another buy of 2,000 shares at $14^{7}/_{8}$.

A word of caution: When you are attempting this trade, you must make sure the stock has enough trading volume for you to get in and out quickly. Often, low-volatility stocks may have wide spreads because of a lack of liquidity, or trading volume, in the stock. This can be very dangerous, because it may take hours or even days to unwind a 2,000-share position once you buy it, simply because the stock does not trade actively. My rule of thumb is to make sure the stock has a daily trading volume of a least 20,000 shares. If it doesn't, do not trade it. You don't have to. There are plenty of other stocks out there with more trading activity.

In addition, it helps to watch these stocks carefully for a few hours before you trade them for the first time. That way, you will get a feel for how actively they trade. Eventually this will no longer be a problem because you will have a personal list of stocks that you trade repeatedly because they fit your criteria. But, in the beginning, you must be cautious.

Know Your Fractions. To be able to detect which stocks have wide spreads, it is essential that you memorize your fractions. Many traders find it difficult at first to think of stocks in terms of ⅛s and ¹⁄₁₆s. Over time it will become second nature. For now, take some time to memorize Table 10.1.

Let's assume you have enough trading capital to trade more than just 2,000 shares of NMK at this point. What other stocks look good right now? Looking down the list, which other names have wide bid-ask spreads? There are several other stocks that look ripe for a trade right now. Look at #6, Dreyfus High Yield Strategies Fund (DHF), a closed-end bond fund (see Figure 10.4). This also has a wide spread. And, so far, it fits the two other criteria: It is only up ⅛ on the day, and it has traded a decent volume (203,900 shares).

The market is as follows:

$$DHF \quad 13–13^{3}/_{16} \quad 145 \times 70 \quad 203,900$$

Table 10.1   Chart of ¹⁄₁₆s.

$\frac{1}{16} = 0.0625$

$\frac{1}{8} = 0.125 = \frac{2}{16}$

$\frac{3}{16} = 0.1875$

$\frac{1}{4} = 0.25 = \frac{4}{16}$

$\frac{5}{16} = 0.3125$

$\frac{3}{8} = 0.375 = \frac{6}{16}$

$\frac{7}{16} = 0.4375$

$\frac{1}{2} = 0.50 = \frac{8}{16}$

$\frac{9}{16} = 0.5625$

$\frac{5}{8} = 0.625 = \frac{10}{16}$

$\frac{11}{16} = 0.6875$

$\frac{3}{4} = 0.75 = \frac{12}{16}$

$\frac{13}{16} = 0.8125$

$\frac{7}{8} = 0.875 = \frac{14}{16}$

$\frac{15}{16} = 0.9375$

Figure 10.4   Finding more stocks with wide bid-ask spreads.

	Symbol	Last	Change	Volume	Bid	Ask	Bid Size × Ask Size
1	ADF	10⅜	+⅛	47,600	10⅜	10$\frac{7}{16}$	11 × 120
2	EE	9	+⅛	52,100	9	9$\frac{1}{16}$	4 × 9
3	NMK	14⅞	−$\frac{3}{16}$	301,400	14$\frac{13}{16}$	15	50 × 100
4	BS	9¼	−$\frac{3}{16}$	470,500	9$\frac{3}{16}$	9¼	409 × 220
5	JEQ	8⅛	−$\frac{3}{16}$	62,000	8$\frac{1}{16}$	8¼	10 × 100
6	DHF	13⅛	+⅛	203,900	13	13$\frac{3}{16}$	145 × 70
7	ACG	9$\frac{9}{16}$	+⅛	38,700	9$\frac{7}{16}$	9$\frac{9}{16}$	116 × 79
8	GCH	7¼	−⅛	57,100	7$\frac{3}{16}$	7¼	10 × 36
9	WEC	30$\frac{13}{16}$	−$\frac{3}{16}$	204,400	30⅝	30$\frac{13}{16}$	200 × 10
10	CV	10⅝	0	11,100	10$\frac{9}{16}$	10⅞	22 × 5
11	NHP	22⅛	+⅛	32,100	22$\frac{1}{16}$	22$\frac{3}{16}$	10 × 16
12	TCO	13$\frac{5}{16}$	+$\frac{1}{16}$	11,800	13¼	13⅜	100 × 50
13	UDR	11⅜	−$\frac{1}{16}$	171,400	11⅜	11½	11 × 45
14	WRE	17$\frac{13}{16}$	+$\frac{1}{16}$	20,500	17¾	17⅞	10 × 5
15	GRT	16$\frac{13}{16}$	−$\frac{1}{16}$	43,800	16¾	16$\frac{15}{16}$	29 × 5
16	FRT	23⅛	+¼	48,500	23	23¼	10 × 14

Real-time data courtesy of Paragon Software, Inc. (InterQuote), 1-800-311-1516, www
.interquote.com.

Enter the Fertile Ground.   Like NMK, DHF has a wide spread at this point in the trading day. This gives you ample room to work with. The market is 13 bid, offered at 13$\frac{3}{16}$. The bid-ask spread is $\frac{3}{16}$ wide. Just as with the NMK trade, your goal is simple: to get between the spread.

The plan is simple: Buy 2,000 shares and resell them for a quick $\frac{1}{16}$-point profit. But where should you attempt to buy stock? The middle ground, the sweet spot. In other words, $\frac{1}{16}$ point higher than the highest bid. You will attempt to buy 2,000 shares at 13$\frac{1}{16}$.

You enter a buy of 2,000 shares at 13$\frac{1}{16}$ and the market changes as follows:

$$13\tfrac{1}{16}\text{–}13\tfrac{3}{16} \quad 20 \times 70 \quad 203,900$$

You are now the highest bid, and the game of waiting begins. You will sit tight until someone agrees to sell you stock at your price—13$\frac{1}{16}$. The next time someone enters a sell at the market, the stock will trade at 13$\frac{1}{16}$, and you will be the buyer.

Several seconds later, the market changes to:

13–13³⁄₁₆   145 × 70   205,900

What happened? Look at the bid. The highest bid is now back down to 13 again. Your bid was hit. You bought your stock at 13¹⁄₁₆.

Now that you have bought 2,000 shares at 13¹⁄₁₆, it is time to resell the stock for a teenie. So you enter the sell at 13⅛, the market changes to:

13–13¹⁄₈   145 × 20   205,900

And the waiting game begins again. Your stock is for sale at 13⅛. Now you need a buyer to step forward to lift your stock at 13⅛. So you wait a few minutes, check the market again, and see that the bid-ask spread has changed once again. It is now:

13–13³⁄₁₆   145 × 70   205,900

What happened to your 13⅛ offer for 2,000 shares? It was lifted. You sold your stock. The trade was completed. Another $125 for only a few minutes' work in a stock that didn't move. This is what you will try to repeat all day long.

You might be asking why anyone would pay 13⅛ for the stock if they could buy it at 13¹⁄₁₆, the same way you did, with a little bit of patience. The answer is that, in the short term, the markets are inefficient. Trading takes a certain degree of skill. The buyers and sellers of these stocks at the market are all long-term investors, most of whom are unaware that a better price can be negotiated for the stock than where it is for sale. This inefficiency is what allows you to make a living as a trader.

In a sense, the wide bid-ask spread is the bargaining table that allows you ample room to negotiate and haggle for better prices. When you bought the stock at 13¹⁄₁₆, it was only because no one else was willing to pay as high a price as you were. When a seller came along, you were willing to give that seller the best price available for the stock. It's just like an auction: You were the highest bidder. Then, when you sold the stock at 13⅛, it was only because no one else was willing to sell the stock for as cheap a price as you were. You had the best sale price in the entire market in this particular stock. The fact that you bought the stock only minutes earlier at a cheaper price than you sold it is of no relevance to the fact that you had the best sale price.

Think of a car dealership. When a dealer offers the best prices, buyers come out of the woodwork to buy that person's cars. It's no different with stocks. You always have to be the cheapest seller to get the stock lifted quickly. In this case, if you wanted to be greedy, you could have held out for ⅛ by selling at 13³⁄₁₆. But there is no telling how long it would have taken. What good is a ⅛-point profit if it takes eight hours to get the trade done? Maybe in the time it took to squeeze out that ⅛, you could have made four or five teenies in the same stock, because you didn't get greedy.

And remember, the only reason you were able to buy the stock cheaper than the sale price was because you negotiated a better price. There was no guarantee you would definitely buy the stock at 13¹⁄₁₆. What if no one agreed to sell it to you there? That is the risk you must take. But it is a risk worth taking because it is a no-lose proposition. Either you buy the stock at your price, or you don't buy it at all.

Are there any other stocks at this point in the day that catch your eye? Do any other stocks meet the criteria of having wide bid-ask spreads, decent trading volume, and low volatility? Yes, there are several others. Look at #15, Glimcher Realty Trust (GRT) (see Figure 10.5). The real-time market is as follows:

GRT   16³⁄₄–16¹⁵⁄₁₆   29 × 5   43,800

Has the stock moved up or down more than ¼ point? No, it has not. It is down ¹⁄₁₆ on the day.

Is the stock trading actively today? It has traded 43,800 shares, enough volume for you to get in and out efficiently.

Does the stock have a wide bid-ask spread? Yes, it does. The stock is 16¾ bid, offered at 16¹⁵⁄₁₆. The spread is ³⁄₁₆ wide. This gives you plenty of room to work with.

The plan of action is to bid for 2,000 shares at 16¹³⁄₁₆, and then, if you buy the stock, to offer it out for sale at 16⅞. You are attempting to make a trading profit of $125 by getting between the spread.

As you can see, this kind of strategy can be repeated throughout the trading day, regardless of the stock, provided the stock has a low volatility. Wide bid-ask spreads are one of the market's many short-term inefficiencies. As such, they never last for long. Eventually, a scalper will take advantage of the situation. When the scalper attempts to exploit the bid-ask spread, the spread will inevitably close. Your goal is to be alert and beat the other scalpers to the punch. If you can do

Figure 10.5 Checking stocks for our trading criteria.

	Symbol	Last	Change	Volume	Bid	Ask	Bid Size × Ask Size
1	ADF	$10\frac{3}{8}$	$+\frac{1}{8}$	47,600	$10\frac{3}{8}$	$10\frac{7}{16}$	11 × 120
2	EE	9	$+\frac{1}{8}$	52,100	9	$9\frac{1}{16}$	4 × 9
3	NMK	$14\frac{7}{8}$	$-\frac{9}{16}$	301,400	$14\frac{13}{16}$	15	50 × 100
4	BS	$9\frac{1}{4}$	$-\frac{3}{16}$	470,500	$9\frac{3}{16}$	$9\frac{1}{4}$	409 × 220
5	JEQ	$8\frac{1}{8}$	$-\frac{3}{16}$	62,000	$8\frac{1}{16}$	$8\frac{1}{4}$	10 × 100
6	DHF	$13\frac{1}{8}$	$+\frac{1}{8}$	203,900	13	$13\frac{3}{16}$	145 × 70
7	ACG	$9\frac{9}{16}$	$+\frac{1}{8}$	38,700	$9\frac{7}{16}$	$9\frac{9}{16}$	116 × 79
8	GCH	$7\frac{1}{4}$	$-\frac{1}{8}$	57,100	$7\frac{3}{16}$	$7\frac{1}{4}$	10 × 36
9	WEC	$30\frac{13}{16}$	$-\frac{3}{16}$	204,400	$30\frac{5}{8}$	$30\frac{13}{16}$	200 × 10
10	CV	$10\frac{7}{8}$	0	11,100	$10\frac{9}{16}$	$10\frac{7}{8}$	22 × 5
11	NIIP	$22\frac{1}{8}$	$+\frac{1}{8}$	32,100	$22\frac{1}{16}$	$22\frac{3}{16}$	10 × 16
12	TCO	$13\frac{5}{16}$	$1\frac{1}{16}$	11,800	$13\frac{1}{4}$	$13\frac{3}{8}$	100 × 50
13	UDR	$11\frac{3}{8}$	$-\frac{1}{16}$	171,400	$11\frac{3}{8}$	$11\frac{1}{2}$	11 × 45
14	WRE	$17\frac{13}{16}$	$+\frac{1}{16}$	20,500	$17\frac{3}{4}$	$17\frac{7}{8}$	10 × 5
15	GRT	$16\frac{13}{16}$	$-\frac{1}{16}$	43,800	$16\frac{3}{4}$	$16\frac{15}{16}$	29 × 5
16	FRT	$23\frac{1}{4}$	$+\frac{1}{4}$	48,500	23	$23\frac{1}{4}$	10 × 14

Real-time data courtesy of Paragon Software, Inc. (InterQuote), 1-800-311-1516, www .interquote.com.

that consistently, you will be profitable. Not to mention that it certainly helps when you stick with trading stocks that are ignored by the rest of the trading community.

Method 3: Shadow the Specialist

Finding a wide bid-ask spread is the easiest way to identify stocks that are ripe for a quick trade. On any given day, however, it may be difficult to find stocks that fit your strict criteria. You may find wide spreads, but they might be in stocks that don't trade actively. Or, you may find that all your stocks are trading in tight $\frac{1}{16}$ spreads. Remember, a wide spread in a liquid stock that doesn't move is an aberration, and it will not last. This means that most of the time, wide bid-ask spreads will appear and disappear quickly.

But do not panic. There is more than one way to trade for teenies. The second best trading method is to pick a stock with a tight spread of $\frac{1}{16}$—if and only if the specialist is on both sides of the market. Why do you want to find the specialist? As mentioned in previous chapters, the role of the specialists is to maintain an orderly market. By risking their own trading capital, specialists ensure that there is always someone there to take the other side of customer buy and sell orders at the market. Specialists will only risk their capital when they feel their chances for profit are good. And they know the market in their particular stock better than anyone. Remember, the specialist is the best day trader in the world. So, if the specialist is willing to buy stock at 15, that is all you need to know. You should attempt to buy stock at 15 as well.

Stepping in Front of the Specialist.   There is a more important reason as well. If the specialist is the only one bidding or offering stock at a given price level, and you enter an order at the same price, the specialist has to give your order priority over his or her own. You will be entitled to the first stock that trades at your price, even if the specialist is willing to pay the same price. This rule will allow you to undercut the specialist on every trade. It should be noted, however, that if another customer order reaches the specialist before yours, you will have to get in line behind the customer, and you will not have priority. If you are actively trading, you don't want to get in the habit of waiting in line behind other customers, because in these stocks, if you are not first in line, you may wait all day before you buy stock at your price level. To ensure that this doesn't happen, stick with stocks with low bid sizes and ask sizes.

How do you know where the specialist is? Look at the bid size and the ask size. My rule of thumb is to look for stocks with bid sizes and ask sizes of 1,000 shares or less. Generally, this will be the specialist. If it is a customer, it is of no consequence, because the line you are getting in is not that long. Either way, it is a favorable trade for the day trader. Let's look at an example.

Once you have taken advantage of all stocks with wide spreads, it is time to exploit stocks with tight spreads: When you scroll down the list of 16 stocks, concentrate on those stocks that are trading in tight $\frac{1}{16}$-point spreads. There are numerous examples of this. But the tight spread is not the important factor, the bid size and the ask size are. Look at #2, El Paso Electric (EE) (see Figure 10.6). The market is 9 to $9\frac{1}{16}$, 400 shares by 900 shares. This is perfect. The bid-ask spread is $\frac{1}{16}$ point wide, 9 to $9\frac{1}{16}$. And there are only 400 shares willing to be bought and only 900 shares willing to be sold. In other words, the line is short on both the bid and the ask. Is it a customer or the specialist? Always

Figure 10.6 Checking for stocks with tight bid-ask spreads and low bid and ask sizes for trading.

	Symbol	Last	Change	Volume	Bid	Ask	Bid Size × Ask Size
1	ADF	10 3/8	+1/8	47,600	10 3/8	10 7/16	11 × 120
2	EE	9	+1/8	52,100	9	9 1/16	4 × 9
3	NMK	14 7/8	−3/16	301,400	14 13/16	15	50 × 100
4	BS	9 1/4	−3/16	470,500	9 3/16	9 1/4	409 × 220
5	JEQ	8 1/8	−3/16	62,000	8 1/16	8 1/4	10 × 100
6	DHF	13 1/8	+1/8	203,900	13	13 3/16	145 × 70
7	ACG	9 9/16	+1/8	38,700	9 7/16	9 9/16	116 × 79
8	GCH	7 1/4	−1/8	57,100	7 3/16	7 1/4	10 × 36
9	WEC	30 13/16	−3/16	204,400	30 5/8	30 13/16	200 × 10
10	CV	10 5/8	0	11,100	10 9/16	10 7/8	22 × 5
11	NHP	22 1/8	+1/8	32,100	22 1/16	22 3/16	10 × 16
12	TCO	13 5/16	+1/16	11,800	13 1/4	13 3/8	100 × 50
13	UDR	11 3/8	−1/16	171,400	11 3/8	11 1/2	11 × 45
14	WRE	17 13/16	+1/16	20,500	17 3/4	17 7/8	10 × 5
15	GRT	16 13/16	−1/16	43,800	16 3/4	16 15/16	29 × 5
16	FRT	23 1/8	+1/4	48,500	23	23 1/4	10 × 14

Real-time data courtesy of Paragon Software, Inc. (InterQuote), 1-800-311-1516, www.interquote.com.

assume that when the bid size and the ask size are small it is the specialist on both the bid and the ask. There is no way to tell for sure, but in this case it really doesn't matter anyway. The line is short.

The plan is to buy 2,000 shares on the bid, and then, if you are lucky enough to buy, to attempt to sell 2,000 shares on the ask. In other words, using limit orders, you will attempt to do exactly what the specialist is doing: to buy stock at 9 and sell stock at 9 1/16. But, unlike the specialist, you are going after 2,000 shares.

As mentioned before, you do not need the stock to move for you to make a teenie. Remember, you are not attempting to outsmart the market. You are not making a prediction that EE is a good long-term investment. You are simply acting as a middleman. You are positioning yourself ahead of the random buying and selling in the stock. In a sense, the price at which you buy the stock at is not your concern; the ability to make a quick teenie is. It doesn't matter if the stock is at 9 or 10 or 11. You just need to sell the stock 1/16 higher than where you bought it.

There is no guarantee that you will buy the stock at your price of $9. What you do know is that, if you are lucky enough to buy the stock at $9, there is an excellent chance you will be able to sell the stock at 9$\frac{1}{16}$ for a $125 profit. So you set your trap and wait. You bid for 2,000 shares at 9. If a sell order reaches the floor of the exchange for 2,000 shares at the market, the seller will hit your bid. The stock will trade at 9, and you will be the buyer. And, as you know by now, the second the stock is in your position, you enter a sell order at 9$\frac{1}{16}$. It is the same procedure as before. You are not getting greedy. Take your teenie and run!

The Process of Elimination.   In the universe of low-volatility stocks, it is not going to be that hard to find stocks trading in bid-ask spreads of $\frac{1}{16}$s. However, not every stock that trades in $\frac{1}{16}$-point spreads is going to be a good trade. It is very easy to weed out the bad candidates, though. One of the first things to look for when eliminating a stock is the size of the bid and the size of the ask. If you are buying on the bid and selling on the ask, you must make sure you have first position over the other buyers and sellers. In other words, if the bid size or ask size is large, that is another way of saying the line is long. You will not have first position. Why not? Because other customers or traders have beaten you to the punch. Let's look at an example from our group of 16 stocks.

Look at stock #4, Bethlehem Steel (see Figure 10.7). The bid-ask spread is $\frac{1}{16}$ point wide—9$\frac{3}{16}$ to 9$\frac{1}{4}$. If you are just looking at the bid-ask spread, you may think there is the chance to make a teenie by buying 2,000 shares at 9$\frac{3}{16}$ and selling them at 9$\frac{1}{4}$. But notice the size of the market. There are 40,900 shares willing to be bought at 9$\frac{3}{16}$ already. And there are 22,200 shares willing to be sold at 9$\frac{1}{4}$. There is no way you will be able to trade this stock for a $\frac{1}{16}$-point profit. Why not? Because for you to be able to buy 2,000 shares at 9$\frac{3}{16}$, you have to get in line behind the 40,900-share order that arrived first. That means that, before you can buy even 1 share of stock, 40,900 shares have to trade first at 9$\frac{3}{16}$. The only way it is possible to cut in line is if that entire 40,900-share bid is the specialist, and the chances of that are highly unlikely. If the specialist were really willing to buy 40,900 shares at 9$\frac{3}{16}$, he or she would certainly not advertise this intention to the entire world. That is why the bid size and the ask size are so important in determining the likelihood of a profitable trade.

Please note that the bid size and the ask size are not a problem if the bid-ask spread is wide. Why not? Because you are not getting in line with the other bidders. Instead, you are outbidding them by $\frac{1}{16}$. That

Figure 10.7 Eliminating stocks with large bid and ask sizes.

	Symbol	Last	Change	Volume	Bid	Ask	Bid Size × Ask Size
1	ADF	10⅜	+⅛	47,600	10⅜	10 7/16	11 × 120
2	EE	9	+⅛	52,100	9	9 1/16	4 × 9
3	NMK	14⅛	−3/16	301,400	14 13/16	15	50 × 100
4	BS	9¼	−3/16	470,500	9 3/16	9¼	409 × 220
5	JEQ	8⅛	−3/16	62,000	8 1/16	8¼	10 × 100
6	DHF	13⅛	+⅛	203,900	13	13 3/16	145 × 70
7	ACG	9 9/16	+⅛	38,700	9 7/16	9 9/16	116 × 79
8	GCH	7¼	−⅛	57,100	7 3/16	7¼	10 × 36
9	WEC	30 13/16	−3/16	204,400	30⅝	30 13/16	200 × 10
10	CV	10⅝	0	11,100	10 9/16	10⅞	22 × 5
11	NHP	22⅛	+⅛	32,100	22 1/16	22 3/16	10 × 16
12	TCO	13 5/16	+1/16	11,800	13¼	13⅜	100 × 50
13	UDR	11⅜	−1/16	171,400	11⅜	11½	11 × 45
14	WRE	17 13/16	+1/16	20,500	17¾	17⅞	10 × 5
15	GRT	16 13/16	−1/16	43,800	16¾	16 15/16	29 × 5
16	FRT	23⅛	+¼	48,500	23	23¼	10 × 14

Real-time data courtesy of Paragon Software, Inc. (InterQuote), 1-800-311-1516, www.interquote.com.

ensures that you have first priority over other customers. When the bid-ask spread is only 1/16, however, you will not have this luxury, because there will be no wiggle room to buy the stock for any price other than the bid. That is why a wide bid-ask spread, if found, is an easier trade.

APPLYING WHAT YOU HAVE LEARNED

Figure 10.8 is another screen shot of the list of 16 low-volatility stocks as it appeared in real time on a different day than the previous example—the afternoon of November 20, 1998. Now you will use the rules and strategies you have learned and apply them to this situation in the hopes of making a quick teenie. What is the best trade here?

Obviously, once you have eliminated stocks that are up or down ¼ point, and stocks that have low trading volume under 20,000 shares, you will look for a wide-bid ask spread. Look at #5, Japan Equity (JEQ),

Figure 10.8 Screen shot of selected low-volatility stocks on the afternoon of November 20, 1998.

	Symbol	Last	Change	Volume	Bid	Ask	Bid Size × Ask Size
1	ADF	10 3/16	−1/16	49,600	10 1/8	10 3/16	42 × 10
2	EE	9 7/16	−1/16	25,900	9 3/8	9 1/2	5 × 19
3	NMK	15 1/8	+0	231,200	15 1/16	15 3/16	250 × 139
4	BS	8 3/4	+1/16	293,100	8 11/16	8 3/4	200 × 250
5	JEQ	8 13/16	+0	62,200	8 3/4	9	110 × 256
6	DHF	12 11/16	+1/8	179,400	12 5/8	12 11/16	52 × 4
7	ACG	9 9/16	+0	84,000	9 9/16	9 5/8	68 × 67
8	GCH	7 3/8	−1/8	54,500	7 3/8	7 7/16	5 × 58
9	WEC	30 13/16	+1/8	236,400	30 5/8	30 7/8	16 × 200
10	CV	11	+1/16	14,600	11	11 1/16	40 × 13
11	NHP	22 5/16	+1/8	34,300	22 1/8	22 5/16	10 × 10
12	TCO	13 7/16	−1/16	26,400	13 3/8	13 1/2	100 × 50
13	UDR	10 11/16	+3/16	408,300	10 9/16	10 11/16	12 × 47
14	WRE	17 5/16	+1/8	12,900	17 1/4	17 5/16	10 × 5
15	GRT	15 13/16	−3/8	89,100	15 13/16	16	7 × 20
16	FRT	22 3/4	+1/8	46,900	22 5/8	22 15/16	5 × 5

Real-time data courtesy of Paragon Software, Inc. (InterQuote), 1-800-311-1516, www .interquote.com.

a closed-end stock fund. The stock is unchanged on the day and has traded 62,200 shares. The bid-ask spread is ¼ point wide, 8¾ bid to 9. As a day trader, you cannot ask for a better situation than this one. Remember, wide bid-ask spreads in low-volatility stocks will not last. That is why, when you see an opportunity, you must not hesitate to act.

The plan of action is to get between the spread. You are going to bid ⅟₁₆ point higher than the current bid of 8¾. Therefore, you will bid for 2,000 shares at 8¹³⁄₁₆. If you are lucky enough to buy the stock at your price, you will attempt to sell those 2,000 shares at 8⅞. That is how you will be able to make ⅟₁₆, or $125, in the stock.

Assume you have enough trading capital to trade more than 2,000 shares of JEQ. Of the other 15 stocks on our list, which looks best? Notice the highlighted stock in Figure 10.9, ACM Government Income Fund (ACG), a closed-end bond fund. Is this a good trade right now? No, it is not. To find out why, use the four-step screening process shown in Table 10.2.

Figure 10.9 Applying the four-step screening process.

	Symbol	Last	Change	Volume	Bid	Ask	Bid Size × Ask Size
1	ADF	$10\frac{3}{16}$	$-\frac{1}{16}$	49,600	$10\frac{1}{8}$	$10\frac{3}{16}$	42 × 10
2	EE	$9\frac{7}{16}$	$-\frac{1}{16}$	25,900	$9\frac{3}{8}$	$9\frac{1}{2}$	5 × 19
3	NMK	$15\frac{1}{8}$	+0	231,200	$15\frac{1}{16}$	$15\frac{3}{16}$	250 × 139
4	BS	$8\frac{3}{4}$	$+\frac{1}{16}$	293,100	$8\frac{11}{16}$	$8\frac{3}{4}$	200 × 250
5	JEQ	$8\frac{13}{16}$	+0	62,200	$8\frac{3}{4}$	9	110 × 256
6	DHF	$12\frac{11}{16}$	$+\frac{1}{8}$	179,400	$12\frac{5}{8}$	$12\frac{11}{16}$	52 × 4
7	ACG	$9\frac{9}{16}$	+0	84,000	$9\frac{9}{16}$	$9\frac{5}{8}$	68 × 67
8	GCH	$7\frac{3}{8}$	$-\frac{1}{8}$	54,500	$7\frac{3}{8}$	$7\frac{7}{16}$	5 × 58
9	WEC	$30\frac{13}{16}$	$+\frac{1}{8}$	236,400	$30\frac{5}{8}$	$30\frac{7}{8}$	16 × 200
10	CV	11	$+\frac{1}{16}$	14,600	11	$11\frac{1}{16}$	40 × 13
11	NHP	$22\frac{5}{16}$	$+\frac{1}{8}$	34,300	$22\frac{1}{8}$	$22\frac{5}{16}$	10 × 10
12	TCO	$13\frac{7}{16}$	$-\frac{1}{16}$	26,400	$13\frac{3}{8}$	$13\frac{1}{2}$	100 × 50
13	UDR	$10\frac{11}{16}$	$+\frac{3}{16}$	408,300	$10\frac{9}{16}$	$10\frac{11}{16}$	12 × 47
14	WRE	$17\frac{5}{16}$	$+\frac{1}{8}$	12,900	$17\frac{1}{4}$	$17\frac{5}{16}$	10 × 5
15	GRT	$15\frac{13}{16}$	$-\frac{3}{8}$	89,100	$15\frac{13}{16}$	16	7 × 20
16	FRT	$22\frac{3}{4}$	$+\frac{1}{8}$	46,900	$22\frac{5}{8}$	$22\frac{15}{16}$	5 × 5

Real-time data courtesy of Paragon Software, Inc. (InterQuote), 1-800-311-1516, www.interquote.com.

1. Is the stock up or down less than $\frac{1}{4}$ point on the day? Yes: It is unchanged on the day.
2. Has the stock traded at least 20,000 shares today? Yes: It has traded 84,000.
3. Does the stock have a wide bid-ask spread? No: It is trading in a $\frac{1}{16}$-point spread, $9\frac{9}{16}$ to $9\frac{5}{8}$.
4. If the stock has a narrow bid-ask spread, are the bid size and ask size low? No: The bid size is 6,800 and the ask size is 6,700. In other words, there are 6,800 shares willing to be bought at $9\frac{9}{16}$, and 6,700 shares willing to be sold at $9\frac{5}{8}$.

This is why ACG is not a good trade right now. The line is too long. Another trader or traders have beat you to the punch. When the bid-ask spread is only $\frac{1}{16}$ point wide, it is essential that the bid size and ask size be small. Think about it. The stock is not going anywhere. It is unchanged on the day. The only way to make a profit is to buy on the

---

Table 10.2   Cutsheet for exploiting the bid-ask spread on the New York Stock Exchange.

Step 1: Eliminate any stock that is up or down more than ¼ point on the day. This will limit your risk of loss because it will force you to stick with the most stable stocks on that given trading day.

Step 2: Eliminate any stock that is trading fewer than 20,000 shares of volume by the end of the day. The reality is that many low-volatility stocks simply don't trade enough during the day to enable you to get in and get out efficiently. If you get stuck in a stock that doesn't trade often, it may take the better part of the day to unload the stock at your price. If you have limited trading capital, this will tie your money up for extended periods, preventing you from jumping on better opportunities when they arise.

Step 3: Find a stock that has a wide bid-ask spread of at least ³⁄₁₆—for instance, 11 to 11³⁄₁₆. Immediately enter a buy order for 2,000 shares ¹⁄₁₆ point higher than the bid. If you buy the stock, then offer the stock out for sale ¹⁄₁₆ point higher.

Step 4: If you are unable to find any stocks that have wide bid-ask spreads, look for a stock with a ¹⁄₁₆-point spread—11 to 11¹⁄₁₆, for example. But be careful. You should not trade the stock unless both the bid size and the ask size are small. Chances are, you will be stepping in front of the specialist on both the buy and the sell. Buy on the bid, and then sell on the ask. If the market is 11 to 11¹⁄₁₆, bid for 2,000 shares at 11, and then if you buy the stock, sell 2,000 shares at 11¹⁄₁₆.

---

bid and sell on the ask. How will you do that? By getting in line behind the other buyer at 9⁹⁄₁₆. But the bid size is 68. A total of 6,800 shares must trade at 9⁹⁄₁₆ before you can buy even 1 share at that price. In a stock that has only traded 84,000 shares all day, it may take four hours or more to buy the stock. Or it could take all day.

Then, once the stock is bought, that is only half the battle. You will be faced with the same obstacle when you try to sell the stock at 9⁵⁄₈. Someone is already in line to sell 6,700 shares at 9⁵⁄₈. That means that for you to sell at 9⁵⁄₈, all of this stock would have to trade first—not a likely scenario.

The market in ACG is a good example of how important it is to be the first one in on a stock when the opportunity arises. In these slow-moving issues, there is not going to be room for more than one trader at a time. In this case there is a very good chance that it is the same trader on both the bid and the ask. Imagine the profit that trader will make by buying 6,800 shares at 9$\frac{9}{16}$ and selling 6,700 shares at 9$\frac{5}{8}$. That person will have made a teenie on 6,700 shares—a profit of $418.75 in a stock that was unchanged on the day. The profit was the direct result of the fact that the trader saw this opportunity before anyone else did, and acted on it.

HOLDING OVERNIGHT POSITIONS

Imagine that, even in light of the conditions in the stock, you entered a buy order for 2,000 ACG at 9$\frac{9}{16}$. What would happen if you bought the stock at 9$\frac{9}{16}$, but were unable to sell it at 9$\frac{5}{8}$ by the end of the trading day? This presents a real dilemma. Do you take the risk of holding the stock overnight? Or, do you unload the stock at 3:59 at the market at whatever price you can find a buyer, even if it is at a loss? The answer to this question sheds some light on why you should stick with low-volatility stocks in the first place. As long as the stock is stable, you have to accept the fact that sometimes you will be forced to hold overnight positions.

When you are exploiting the bid-ask spread, you are constantly going to turn over the stock positions in your account. It is a continual process of buying and selling. If possible, every trader would prefer to be flat, or without a position, by the end of every trading day. In our game of trading slow-moving stocks, that is a fantasy. The reality is that you are not going to be able to sell all of your positions by the end of the trading day all the time at your price. This means that there are going to be times when you are forced into carrying a 2,000-share position overnight.

In the world of day trading high-volatility stocks, many traders refuse to hold any stocks overnight. They consider this practice extremely risky, because the majority of price movement occurs when stocks gap up or gap down on the open of trading the next morning. Imagine buying 2,000 shares of IBM and holding the stock overnight. To your horror, you awake the next morning to a front-page article in *The Wall Street Journal* that says IBM's earnings estimates have been downgraded significantly. Bad news like this could easily cause the stock to open down 10 points the next trading day. If the stock closed at 100, it might open the next morning at 90. The same is true of good news: It could easily make the stock open up 10 points. The minute you get into the habit of taking overnight positions in volatile stocks, factors come into play that are entirely out of your hands. That is exactly the point: Holding volatile stocks overnight leaves too much to chance. Remember, if trading is your livelihood, luck and chance will not put food on your table.

In the world of low-volatility stocks, however, a gap opening is unlikely. It is not out of the realm of possibility, however. Closed-end bond funds will very rarely be in the news. Electric utilities and real estate investment trusts, on the other hand, will be. Every trader must face the choice between holding the stock overnight or liquidating it at a loss before the market closes. I prefer to hold the stock overnight on the belief that, over the course of the year, the good and bad effects of taking overnight positions will balance out. Remember, trading is not without some degree of risk. You must do all you can to limit that risk, but sometimes there is nothing you can do. Taking risks is as much a part of trading as making profits.

If you are uncomfortable with taking overnight positions, the only thing you could do is refrain from entering any buy orders after a certain time (2:00 P.M., for instance). This will give you at least two full hours to sell any position you might own before the market closes, eliminating the risk of buying a stock at 3:45 in the afternoon and not being able to sell it for a profit before 4:00 when the market closes.

THE SCREENING PROCESS

It is my hope that you now have a good feel for the mechanics behind exploiting the bid-ask spread. The next step is to apply the strategy, and that is a matter of picking the appropriate stocks. Table 10.3 provides an extensive list of such stocks that have two things in common: They are in market segments that historically have low volatility, and they trade on the New York Stock Exchange (and several on the American Stock Exchange). None of the stocks in these lists are NASDAQ stocks.

A word of advice: I would caution against trading any electric utilities, real estate investment trusts, or closed-end stock funds that are priced at over $30 per share. Higher-priced stocks typically have more volatility and trade in a wider range than lower-priced ones. And, as you know, when trading for teenies, you want to eliminate volatility as

Table 10.3   Day trader's sample list of appropriate stocks for trading.

Closed-End Bond Funds

AAT	ACG	ADF	AMF	AMU	APX	ARK	AWF	AWG	AXT
BKN	BMN	BMT	BNA	BRM	CFD	CIF	CIM	CMK	CMU
COY	CXE	CXH	CYE	DBS	DBU	DHF	DHY	DMF	DSI
DSM	DSU	DUC	EDF	EFL	EMD	FAX	FBF	FBI	FCO
FMI	FT	GDF	GHI	GIM	GSF	GSI	HIS	HIX	HYB
HYF	IIM	IMS	IMT	IQI	JHS	KBA	KMM	KST	KTF
KYT	LBG	LEO	MCR	MEN	MFM	MGB	MGF	MHD	MIF
MIN	MMT	MMU	MQT	MQY	MSD	MSY	MTU	MUS	MVF
MVT	MYD	MYI	NIF	NIO	NMA	NMO	NPF	NPI	NPM
NPP	NPT	NPX	NQI	NQM	NQU	NUV	NXQ	NXR	OIA
OIB	OMS	PGM	PHF	PIA	PIF	PIM	PMG	PMH	PMM
PMO	PMT	PPM	PPT	PYM	RCS	SBG	SBW	SEL	SGL
3I	SQF	TEI	TFA	TFB	TGG	VGM	VKA	VKI	VKQ
VKV	VMO	VMT	VOT	WDV	XAA	YLD	YLT	ZTR	

Real Estate Investment Trust

ACN	ACP	ACR	AEC	AER	AHE	AIC	AKR	AMB	AML
ARI	ASN	AXM	BDN	BED	BFS	BNP	BOY	BPP	BRE
BRI	BTR	CAX	CBG	CBL	CDC	CDX	CEI	CLI	CMM
CMO	CNT	CPJ	CPP	CPT	CRE	CT	CWN	DDR	DRE
EGP	EIN	ENN	EOP	EPR	EQY	FCH	FFA	FR	FRT
FRW	FUR	GB	GBP	GLB	GLR	GRT	GTA	GTY	HCM
HCN	HIW	HME	HPT	HR	HTL	IAC	ICH	IMH	IND
INV	IRS	JDN	JPR	KIM	KPA	KRC	KRT	LFT	LHO
LMM	LRY	LTC	LXP	MAA	MAC	MDN	MHX	MRR	MT
NDE	NFI	NHI	NHP	NLY	NNN	NXL	OAC	PAG	PAH
PEI	PGE	PKY	PLD	PNP	PP	PPS	PRT	PSA	PSB
PW	PZN	REA	REG	RFS	RPI	RWT	SEA	SHU	SIZ
SKT	SLG	SMT	SPG	SSS	TCC	TCO	TCR	TCT	TEE
TMA	TOW	TRI	TZH	UDR	UHT	UMH	USV	WDN	WEA
WIR	WKS	WRE	WRP	WXH					

Lower-Priced Electric Utilities

BGR	CIV	CPN	CSR	CTP	CV	CZN	DPL	EE	EIX
EUA	GMP	ILN	KEP	LGE	NMK	NSP	NU	NVP	OGE
PNM	POM	PPL	PPW	PSD	TE	UNS	WWP		

Table 10.3 *(Continued).*

Closed-End Stock Funds								
ASG	BKF	BLU	BTO	BZF	CVT	CWF	DDF	
DIV	DNP	EMG	EQS	ETF	FAK	GAB	GCH	
GCV	GGT	GHS	GRF	GRR	HQL	IF	IFN	
JEQ	JFC	JOF	KEF	KF	MF	MGC	NBM	
PCF	PGD	RIF	RVT	SBF	TC	TMF	TTF	USA

much as possible. For instance, 2,000 shares of a $10 utility are going to be a safer trade than 2,000 shares of a $50 utility.

That is why the lists on the following pages leave out numerous issues trading in the higher price ranges. Obviously, market conditions and stock prices will have changed to some degree by the time this book reaches the shelves. Regardless, there are simply too many lower-priced issues you could trade instead of taking the added risk of higher-priced stocks. Not to mention that if you have limited trading capital, you will be forced to trade lower-priced stocks if you want to trade 2,000 shares at a time as I suggest. In addition to the following lists, I recommend you check your newspapers each morning for any NYSE-listed stocks that are trading below $10 per share. The low price alone will be a shield against volatility to a certain degree, thus allowing the potential for a quick trade.

It is important to remember that, of the hundreds of stocks listed in Table 10.3, not every one will necessarily be ripe for a trade at all times. As stated earlier, you should only trade when the odds are in your favor. Sometimes this means looking at 20 or 30 stocks before you find one that fits your criteria. In the beginning, I suggest you start with about 5 to 10 different names. Even if you don't make any trades, familiarize yourself with how these particular stocks trade. It really doesn't matter which names you pick. After a while, you will start to develop a feel for how a particular stock acts, and that is when you will be able to start trading the stock profitably.

One of the great things about trading stocks from these lists is that, at any given time of any given day, you might be the only speculator in the stock other than the specialist. These stocks are generally ignored by the rest of the day trading community. Without outside competition, it is a head-to-head battle between you and the specialist, and thus it is much easier to make teenies than if other market players were involved.

Due to mergers or other unforeseen economic events, some of these names may be unsuitable—specifically, too volatile—for our trading strategy at the time of publication. This is only a sample list. Proceed with caution.

Please note that Table 10.3 shows only a sampling of closed-end bond funds. There are literally hundreds of other issues that have been left out. As you know, the danger in day trading these bond funds is not volatility but lack of trading volume. You do not want to get stuck in a position that does not trade often. That is why you must make sure the stock has traded at least 20,000 shares that day before you consider entering a buy order.

There are many more issues in the universe of electric utilities than the ones listed in Table 10.3. Issues trading above $30 per share at the time of publication have been intentionally left out. The risk with some electric utilities is generally not a lack of trading volume, but occasional volatility. Stick with the lower-priced issues. As mentioned earlier, there is much less risk involved in buying 2,000 shares of an $8 stock than in buying 2,000 shares of an $80 stock.

Closed-end stock funds are more volatile than closed-end bond funds. Many of these stock funds have overseas exposure. For this reason, I cannot stress enough the importance of only trading issues that are up or down less than ¼ point from the previous day's close. This will serve to screen out any issues that do not fit the low-volatility criteria.

IN SUMMARY

As a day trader, you must keep your strategy in the back of your mind at all times. Essentially, you look to do one thing, and one thing only: to buy stock at price levels where you are almost certain you can turn around and sell the stock for a profit. Either you buy the stock at your price or move on to another stock. You pick and choose your opportunities carefully. Not every stock is ripe for a trade, and that is why you must only trade when the odds are in your favor.

It is important to keep day trading in perspective. Remember, the day trader is a middleman and nothing more. By exploiting the bid-ask spread, day traders are able to extract tiny profits out of the market.

This kind of trading strategy only works because day traders are fulfilling a need the market has: being buyers when the market needs buyers, and sellers when the market needs sellers. As a day trader, you fill the gap between supply and demand. All the while, as long as you can shield yourself from volatility, it is not necessary to know anything more about the stocks you trade. You are not an analyst, nor are you an investor. You are a trader.

SECTION V

Trading the Momentum

Dow Stocks, NASDAQ, and Event-Driven Trading

Day traders who want to last in this game must limit their risk. But taking risk is as much a part of trading as it is a part of everyday life. While some situations call for prudence, others call for guts. There are certain rare times when the odds are overwhelmingly in the trader's favor, when taking a big risk is justified. When this happens, it is no longer about trading for teenies. This is not about trading utilities, real estate investment trusts, or closed-end funds. Instead, this is the domain of the high flyers: IBM, Microsoft, Dell, Intel, Yahoo!.

The minute you begin to venture into this arena, you enter a different sort of battlefield entirely, with different rules, strategies, and risks. This is a high-stakes game, and the pace is lightning fast. And there are land mines everywhere. What is the worst that can happen? You will step on one of these land mines, and it will wipe you out. It can happen to anyone, even the most careful of traders. Has it happened to me? Yes, it has. I once lost over $12,000 in about 24 hours trading this way.

There is nothing more exciting than getting on the right side of a stock that is flying. And there is nothing more terrifying than being on the wrong side of a stock that is plummeting. Day traders who *choose to trade these stocks will face this every single day. Momentum trading is not for the faint of heart, nor is it for those with weak stomachs. But pass this test and you will be among an elite group. The people that excel here can make and lose more money in a single day than most people could in several weeks trading for $\frac{1}{16}$s.*

CHAPTER 11

The Momentum Game

Momentum trading requires an entirely different set of skills and strategies than the ones involved in exploiting the bid-ask spread for teenies. If that strategy required more brains, this one requires more guts. If that was a chess match, this is a high-stakes game of poker. You must be forewarned: The people you are trading against in the land of momentum are the best in the business. These are high-volatility stocks, and the risk is extremely high. Fortunes are made and lost in the blink of an eye. You must remember that in this game, online day traders are not on the inside, they are on the outside. What does this mean? It means that, unlike in the trading of low-volatility stocks, the odds favor the house, not the day trader.

When I trade high-volatility stocks, often I can feel my heart race. Why? Because I know the terror and hardship this kind of trading can inflict on you if you are not careful. Let your guard down for even one second and you will get crushed. Step away from your computer for a few minutes, and you might lose a week's or a month's worth of hard-earned profits. But, as with everything else, you can beat the system. How? By only trading momentum stocks when the odds are in your favor.

THE DANGERS OF SLOW EXECUTION

Until now, the majority of this book has been devoted to trading low-volatility stocks. The rest will be spent detailing the pros and cons of trading higher-volatility issues, such as Dow stocks and NASDAQ tech stocks. These are the kind of stocks that can easily move ½ point or more in a matter of only a few seconds. When you are trading stocks that move drastically, the speed of your execution means everything. Even being one or two seconds too slow could mean the difference between making and losing several thousand dollars. As online traders, you and I do not have the luxury of a fast execution. When placing trades over the Internet, a slow execution is a fact of life, which is exactly why I prefer to trade lower-volatility stocks, where it is not execution speed but trading strategy that is the determining factor. That is the only way I have been able to consistently overcome the disadvantage that I face by trading from home and thus make a living as an online day trader.

But that is not to say you can't make money trading high-profile, high-volatility stocks over the Internet. You can. And, when you are right, the amount of money you will make on these stocks is staggering. But, when you are wrong, the amount of money you will lose is also staggering. That is why you must proceed cautiously.

As you know, when you place trades over the Internet, the reality is that your execution is going to be much slower than that of your trading counterparts on Wall Street. There is absolutely nothing you can do about this. The only thing you have control over is your trading strategy. In low-volatility stocks, a slow execution is not a problem because the stocks being traded aren't moving. But what about stocks that are moving? You have to accept the fact that, when you trade high-volatility stocks, you are going to be leaving money on the table every time you trade. You are not going to be able to pick tops and bottoms on stocks, nor are you going to get filled at the best possible prices. You are not going to be the first one in, and you are certainly not going to be the first one out.

But that does not mean you can't trade these high flyers profitably. You just have to pick and choose your opportunities carefully. If you trade these stocks all the time, the odds are going to be against you as long as you are trading over the Internet. So how do you tip the odds in your favor? By being extremely selective when determining which stocks to trade and when. Every so often, there are going to be times when all the forces align to enable you to hit a home run. But these instances are going to be few and far between. When they do arise, you must capitalize on them. When they do not, you should stay as far away from this segment of the market as possible.

WHAT IS MOMENTUM TRADING?

Momentum trading is the strategy of buying and selling stocks that are in motion. In simpler terms, when a stock looks like it is moving up, you buy it. This is the exact opposite of the trading methods outlined earlier in the book. When you were trading for teenies in low-volatility stocks, you didn't need the stock to move to make money. In momentum trading, it is absolutely essential that the stock be moving. That is why you have to stick with the high-flying, high-profile names: technology stocks, blue-chip issues, stocks making headlines, market leaders. These are the stocks of choice. These stocks may trade 10 million shares in a single day. Compare that to some of our closed-end bond funds, which may only trade 20,000 shares in a day. The momentum trade is all about movement. And the goal of this kind of trading strategy is not to make $\frac{1}{16}$s, but $\frac{1}{2}$s, whole points, and even higher, because that is what you can lose if the trade goes against you. In essence, you are taking on a higher degree of risk in the attempt to make much higher profits.

We will highlight two different types of momentum trading: New York Stock Exchange–listed stocks and NASDAQ stocks. Until now, the entire book has been devoted to trading stocks that are listed on the New York Stock Exchange and the American Exchange. But the NYSE and AMEX are only half of the world of online stock trading. The other half is trading the over-the-counter or NASDAQ stocks. The over-the-counter market is a different animal entirely, and it requires slightly different strategies.

Before we get into the specific strategies, we must paint some broad strokes about the principles of momentum trading. Though NASDAQ and NYSE trading is slightly different, there are certain common threads that you must understand before you begin to trade high-volatility stocks.

THE HOUSE EDGE AND THE DANGERS
OF MOMENTUM TRADING

As you know by now, the bid-ask spread is Wall Street's form of the house edge. When you are trading low-volatility stocks, you overcome this edge by exploiting the bid-ask spread through the use of limit orders. This enables you, like the specialists, to make teenies by taking the other side of the random customer buy and sell orders that occur throughout the trading day at the market. The prerequisite for the success of that trading strategy is that the stock not move. These are low-risk trades that produce consistent profits, and as long as you are on top of your market, the specialists are of no consequence. You have the edge. You are taking money out of the specialists' pockets and there is nothing they can do about it. Essentially, you are beating the specialists at their own game.

But what about high-flying stocks? When you are trading Intel, Cisco, Compaq, and America Online, how can you beat Wall Street at its own game? How can you take food out of the specialists' mouths? The reality is that the house edge is more amplified, more exaggerated, and more powerful in volatile stocks than in slow-moving stocks. This means that if you get in the way of the market makers and the special-ists, they will destroy you. They are not going to let you in on their feast. You are forced to play by their rules, not yours. This is a fact of life and there is nothing you can do about it. But you do have one defense: You can refrain from trading until the odds are in your favor.

THE DANGER OF USING LIMIT ORDERS ON MOMENTUM TRADES

So, if exploiting the bid-ask spread works so well in low-volatility stocks, can it work for volatile stocks, where the house edge is more powerful? Absolutely not. Unlike trading low-volatility stocks, momen-tum trading requires that you use market orders, not limit orders. It is very difficult to exploit the bid-ask spread consistently in these stocks because the specialists and the market makers have the upper hand. You have a slow execution, they have a fast one. If you attempt to take food out of their mouths by using limit orders, they will use their upper hand to take advantage of you. If you try to buy on the bid, you will only buy your stock when it is headed lower. And if you try to sell on the ask, you will only sell your stock when it is headed higher. Either way, the stock will inevitably trade through your price. This is a surefire way to lose money. That is why your chance for success only lies in buying and selling at the market when you are trading high-volatility stocks.

Why is the house edge more amplified in high-profile stocks? Because bid-ask spreads are wider in volatile stocks than they are in slow-moving stocks. Remember, if the future direction of the stock is uncertain, the market markers, or specialists, will not put themselves at risk by keeping a tight spread. They will keep the bid-ask spread as wide as possible, both to maximize their profits and to protect themselves from losses in the event the stock moves against them.

But that does not tell the whole story. Wide bid-ask spreads help you when you are exploiting the spread in less volatile stocks. So why wouldn't they help you make money in momentum stocks? Because it is next to impossible to get between the spread profitably in high-volatility stocks. That fact alone forces you to use market orders. By now, you know how wide spreads will hurt you when you are buying and selling at the market. This is the problem momentum trading poses. Because of your slow execution over the Internet, and because of the fact that these stocks move so fast, you will not accomplish your goal if you attempt to buy and sell using limit orders.

Typically, in momentum trading, you should be buying stocks when they are running. If you use limit orders, you will miss the stock. In other words, the stock will move higher before you get a chance to buy it. What happens if the stock reverses its move? You will not be able to cancel your order fast enough before you get filled, even when you see it coming. You will miss the stock when it runs, and you will end up buying it at the precise moment that it drops. That is not a formula for success: It is a recipe for disaster. That is why your only chance for success lies in using market orders.

So in momentum trading you must walk a fine line. On the one hand, you know full well the dangers of entering orders at the market. You know you are leaving money on the table every time you enter a market order. But you also know the even greater danger of using limit orders in volatile stocks. This is the problem. There is no such thing as a break-even trade. If you are right, you can make big money. If you are wrong, you lose and lose big. And, if the stock doesn't move, you still lose big, because you are at the mercy of wide bid-ask spreads.

CENTERING YOUR TRADING STRATEGY AROUND SLOW EXECUTION

As discussed before, having a slow execution is the momentum trader's biggest handicap. Remember, we are not talking about "slow" in the absolute sense, but in the relative sense. On Wall Street, "slow" could mean the difference between a trade that took one second to get executed and one that took two seconds. When you place a trade over the

Internet, it is typically going to be a split second slower than those placed by traders at the big firms on Wall Street. And, when you are looking at the same buy and sell signals the Wall Streeters are, the difference between making money and losing money is not trading ability, it is execution speed. Wall Street will be in the stock before you, and will be out before you. That is the reality of trading from home over the Internet.

The fact that your execution is so slow will change the way you approach trading these momentum stocks. You do not have the precision, split-second trade executions the faster players have. When you are trading from home, you are not going to be able to buy and sell at the precise moment everyone else is. You have to be smart. You have to pick your entry and exit points carefully. What does this mean? It means the textbook buy and sell signals that all momentum traders use will not work for you as an online trader, because of your slow execution. It means you will have to be two to three seconds ahead of everyone else. You will not have the luxury of waiting until the stock begins to run before you buy it. Why? Because the second it begins to run, everyone else will be jumping on it, and you will get filled last. And when you get filled last, you get the worst possible price. It is hard enough to predict when a stock is going to move, but it is even harder to get a good execution when you are trading from home.

Let's take a real life example that happened to me in May of 1997.

It was Tuesday at around 2:10 P.M. That day was a special one because the Federal Reserve was set to announce the results of its Federal Open Market Committee (FOMC) meeting. The FOMC is the group that meets to decide what to do with interest rates. I was watching CNBC very carefully. The market consensus was split 50-50 between keeping interest rates unchanged and raising them. Anytime the market consensus is split, there will always be a big move the second the announcement is made. If the FOMC left rates unchanged, the market would soar. If rates were raised, the market would sell off.

My plan was simple: If rates were unchanged, I would buy 1,000 shares of Travelers (TRV) the second I heard the announcement. I would have to do so at the market, because the market would be moving too fast for a limit order. If rates were raised, I would refrain from placing any trades. At approximately 2:16, the announcement was made: "Fed leaves rates unchanged." As fast as I could, I entered a buy of 1,000 TRV at the market over the Internet. At the precise time my order was entered, the quote in TRV read 55⅜ to 55½. And the market was soaring. I was horrified when I got my fill report back. I was filled at 56½, up a full point from where my quote indicated the stock was trading.

What exactly was going on? I remember feeling as though I had been robbed! How could I have possibly been filled up at 56½ if the stock was trading at 55½? I was angry, and I needed an answer. I quickly called the customer service department of my online broker and demanded an explanation. It turned out it was a fair fill. The stock was trading up at 56½, not 55½. The influx of buy orders at 2:16 P.M. had caused the stock to trade up a full point in only a few seconds. The market had moved so fast that my quote screen could not update fast enough. I had made a huge error: I thought I could beat the other traders to the punch. That was the last time I ever tried to outsmart the market in a spree of panic buying.

I learned a valuable lesson from that experience. What was I thinking? In retrospect, I had made a mistake every online trader makes at least once: In my arrogance, I thought I could outsmart Wall Street. I thought I could get a jump on all the other traders who were looking at the same exact thing as I was. I thought that, by trading through an online broker, I would be assured an instantaneous execution before everyone else. What I learned is that no one will ever make any money by entering buy orders simultaneously with the rest of the investing world. Remember, the whole world knew the market would go higher if the Fed kept rates unchanged. But no one knew for certain that keeping rates unchanged would be the outcome. So all the traders on Wall Street waited until after the announcement was made to enter their buy orders. This was a classic case of panic buying. And when there is panic buying, guess who gets filled last? The novice who is trading over the Internet. Had I had a faster system, I might have been filled at 55¾ or better. Instead, I was filled at 56½. A difference of half a second probably cost me $750. That is the reality of trading a stock that can literally move a full point in only a few seconds.

This was an extremely dangerous trade. Remember, for every buyer there is a seller. And this was a market order. Who was taking the other side of this trade, and at what price? The specialist was on the other side, selling when the rest of the investing world was blindly buying. But the specialist was selling on his or her terms, and at his or her price. Do you really think the specialist would be so stupid as to sell to me at a good price, knowing the market was heading higher? Of course not. Specialists are not in the business of leaving money on the table. That is exactly why the stock gapped up a full point in a few seconds. I got filled at 56½ simply because that was the price where the specialist was willing to take the other side of my trade.

I hope this example paints a good picture of the inherent danger involved when momentum turns into panic buying. The strategy simply does not work with a slow execution. Internet day traders will be the last in and the last out, and will lose money 9 out of 10 times. The only remedy is to refrain from trading high-volatility stocks in these kinds of situations, when the odds of a profitable trade are not in the day trader's favor.

KEEPING YOUR FINGER ON THE PULSE OF THE MARKET

In the arena of low-volatility stocks, such as utilities, closed-end funds, and real estate investment trusts, the conditions of the overall market do not play a vital role in the movement of the stocks. Because of their stability, these slow-moving stocks are not directly affected by wide swings in the overall markets. If the Dow is up or down 100 points, many of these low-volatility issues might not move even ⅛ point. Successfully trading these slow-moving stocks does not require having a real awareness of what the overall market is doing, because you are mainly concentrating on the bid-ask spread, not the market averages.

This is not true of higher-volatility issues. If you want to trade momentum stocks, it is absolutely essential that you keep your finger on the pulse of the market at all times. What does this mean? It means knowing exactly where the Dow Jones Industrial Average, Standard & Poor's (S&P) 500 Average, and the NASDAQ Composite are at all times. Why? Because these high-profile issues are the market. These stocks will generally move with the momentum of the overall market. If the market averages are up, most of these stocks will be up as well. If the market averages are down, most of these stocks will trade down with the averages. It will be rare for IBM, Microsoft, or Dell to be down when the overall market averages are up.

There are essentially three main market indexes you should use when gauging the strength or weakness of the overall market: the Dow Jones Industrial Average, the NASDAQ Composite, and the S&P 500 Index. These will be your road map and your point of reference when you are trading high-volatility stocks.

The Dow Jones Industrial Average: This is the most famous market index in the world. It is composed of 30 market-leading companies that trade on the New York Stock Exchange—companies like General Motors, Johnson & Johnson, Exxon, and General Electric. This is often used as a barometer for the health of our overall economy.

The NASDAQ Composite: The NASDAQ Composite is a benchmark index of the stocks in the over-the-counter, or NASDAQ, market. It is heavily weighted in technology issues, and as such is typically used as a barometer for the health of the technology sector.

The S&P 500 Index: This index is a benchmark of the 500 largest stocks, by market value, that trade on the New York Stock Exchange, the American Stock Exchange, or NASDAQ. This is the main benchmark against which money managers and mutual funds judge their relative performance.

KEEPING THINGS SIMPLE

This is where the beginning trader can really get lost in the maze of information. I could easily write 300 pages on the principles of momentum trading alone. My goal here is to paint a few broad strokes that will enable you to weed out bad situations. Like trading for teenies, momentum trading also requires that you refrain from trading if the odds are not overwhelmingly in your favor. This means looking at 20 different situations and possibly only choosing to trade 1. That is why you need the self-discipline to refrain from making a trade unless your criteria are met. When you are trading for teenies, you have very strict criteria to determine when to trade. Because the risks are so much higher in momentum stocks, your criteria must be even stricter for them. Before we get into the specifics of trading the Dow 30 and NASDAQ issues, we must first say a few words about trading psychology.

TRADING PSYCHOLOGY

One of the major differences between trading for $\frac{1}{16}$s in low-volatility stocks and trading momentum stocks is the risk of loss. What do you do if a trade goes against you? How do you limit your losses? The way you handle your losses is an integral part of trading high-volatility stocks. When you are trading for teenies, the issue of having a stock move against you can be dealt with rationally, because you are trading slow-moving stocks. But in the momentum arena, if you get caught on the wrong side of a trade, the stock could easily move 1, 2, or 3 points lower than where you bought it in a matter of only a few minutes. Panic can set in. That is why it is absolutely essential that you have a strategy for limiting your risk if and when a trade goes against you.

CUTTING YOUR LOSERS AND RIDING YOUR WINNERS

No one is right all the time. Over time I have found that when I trade low-volatility stocks for $\frac{1}{16}$s, I can turn a profit on at least 8 of every 10 trades I place. But when I trade high-volatility stocks, my success rate is much lower. In fact, sometimes I may turn a profit on only 5 of every 10 trades in high-profile stocks. Why? Because it is very difficult to be right on 8 of every 10 trades when buying and selling at the market. The house edge is simply too strong. And it doesn't help matters to have a slow execution. So what is the key to success? Remember, limit orders will not overcome the house edge in high-volatility stocks. And if limit orders don't work, and you are forced to use market orders, how can you consistently make money as a momentum trader? Success lies in your ability to ride your winners and cut your losses.

The forces of human nature seem to be at odds with the psychology of momentum trading. The minute a stock goes against you, the natural human tendency is to want to hold on to that stock until it rebounds. What inevitably happens is that, as the stock heads lower, it becomes harder and harder to sell because the loss becomes bigger and bigger. In other words, as the stock heads lower, your refusal to take the loss will take on a life of its own. A $1,000 loss becomes a $2,000 loss. Then a $2,000 loss becomes a $3,000 loss. The larger the loss becomes, the less likely you are to sell. This is how traders can lose their life savings in a single afternoon.

If you trade momentum stocks, the only way to be successful is to fight this tendency. Look at the traders who consistently make money trading these stocks. Profitable traders are not emotionally attached to the stocks they trade. If the stock goes against them, they sell. They admit they are wrong, and they take the loss. No questions asked. There are too many other opportunities out there to get hung up on one bad trade.

My rule of thumb is that, if the stock goes against me by ¼ point or more, I sell immediately. If I am wrong, and the stock begins to head higher after I sell, I simply buy the stock back, even if I have to pay a higher price than I sold the stock for the first time around. Remember, this game is not about absolute price levels. The price paid for the stock doesn't matter. Whether the stock is overvalued or undervalued means nothing in the short term. The day trader is a middleman. The only thing that matters is the ability to sell the stock at a higher price than where it was bought.

The same destructive tendencies of human nature are at play on winning trades. While day traders are naturally inclined to ride losses, they also have the tendency to cut winners. In other words, if they are on the right side of the trade, they want to book their profits immediately instead of letting them run. This is a very bad way to trade. How is it possible to be successful over the long term if you ride losing positions into the ground and sell winning positions before they have run their course?

That is why you must let winning positions run. If you are on the right side of the trade, you must let the stock do its job of making money for you. Remember, trading high-volatility stocks entails taking a very large risk. You will lose money if the trade goes against you. You must put yourself in the position to garner the rewards of the risk you have taken when the trade goes with you. If your tendency is to lock in your profits on these trades, you will not be doing yourself justice. If you are lucky enough to be on the right side of the trade, let the trade work for you. You have to remind yourself of one question: Why were you in the stock in the first place? Was it to make ¹⁄₁₆, ⅛, or ³⁄₁₆? No, that is not why you took all that risk. It was to make ½ point, ¾, or higher. And, the only way you will be able to do that is to let the momentum run its course.

PICKING THE CORRECT NUMBER OF SHARES TO TRADE

I strongly advise that you trade high-volatility stocks in 100- or 500-share lots. Do not trade 2,000 shares at a time. The reality of momentum trading is that these stocks fluctuate so much in the course of the day that it is not necessary to trade 2,000 shares at a time. When you are trading for teenies, trading in 2,000-share lots is a necessity be-cause the profit margin per trade is only $\frac{1}{16}$. In addition, you feel com-fortable because the stocks are stable and the risk of loss is low. You also need to trade 2,000 shares at a time to overcome the commission costs. In momentum trading, however, the potential profit and loss on each trade are much higher. That is why you do not want to risk trad-ing large blocks of stock. If the trade goes against you, you can lose a small fortune if you are trading 2,000-share lots at a time. Any of these momentum stocks can easily drop $\frac{1}{2}$ point in a few seconds. This means that on 2,000 shares, you could be down $1,000 in that short time. It is simply too risky. Take my advice: You will be much better off if you stick with 100 or 500 shares at a time instead.

CHAPTER 12

Riding the Market's Momentum

It is extremely difficult for online day traders to be consistently profitable by entering market orders in high-volatility stocks. Wide bid-ask spreads, slow executions, and lightning-fast market movements all work against these traders. Given the time it takes to enter orders over the Internet, day traders are simply not fast enough to get in and out before the other players do. However, the dilemma is that even in this situation, market orders are the only way day traders can trade momentum stocks. Limit orders simply will not work. In the land of momentum, the only defense day traders have is to pick and choose their opportunities carefully and to use every market inefficiency to their advantage.

THE SPECIALIST AND THE UPPER HAND

In the domain of trading high-volatility NYSE-listed stocks (see Figure 12.1), the house edge is extremely powerful. This is because of the presence of the specialist. As stated earlier, on the New York Stock Exchange the specialist is required to maintain an orderly market. Each individual stock has one specialist who is assigned to oversee all transactions in that particular stock. The specialist risks his or her own

Figure 12.1   Sample listing of high-volatility NYSE stocks.

	Symbol	Last	Change	Volume	Bid	Ask	Bid Size × Ask Size
	$INDU	9124.53	+68.48	DOW			
	$SPX	1159.58	+6.97	S & P Index			
	$@CCO	1921.16	+1.48	NASDAQ Comp			
	SP8Z	1162.5	+3.80	S & P Futures			
	$TYX	5.21	−0.33	30 year treasury			
	ZB8Z	128 20/32	+22/32	30 yr bond futures			
1	AA	80 5/16	+1	777,400	80 1/8	80 5/16	5 × 2
2	ALD	41 7/16	+1/4	579,200	41 3/8	41 7/16	26 × 100
3	AXP	104 1/16	+2 11/16	1,473,700	103 7/8	104 1/8	41 × 100
4	T	63 3/8	+7/16	3,522,700	63 5/16	63 3/8	10 × 60
5	BA	43 7/16	+5/16	2,418,900	43 3/8	43 7/16	65 × 20
6	CHV	86 1/8	−3/16	1,112,000	86	86 1/4	73 × 100
7	CAT	48 1/16	+1/4	967,000	47 15/16	48 1/16	100 × 25
8	CCI	44 15/16	+1/2	11,889,300	44 7/8	45	200 × 840
9	KO	72 7/16	+1 1/16	2,480,700	72 5/16	72 7/16	33 × 24
10	DIS	28 3/8	+1/16	4,736,300	28 3/8	28 7/16	600 × 20
11	DD	60 1/2	−3/16	1,227,500	60 1/2	60 9/16	25 × 1
12	EK	76 1/8	−1/16	1,096,400	76 1/16	76 1/8	38 × 1
13	XON	71 5/8	+1 3/4	3,825,600	71 9/16	71 11/16	19 × 20
14	GE	92 3/16	−3/8	3,849,700	92 1/8	92 1/4	10 × 15
15	GM	72 1/16	−1/2	2,338,800	72 1/16	72 3/16	10 × 10
16	GT	56	+7/16	438,400	55 15/16	56	19 × 3
17	HWP	58	−1 1/16	5,469,600	57 15/16	58	15 × 200
18	IBM	159 1/8	+9/16	2,427,200	159 1/16	159 1/8	10 × 10
19	IP	45 3/4	+1/2	442,700	45 5/8	45 13/16	60 × 52
20	JNJ	88 1/8	+1 1/2	1,409,900	88 1/16	88 1/8	6 × 37
21	MCD	70 7/8	−3/16	1,785,300	70 13/16	70 7/8	28 × 52
22	MRK	150 7/16	+1/8	1,779,800	150 3/8	150 1/2	52 × 60
23	MMM	82 1/2	−3/16	1,035,900	82 1/2	82 9/16	21 × 5
24	JPM	109 1/2	+3 1/8	901,400	109 3/8	109 1/2	13 × 18
25	MO	55 11/16	+5/16	6,199,600	55 9/16	55 3/4	96 × 50
26	PG	90 13/16	+1 3/16	1,525,200	90 13/16	90 15/16	10 × 30
27	S	48 1/16	+3/8	749,400	48	48 1/16	10 × 5
28	UK	44 7/16	+1 1/16	453,600	44 3/8	44 1/2	50 × 65
29	UTX	103 3/16	+2 5/16	705,900	103 1/8	103 5/16	10 × 17
30	WMT	73 1/4	+1/4	2,304,100	73 3/16	73 5/16	15 × 50

Real-time data courtesy of Paragon Software, Inc. (InterQuote), 1-800-311-1516, www .interquote.com.

capital to ensure that customers receive fair and instantaneous executions when buyers cannot be matched with sellers, provided the orders are market orders. As you know, specialists will only risk their trading capital at a price level that is advantageous to them. In other words, when they risk their trading capital, they do so at a price where they think they can turn a profit on the trade. Remember, the specialist is the best day trader of all.

In slow-moving stocks, you are able to trade with the house by buying and selling at the same price levels as the specialist. Your reasoning is that, if the specialist is willing to risk his or her capital to buy stock at a certain price, it must be a good price level to buy stock. So you enter your buy order at the same exact price as the specialist. Where the specialist is buying, so are you. This rule enables you to make the same small profits as the specialists off the buying and selling public. In essence, you are taking food out of the specialists' mouths by copying their trading strategy. And the rules are on your side because specialists must let customer buy and sell orders take priority over their own intentions, if the customers are willing to buy and sell at the same price level as the specialists are.

Taking food out of the specialists' mouths is a very dangerous way to make a living. Why? Because the specialists do not like it when day traders take profits out of their pockets. You can be sure of one simple fact going in: The specialists will trade against you every chance they get. If you are off your market, the specialists will take advantage of you. You can counteract this risk, however, by sticking with slow-moving, low-volatility stocks. This essentially eliminates your disposition. There is no real threat of specialists trading against you, because the stocks don't move. In other words, there is nothing the specialists can do to get rid of you.

However, the minute you enter the arena of high-volatility stocks, the rules change. There is no way for you to consistently make money by exploiting the bid-ask spread in volatile stocks. The specialists have the upper hand, and you cannot get in their way. If you do, you will lose money. Why? Because the specialists have a lightning-fast execution, and online day traders have a slow one. In high-volatility stocks, this slow execution will prevent day traders from trading with the specialists. The online day traders will always be one step behind. And, when seconds are the difference between making and losing money, being one step behind always means losing money.

It is important to remember one of the major themes of this book: You never want to bet against the house. Over the long term, you will not make a living as a day trader if you attempt to do this. Over time, the house edge will destroy you. As you know, when you trade for teenies, you are never betting against the house: You are always betting with the house, by buying on the bid and selling on the ask. You are working the bid-ask spread to your advantage, something you will be unable to do in high-volatility stocks.

So, if you can't trade with the house all the time, how can you possibly make any money by day trading volatile New York Stock Exchange stocks? If you recklessly throw your money at every trade, the answer is that, most of the time, you cannot. Outside of a few rare instances that I will mention in the next few pages, I honestly do not know if there is any way to consistently day trade these issues profitably if you are trading from home over the Internet, and if you do not screen your opportunities carefully. Remember, there is a whole world on Wall Street of day traders who trade these stocks for a living. What is the difference between them and you? How do they make a living trading these issues, and if they can, why can't you? It is because they have high-tech systems and lightning-fast executions. It is not that they are necessarily better traders than you. They just have better trading equipment, and in a game of seconds, that is the difference between winning and losing. Why do they have better trading equipment? Because they are not paying $10 or less for each trade. These professional traders generally pay more like $20 or $30 to get the trade executed on the floor of the exchange. They pay more money because a better trade execution costs more. It's that simple. As we said before, the cheap commissions and the luxury of trading from home come with a cost: a slow execution.

With this in mind, I have only come across one type of momentum trade that is a pure way to trade with the house—to be on the same side of the trade as the specialist without being at a real disadvantage for having a slow execution. In a fast-moving stock, this is the only time the odds are truly in the day trader's favor. This is when the day trader must go for the jugular, because these kinds of opportunities do not come around often.

PLAYING THE GAP OPEN—THE ONLY PURE WAY TO TRADE WITH THE HOUSE

The only pure way to trade with the house on volatile NYSE stocks is to be on the same side of the trade as the specialist when the stock opens.

Remember, the role of the day trader is that of middleman. The day trader is a buyer when the market needs buyers, and a seller when the market needs sellers. A supply-demand imbalance offers a great chance for a profitable trade. Imagine a company that has just released bad news. The bad news will inundate the stock with sell orders. For the stock to open, the sell orders must be matched with buy orders. If the stock opens down 15 points on the news, the specialist will generally be forced into being the buyer of last resort. Why? Because no one wants the stock in light of the bad news. The important thing is that when this happens, the specialist will set the price at which he or she buys the stock. And, as you know by now, specialists will only risk their capital when they feel they can make money consistent with their role of maintaining an orderly market.

BUYING ON BAD NEWS

How does the day trader trade with the house when this happens? By joining the specialist in buying the stock from the investing public on the opening print, with the intention of reselling the stock minutes later for a profit. The reasoning is that, if the specialist is risking his or her capital to buy the stock, it must be a good price level at which to buy. This trading strategy has worked very well for me over the years, but it only works on New York Stock Exchange stocks.

Let's look at an example. On the morning of July 22, 1998, Computer Associates (CA) issued a press release warning that earnings for the year would be far below expectations. This news came as a major surprise to the analysts that cover the stock. The result was that the stock was downgraded from a strong buy to a hold at several major brokerage firms. When a stock is downgraded to a hold, investors usually do not wait around for conditions to improve. They rush for the exits and sell. This is a true panic situation.

What the investing public doesn't realize is that when bad news is released before the market opens, the stock will immediately reflect the news. In other words, the price level at which the stock opens for trading that morning will have the bad news priced in. In this case, by 9:30 A.M. and the open of trading, it was fair to say that this bad news had reached everyone it needed to reach. In addition to being on the front page of all of the major financial newspapers, including *The Wall Street Journal* and *Investor's Business Daily,* it was talked about continuously on CNBC's *Squawk Box* from about 7:00 A.M. to the open of trading. In other words, the information was fully disseminated before the stock had opened for trading.

Anytime there is panic selling, the sellers do not care about the price at which the stock trades. They just want to get out of the stock at any price. This is an extreme case of a supply-demand imbalance. Remember one thing: For every buyer there is a seller. This means the stock must open for trading at the price at which the influx of sell orders can be matched with buyers.

By 9:25 A.M., five minutes before the opening bell, the stock had over 2 million shares of sell orders at the market on the books. This means that all these orders had to be filled on the opening print of the stock. In other words, the specialist now had an order in hand to sell a total of 2 million shares at the market. But who in their right mind would want to buy a stock when it is this lopsided? Conventional wisdom would tell anyone to stay away from the stock. But conventional wisdom never put any money in the day trader's pocket.

This is where the role of the specialist becomes very important. The specialist assigned to Computer Associates is obligated to maintain an orderly market. This means that, as long as the 2 million shares to be sold were entered at the market, the specialist is required to give them an execution at some price. If the specialist cannot match the sell orders with buyers, he or she becomes the buyer of last resort. And, as you know, the buyer of last resort holds one advantage over the investing world: He or she determines the price at which the stock will be sold.

Think of the significance of this situation for one moment. Imagine being at a bargaining table where you are the only buyer and the sellers are in a state of panic. They want out at all costs. They tell you, as the only buyer, to name your price. Think of the edge you have over the sellers. They will accept any price you give them. This is what the specialist is faced with on a gap opening.

BETTING THE FARM ON THE SPECIALIST

If I were a gambler, I would bet the farm on the specialist in this kind of situation. When the specialist has over 2 million shares to be sold, and cannot find buyers, he or she will be forced to step up to the plate. As the buyer of last resort, the specialist will be called on to buy a large percentage of that 2-million-share sell order at his or her price. Maybe the specialist will have to buy upward of 1 million shares. Think about this. If you were forced to buy 1 million shares of stock, but you could name your price, what price would you arrive at? Would it be high or low? In whose best interests would that price be? Yours or the seller's? That is exactly my point. In this type of trade, the odds are overwhelmingly with the specialist.

The beauty of this kind of situation is that you don't have to be a gambler to bet the farm on the specialist. By placing a buy order in the stock before it opens for trading, you have placed your bet on the specialist. You are risking your trading capital on your trust in the trading abilities of the specialist. When you enter a buy order at the market, provided it is entered before the stock opens for trading, you will buy your stock on the opening print at the exact same price and the exact same time as the specialist. You will join the specialist as a buyer of last resort.

One of the great things about this trade is that you do not need a split-second execution for it to be profitable. This is because your decision to buy the stock is made before the stock opens. It is not a race among day traders as to who gets the stock first. Whether you have a slow execution or a fast one, if you get the buy order in before the stock opens, you will get in on the action.

AN EXTREME CASE OF BUYING ON THE BID

In the case of Computer Associates, there was such a strong sell imbalance that the stock was delayed until 9:54 A.M., a full 24 minutes after the stock market opened for trading. The opening print was at 39⅛, down over 15 points from where the stock closed the day before. Over 2.5 million shares changed hands on the opening trade. I bought 1,000 shares for myself. The ironic thing about this kind of trade is that, although it is entered at the market, it is much more like a limit order than a market order. This is buying on the bid in its most extreme form. How are you buying on the bid? Because you are getting filled at the same exact price as the specialist, the result of both of you being on the same side of the trade. In other words, in the case of Computer Associates, I bought 1,000 shares at 39⅛ and I would bet that the specialist bought at least 1 million at 39⅛ as well. Provided an order is entered at the market, both buyer and seller will get executed on the opening print. That is exactly why the stock was delayed 24 minutes at the open. The specialist had trouble matching buyers and sellers for 2.5 million shares.

The trade went exactly according to plan. Within a few seconds of the stock opening at 39⅛, it was immediately bid for at 39³⁄₁₆. By 9:58, the stock was trading up at 39¾, and by 10:00 it had broken through 40. That is where I sold. I had made $875 in six minutes, and I was out of the stock by 10:00 A.M.

THE SPECIALIST GOOSED THE MARKET

It is very important to understand what happened here. There was a very good reason the stock immediately traded up from its opening print of 39⅛. To comprehend what happened, you have to put yourself in the specialist's shoes. There is a very good chance that the specialist was the buyer of a very large block of that 2.5-million-share piece, quite possibly 1 million or more shares, as it traded at the open. That is a huge position. Obviously, the specialist is not stupid. He or she would not have arrived at an opening price of 39⅛ if he or she thought the stock would trade any lower than that price. Like any other day trader who bought stock on the open, the specialist bought 1 million shares at 39⅛ because he or she thought the shares could eventually be sold at a higher price.

If you had enough trading capital, what is the first thing you would do after you bought 1 million shares of stock? You would try to goose the market. In other words, you would immediately bid the stock up from 39⅛ to make it appear the stock was headed higher. That is why the stock went to 39³⁄₁₆ bid to 39¾ bid to 40 bid in only a few minutes. Who do you think bid the stock up? The specialist. Why? So that other speculators would see that the stock had bottomed at 39⅛ and was now moving higher. These traders would then jump on the momentum. This would create a buying frenzy at these discounted price levels (remember, the stock was trading 15 points higher the day before) that would move the stock higher. The specialist would then sell into this supply-demand imbalance, slowly liquidating the 1-million-share piece for a profit. Imagine making an average of even ¼ point on 1 million shares! That is a $250,000 profit, all for a just a few hours' work.

RIDING ON THE SPECIALIST'S BACK

How was I able to make an $875 profit in only six minutes? By riding on the specialist's back. I was fulfilling a need the market had. Like the specialist, I was a buyer when the market needed buyers, and I was a seller when the market needed sellers. When the selling pressure was most intense, I was a buyer. When buyers finally stepped into the market, I was a seller. That is how I made my money. But that does not tell the whole story. The money was really made because I trusted the specialist. I knew 39⅛ was a safe price to open the stock. I did not know the stock would open at 39⅛, down 15. But the price didn't matter. I was comfortable knowing that, regardless of price, wherever the specialist was willing to risk trading capital by buying stock was a good price level for me to do the same.

THE PARAMETERS OF THE GAP OPENING TRADE

When you attempt to do this kind of trade, you must be very selective in the stock you choose. Anytime you are buying on bad news, you must be extremely careful how you go about doing it. There are a few questions you must ask before entering a buy order.

1. *Is It a Large, Market-Leading New York Stock Exchange Stock?* It is absolutely essential that the stock trade on the New York Stock Exchange. This kind of strategy will not work as well in NASDAQ stocks (for reasons mentioned later). In addition, it must be a market leader. If it is not a household name, I would strongly advise that you stay away from it. Why? The reason is simple. If the stock is a large, recognizable name, there will always be buying interest in it, no matter what the price and no matter how bad the news. The buying interest brings trading volume to the stock. Ideally, this strategy works best if the stock trades several million shares of volume. If it is a smaller, less well known company, one or two large sellers could crush the stock at any time if they decide to unload, because of the lower trading volume. In other words, it is a much more unpredictable situation, because a smaller stock could not absorb the selling pressure as well as a large stock could. As a day trader, you do not want to be in an unpredictable situation. You do not want to leave anything to chance.

2. *Has the Information that Is Moving the Stock Lower Been Fully Disseminated?* This is another very important qualification for this kind of trade. Bad news brings out sellers. Anytime you are buying on bad news, you must make sure you are buying

the stock at the precise moment the selling pressure is highest. As long as the news is released in the morning before the opening bell, the opening trade will undoubtedly be when the selling pressure is most intense. Why? Because anyone who has decided to sell the stock based on the bad news will most likely do so on the open. In a panic situation, people are not likely to wait. This is because the investing public doesn't understand that when they rush for the exits at the same time, as a group, they are their own worst enemy. This is exactly what creates a short-term bottom. How can you tell if the news has been fully disseminated? My rule of thumb is that if it makes the front page of *The Wall Street Journal,* the bad news has been fully disseminated.

3. *Is It an Extreme Supply-Demand Imbalance?* It is essential that you make the distinction between an ordinary sell-off and a panic sell-off. You do not want to use this trading strategy when a stock only opens down a point or two on bad news. You need a true panic sell-off—down 5, 10, 15 points or more. Why? Because the prerequisite for the success of this trade is that all the sellers rush for the exits at the same time—at the open. You need a panic sell-off to scare enough reluctant sellers into selling. This prevents the stock from heading any lower, because anyone inclined to sell will have done so on the open, out of fear. It is this fear that creates the market bottom, enabling the day trader to make a quick profit on the inevitable rebound.

SELL BEFORE THE SECOND WAVE

In my experience with this type of trade, it is best to sell the stock into the first upsurge. This means that your intention should only be to hold the stock for a few minutes. This is because these kinds of situations are prone to a second wave of selling. There is no reason to wait around for this second wave. Take your profits in the initial updraft.

In addition, I have found that this type of trade usually occurs approximately once every few weeks. The best way you can be alert to these kinds of situations is to watch CNBC's *Squawk Box* each morning and also read the headlines in *The Wall Street Journal* and *Investor's Business Daily.* If the company is not well known enough to make the headlines, you should refrain from using this trading strategy.

FEAR AND GREED

When you attempt to trade high-volatility stocks, I cannot stress enough just how fast these stocks will move in a rally. In the blink of an eye, they could easily move ½ point or more. Why do they move so fast? Because fear and greed rule the markets. The forces of human nature are extremely powerful. Market psychology is in a constant transition between these two dangerous forces. Fear brings out sellers, and greed brings out buyers. Think about it. The only reason anyone ever buys a stock in the first place is the belief that it will make them money. Fear usually does not enter the equation until after the stock is bought, when the money is truly at risk. And for every buyer there is a seller. So what you have is a volatile mixture of buyers buying stock on the urges of greed and sellers selling stock on the impulses of fear.

These forces manifest themselves constantly in the movements of the overall market. That is why the financial markets are prone to irrational selling and buying at any time, for no apparent reason. In light of this, regardless of the stock you are trading, you must maintain an awareness of the condition of the market indexes at all times. Typically, if the stock you are trading is a high-profile market leader, it will move in sync with the momentum of the overall market indexes.

TRADING TICK FOR TICK WITH THE MARKET INDEXES

There is a saying on Wall Street that a rising tide lifts all boats. When the overall market is heading higher, 9 out of 10 times the large-cap stock you are trading will move with the market. Why? Because these large stocks *are* the market. That is why it is absolutely essential that you check the market indexes continually while you are trading. Let's look at an example.

In late summer and early autumn of 1998, I was trading IBM, one of biggest and most influential stocks in the Dow Jones Industrial Average. Table 12.1 demonstrates how stocks like this one move in tandem with the overall market indexes.

This snapshot of the market in IBM occurred during a span of about 45 seconds. My point in all of this is to illustrate the fast and orderly way high-profile stocks move with the broader market averages. Look at the Dow Jones Industrial Average. As the Dow began to rally from down 74 points to down only 69 points, IBM traded higher with the Dow step by step.

Table 12.1 Tick for tick—IBM and the Dow.

Market in IBM		Dow Jones Industrial Average
116–116¹/₁₆	*5 × 35*	*−74.06*
Stock is lifted at 116¹/₁₆ as the market begins to rally from down 74 to down 73		
116–116¼	*5 × 10*	*−73.10*
Stock is also lifted at 116¼, and the bid moves higher as the market moves from down 73 to down 69		
116¼–116½	*10 × 10*	*−69*
As the market rallies, the bid-ask spreads widen, and offers disappear		

WHY LIMIT ORDERS DON'T WORK IN A RALLY

As the market was rallying, traders were lifting offers in IBM as the specialist was moving the market higher. Notice the market when the Dow was down 74 points. There were 3,500 shares of IBM for sale at 116¹/₁₆. The split second the Dow upticked, a trader lifted the stock. Now stock was for sale at 116¼. As the Dow began to move higher, IBM was moving higher as well. The stock for sale at 116¼ was also lifted. Buyers will lift offers in market rallies. That is why it is next to impossible to use limit orders in a momentum stock. If the stock is rallying, you must lift offers by buying at the market. You will miss the market if you try to bid for the stock at a cheaper price using a limit order, because other traders will step in front of you and move the market higher themselves. If you attempt to use a limit order, inevitably you will watch the stock move higher before you are able to buy.

Think about this for a second. Imagine if you tried to get cute and bid for IBM at 116. How would you buy the stock? Chances are, if someone were to hit your bid and sell you stock at 116, it would be because the market was heading lower. And, in this case, the market was heading higher, so you would not buy your stock. So, what inevitably happens with limit orders is that you miss the stock when it runs and you get stuck buying it when it falls. If the stock looks like it is reversing its tracks and heading lower, and you have a buy limit order at a slightly lower price, chances are you will be unable to cancel your buy order before your bid is hit. The stock will trade through you and head lower. You will not make a profit this way. That is the problem with limit orders in high-volatility stocks. You have to remember that the strategies used in low-volatility stocks, namely using limit orders, do not work in momentum stocks.

I hope this illustration gives you a good indication of how fast these stocks will move at the slightest indication the market is rallying. A high-profile stock like IBM will typically move faster than you can get your buy order entered over the Internet. The result: Even if you know the stock is headed higher, you will not be able to react fast enough to buy it at a decent price. That is why these high-volatility stocks are so dangerous to trade from home. You can't use limit orders, so you are forced to use market orders. And look how wide the bid-ask spread gets as the stock rallies. You are going to be leaving money on the table every time you trade.

RIDING THE WAVE OF MOMENTUM

So, when can you make money trading these stocks? The answer is simple: when the momentum carries the stock further than where you bought it. Remember, your intention in this kind of trade is not to hold the stock for the entire afternoon. You may even be inclined to sell it several seconds after you have bought it. You need to get caught in the updraft. For this to happen, you need help from the overall market. If you are trading a stock like IBM, the market indexes must continue to rally for your stock to head higher. If the market indexes, like the Dow Jones Industrial Average and the S&P 500 Futures, fail to continue the rally after you have bought stock, your stock is in trouble and you should sell. If you have just bought IBM, but the Dow is beginning to sell off, you must sell the stock immediately. Nine out of 10 times, IBM will trade down when the market sells off.

USING THE S&P FUTURES TO GAUGE THE SUSTAINABILITY OF A RALLY

If you use only the Dow Jones Industrial Average as your gauge of a market rally, you will have trouble predicting if a rally is for real or just temporary. You will need another barometer as a guide in the treacherous world of momentum trading. The other gauge most day traders use is the S&P 500 Futures Contract. The S&P 500 Futures Contract is essentially a contract whose value is linked to the future value of the S&P index. It is traded in the futures pits at the Chicago Mercantile Exchange. As such, it is used as a leading indicator of the future direction of the overall market. If the S&P 500 Futures are rallying, it will ignite a rally in the Dow Jones Industrial Average. If the S&P 500 Futures begin to sell off as the Dow continues to rally, it is usually a sign that the Dow's rally is unsustainable. That is why it is very important to watch this crucial indicator before you place a trade.

THE LIGHTNING-FAST MARKET UPSURGE— HOW OFFERS VANISH IN THE VAPOR TRAIL

One of the most difficult things about trading a high-profile momentum stock is that there are literally thousands of traders looking at the stock at the same time. The competition is fierce. And everyone is looking for the same thing: momentum. Remember, when a stock rallies, there is only a limited amount of stock for sale at each price level. The stock may be inundated with thousands of buy orders simultaneously. It becomes a race among traders to see who gets the stock first. The winner makes money on the trade, and the losers lose money on the trade. It's that simple. That is why these stocks move so fast at the slightest hint of a rally.

Table 12.2 illustrates another example of just how fast a Dow stock will react to the market upsurge during a buying rally. The stock in this case is Citicorp (which after the merger with Travelers is now Citigroup). I recorded this price move when I was trading the stock in the fall of 1998.

One of the most difficult things about trading a stock like Citicorp in an upsurge is that the offers seem to disappear into thin air. I call this the *vapor trail*. Like the last example, this one took place during a very short time frame of only a few seconds.

STOCK FOR SALE BECOMES SCARCE

As you can see, as the market moved higher, stock for sale in Citicorp became scarcer and scarcer. This was done on purpose by the special-

Table 12.2   The vapor trail.

Market in Citicorp		Dow Jones Industrial Average
99–99⅜	*10 × 100*	*+221*

As the stock begins to rally, the specialist cancels his or her offers to sell stock at lower prices and reoffers the stock at a higher level, in this case up ¼ point at 99⅜.

99–99⅝	*10 × 1*	*+224*

In addition, as the market continues to rally, the specialist offers less and less stock for sale at each price level, essentially making buyers pay a higher price if they want to buy more than 100 shares. Originally the specialist had 10,000 shares for sale at 99⅜. Now, a split second later, after canceling that order, he or she has only 100 shares for sale at 99⅜. Less stock for sale, and at a higher price. A double whammy for the day trader who wants to buy a large block of stock.

99½–100	*10 × 100*	*+230*

In a matter of only a few seconds, stock for sale at lower prices seems to disappear into thin air. To buy stock, buyers are now forced to pay 100 per share, when only 10 seconds earlier it was for sale at 99⅜, which was the specialist's intention.

ist, who did not want to get caught short the stock as it ran higher. In other words, the specialist did not want to get picked off by the short-term speculators in the stock. This could lead to huge trading losses for the specialist if the stock continued to run higher and higher as buy orders poured in. Remember, if the orders are market orders, the specialist must fill them at some price.

The point of this illustration is that at any given time, the specialist is fully aware of the situation in the stock. If the day trader who is watching the stock from home knows it is heading higher, the specialist probably knew 10 seconds ago. Specialists are not stupid, and they are always one step ahead of the day trader. They will adjust their markets accordingly. This is typically why high-volatility stocks move so fast in an upsurge. Specialists will keep raising their prices and make it harder and harder for buyers to accumulate stock at cheap levels. If the specialists know the stock is headed higher, they are not going to be foolish enough to sell you their stock at lower prices. They will mark the stock up accordingly because they know the speculators, in their greed, will pay any price to buy the stock. That is exactly how a stock can move a full point in a matter of a few seconds.

As you can see, trading high-volatility New York Stock Exchange stocks can be very difficult because of the speed with which the markets change. But trading high-profile NYSE stocks is only half of the world of momentum trading. There is another segment of the market that we have not talked about as yet: the NASDAQ market.

INTRODUCTION TO THE NASDAQ MARKET—THE ROLE OF THE MARKET MAKERS

Until now, the majority of this book has been devoted to trading stocks that are listed on The New York Stock Exchange. The NASDAQ, or over-the-counter, market (see Figure 12.2) is a slightly different animal. Most of the high-profile momentum stocks you hear about in the news are NASDAQ stocks. Microsoft, Intel, Cisco, Dell, Yahoo!, Sun Microsystems,

Figure 12.2 Sample listing of NASDAQ stocks.

	Symbol	Last	Change	Volume	Bid	Ask	Bid Size × Ask Size
1	$INDU	8811.71	−11.59	DOW			
2	$SPX	1164.53	+1.70	S & P Index			
3	$@CCO	2017.75	+5.15	NASDAQ Comp			
4	SP8Z	1164	+1.20	S & P Futures			
5	$TYX	5	−0.29	30 year treasury			
6	ZB8Z	$129\frac{1}{2}$	$+\frac{10}{32}$	30 yr bond futures			
7							
8	AMZN	$294\frac{3}{4}$	+52	14,902,200	$294\frac{1}{8}$	$294\frac{3}{4}$	10 × 10
9	MSFT	$134\frac{1}{8}$	$+2\frac{1}{4}$	11,256,900	134	$134\frac{1}{4}$	10 × 10
10	DELL	$64\frac{13}{16}$	$-\frac{3}{4}$	11,713,000	$64\frac{3}{4}$	65	18 × 16
11	INTC	$115\frac{9}{16}$	$-\frac{3}{8}$	9,861,900	$115\frac{1}{2}$	$115\frac{3}{4}$	20 × 10
12	CSCO	$83\frac{5}{8}$	$-\frac{1}{8}$	11,248,900	$83\frac{9}{16}$	$83\frac{3}{4}$	10 × 3
13	SUNW	$80\frac{3}{8}$	$+\frac{1}{8}$	3,856,600	$80\frac{1}{4}$	$80\frac{5}{16}$	10 × 3
14	YHOO	$207\frac{3}{16}$	$+9\frac{3}{16}$	6,364,500	$207\frac{1}{16}$	$207\frac{3}{16}$	10 × 11
15	SEEK	$46\frac{1}{4}$	$-1\frac{1}{4}$	4,458,600	$46\frac{1}{4}$	$46\frac{7}{16}$	10 × 2
16	ORCL	39	$-\frac{9}{16}$	8,396,800	$38\frac{15}{16}$	39	15 × 15
17	SYBS	$7\frac{3}{16}$	$-\frac{3}{8}$	457,400	$7\frac{3}{16}$	$7\frac{1}{4}$	10 × 10
18	AAPL	$33\frac{1}{16}$	$-\frac{9}{16}$	3,060,900	33	$33\frac{1}{16}$	10 × 1
19	AMAT	40	$-\frac{5}{8}$	3,860,300	$39\frac{7}{8}$	40	13 × 10

Real-time data courtesy of Paragon Software, Inc. (InterQuote), 1-800-311-1516, www.interquote.com.

and Amazon.com all fall into this category. No day trading book would be complete without mentioning the dimensions of the NASDAQ market.

Unlike the New York Stock Exchange, the NASDAQ exchange does not rely on the specialist system. Instead of having one specialist assigned to maintain an orderly market in a particular stock, NASDAQ uses *market makers,* or member firms that buy and sell on their own behalf. These member firms are linked electronically, and as such there is no physical exchange where the stock changes hands. It is all done in cyber space. But as with the specialist system, these market makers are obligated to maintain an orderly and liquid market in the stocks they trade. Therefore, instead of having one specialist actively trading the stock, a NASDAQ issue may have upward of 10 to 20 different market makers.

In my experience trading NASDAQ stocks, I have found that the market maker system creates much more volatility than the specialist system on the New York Stock Exchange. This is because there is no one individual who is totally accountable for the movements of the stock. Remember, on a New York Stock Exchange stock, any complaints of unfairness fall directly into the specialist's lap. The specialist assumes all the responsibility of maintaining a fair market. Not true on NASDAQ: Instead, the burden falls collectively on the group of market makers. That is why there have been numerous complaints over the years accusing NASDAQ market makers of unfair trading practices from price fixing to collusion.

On a typical trading day, most of the largest movers usually trade on the NASDAQ market. Stocks like Amazon.com, Yahoo!, and Dell Computer can literally have intraday price swings of 20 to 30 points. If you get on the wrong side of this momentum, it can destroy you. That is why I believe the NASDAQ market is extremely dangerous for the day trader trading from home, because of the slow execution. But, as with everything else, there are some times when the odds are in your favor. You must understand the landscape before you proceed, however.

THE STOCK MARKET OF THE NEXT HUNDRED YEARS

The NASDAQ market is often called *the stock market of the next hundred years.* This is because most of the issues that trade on NASDAQ are entrepreneurial in nature. They are usually not seasoned companies like those listed on the New York Stock Exchange, but instead are companies in rapid growth industries, especially technology. This is usually the main culprit for the volatility, as the market tries to gauge the future prosperity of many of these start-up companies. It is not uncommon for some companies, particularly in the Internet sector, to go public without ever having turned a profit. Why would anyone buy stock in these companies? On the belief that they are the next Microsoft, Intel, or Dell. These are typically the kinds of companies whose share prices can double or triple in a matter of only a few days (or hours), only to cancel out all of those gains in a quick bout of panic selling.

THE "REAL" DAY TRADING FIRMS

There is a whole class of day traders who specialize in trading NAS-DAQ stocks. These day trading firms are not in the business of trading over the Internet from home like you and I. Many have rooms of 70 or 80 traders, all looking for one thing: momentum. They have high-powered, high-tech systems that can alert them to profitable opportunities before you and I even see them. These day traders are drawn to NASDAQ stocks because they are so volatile. Remember, when you have a fast execution, volatility creates profits, because you can get in and out of stocks quickly and efficiently. When you have a slow execution, volatility destroys profits. The amount of money these day traders can make in a single afternoon using these trading systems is staggering.

What has allowed these day traders to consistently make profits on NASDAQ stocks? Their lightning-fast execution. When a volatile stock is running, the difference between making and losing money could be a fraction of a second. These people are the ones making money at times when the slower traders, like you and me, could be losing money.

THE SOES BANDITS

When these day trading firms began in the early 1990s, they were nicknamed *SOES bandits*. They got this name because they exploited a NASDAQ loophole called the Small Order Execution System (SOES) to get lightning-fast executions. SOES was designed after the crash of 1987 to give the individual investor an immediate fill on 1,000 shares or less of a NASDAQ stock at the best possible price. What these bandits did was to use SOES to pick off the market makers. The SOES bandits were the single biggest threat to the market makers' profits. The reason was that SOES was not originally intended for professional day traders. In the glory days of SOES trading, it was not unusual to hear stories of SOES bandits making $50,000 or $100,000 in trading profits in a single day. In recent years, changes have been made by the market makers to make it much more difficult for this kind of trading to occur.

TRACKING THE NASDAQ COMP

If you are going to day trade NASDAQ stocks, it is very important that you keep your eyes on the NASDAQ Composite Index (the *NASDAQ Comp*) at all times. Like the Dow Jones Industrial Average to NYSE stocks, this is the main barometer for the momentum of the NASDAQ market. The large, market-leading technology stocks, including Microsoft, Intel, Dell, Sun Microsystems, and Cisco all move in tandem with the NASDAQ Comp. It is extremely volatile, and is prone to breathtaking rallies and gut-wrenching sell-offs even in times when the Dow and the S&P 500 are stable.

A FEW WORDS ON SHORT SELLING

I have yet to mention a trading strategy that is very popular among day traders—the concept of *short selling*. When you short a stock, you are essentially selling the stock before you own it. It is the exact opposite of buying the stock. Instead of buying low and selling high, when you short a stock, you are attempting to sell high and buy low. In other words, you sell the stock first before you buy it. It is a bet that the stock price will decline. If you short a stock at 100 and buy it back at 99, your profit is the same as if you bought the stock first at 99 and sold it later at 100. Why do traders like to short stocks? Because stocks typically fall faster than they rise.

Even in light of this, in my experience, very few of my short positions have ever been profitable. There are many traders who share this belief. Again, the reason comes down to execution. To get a short off, you need a lightning-fast execution. It is a precision trade that requires skill and speed. This is because there are rules in place that prevent you from shorting on a downtick, or on a price lower than the previous trade. On the NYSE, the short must occur on an uptick, or a price higher than the previous trade. This rule was enacted to prevent traders from jumping all over a stock that is falling and driving it into the ground by adding to the selling pressure.

The dangerous thing about shorting stock is that your risk of loss is unlimited. Imagine you short a stock at 15 and, to your horror, the stock opens the next trading day at 100. Though unlikely, this is not out of the realm of possibility. Imagine you own 1,000 shares. On a $15,000 investment, you will lose $85,000 if you *cover* or buy the stock back at 100. It would be no different than buying 1,000 shares at 100 and selling them at 15. That is why shorting stock is a very risky practice.

TAKING FOOD OUT OF THE MARKET MAKERS' MOUTHS

If there is one thing I have learned in my forays into trading NASDAQ stocks, it is that on NASDAQ you will be unable to get between the bid-ask spreads profitably if you have a slow execution. If you want to trade these issues, you will have difficulty buying on the bid and selling on the ask, except when the stock moves against you. Why? Because the market makers control the trading in the stocks. They make the spread, and there is no way they will let you in on the action. They are not bound by the same rules as the specialists on the New York Stock Exchange. On NASDAQ, there is no stepping in front of the specialists because there are no specialists. Here the bid-ask spread will always work against the online day trader. This is a fact of life in the game of momentum trading, and it is why it is very difficult to be consistently on the right side of these trades if you blindly buy and sell anything that moves.

But, even though the house edge is strong, there are a few ways to beat the market makers at their own game. The only way to take food out of the market makers' mouths is to catch them off guard. That is precisely what the high-tech day trading firms have been doing for years. In the game of momentum trading, the market makers will have difficulty maintaining an orderly market if the stock is extremely volatile. Typically, when the stock appears to be poised for a run, the day traders will bombard the stock with buy orders. As they are buying, the market makers are required to sell. What inevitably happens is that the market markers are forced to bid the stock up to protect themselves from getting short the stock as it runs higher, creating a self-fulfilling prophecy. If you want to trade NASDAQ stocks over the Internet, this is what you must look for. You must ride the momentum.

TWO METHODS FOR DAY TRADING NASDAQ STOCKS

There are two primary methods I have relied on to make money day trading NASDAQ stocks. These strategies also work well on high-volatility New York Stock Exchange stocks. As you know, when you trade over the Internet, the slow execution will prevent you from making certain trades. To be profitable, you will have to pick and choose your opportunities very carefully.

BUYING STRONG STOCKS AND HOLDING THEM OVERNIGHT

When you are trading high-volatility stocks on NASDAQ, you have to be very careful about holding positions overnight. Many traders prefer not to carry a position in a stock overnight because of the volatility involved. The reasoning is that many of these high-tech companies can easily gap up or down 10 points on the next open. In other words, there is no way to tell what the stock will do the next day.

But there are certain rare times when the odds of a profitable trade are in your favor when you hold a stock overnight. There are several conditions for such a trade:

1. *Never Hold a Weak Stock Overnight.* Remember, momentum works both ways. A stock that is weak has a natural tendency to open weaker the next day.

2. *Only Hold Stocks Overnight that Go Out Strong.* The only way this trading strategy will be consistently profitable is if you buy a stock that is very strong in the afternoon. The reasoning is that the buying strength will spill over into the next day, as the good news that is moving the stock higher gets fully disseminated.

The strategy here is very simple. You buy the stock, hold it overnight, and then sell it on the open of trading the next morning. Momentum has a funny way of perpetuating itself, and it is a very powerful force. If you can get on the right side of momentum, you can make substantial amounts of money.

SCREENING STOCKS FOR THE OVERNIGHT TRADE

When you are looking for stocks that fall into this category, it is best to keep your eyes out for any stocks that are movers. There are numerous Web sites on the Internet where you can check the day's most actives. CNBC will also keep you informed of this kind of movement. A real-time news service will give you the best up-to-the-minute information to alert you to stocks that are moving.

Remember, when trading from home, you will not be the first one in the stock when it is running. When you are looking for stocks to hold overnight, timing is not as important as picking the right stock. You do not care if the stock has already run 5 points in the afternoon before you bought it. All you care about is being able to ride the momentum through the next morning, so that you can sell the stock for a higher price than you paid for it.

THE MARKET MAKERS GET CAUGHT SHORT

There are two main reasons the momentum that carries a stock higher has a good chance of spilling over into the next trading day:

1. *The Market Makers Get Caught Short the Stock during the Rally.* Remember, for every buyer there is a seller. On NASDAQ, the market makers perform the same function as the specialists on the New York Stock Exchange. This means they are obligated to maintain an orderly market. If the stock is inundated with buy orders, someone must step up to the plate to sell stock to the general public. Many times, a buying spree will flood the market makers, causing them to get short the stock as it is moving higher. In other words, because of a scarcity of sellers, the market makers are forced into selling stock they

do not own. This means they will eventually have to buy the stock back in the open market to cover, even if it is at a higher price. This is a very dangerous situation for the market makers to be in if the stock continues to run higher, as it can lead to significant trading losses.

Usually, a buying panic at the end of the day will catch the market makers off guard. This will cause them to carry substantial short positions in the stock overnight. Market makers are not investors. Like you and me, they are traders. They do not like to carry a short position for an extended period of time, especially in a stock that has strong upward momentum. Getting short a stock that is running is no different than being stuck long a stock that is falling. The market makers will attempt to cover their short positions if they fear the stock is headed even higher the next day. In its own way, this is a panic buying situation, except this time it is the market makers, not the investing public, doing the panicking. This will add additional buying pressure to the stock.

In addition, the market makers do not want to run the risk of accumulating a larger short position if the stock continues to go higher the next day. That is why the stock will tend to gap up on the open. If the market makers are forced into the uncomfortable position of selling more stock short, they will do so at a price that is advantageous for them (i.e., a much higher price). That is why it is not unusual to see a NASDAQ stock open up 10 or 20 points on good news.

2. *The Information Moving the Stock Has Not Been Fully Disseminated.* It is very important to pick and choose your overnight positions carefully. My rule of thumb is to only hold a stock overnight if I think the good news that is moving the stock higher has not been fully disseminated. Why? Because the good news is the fuel that will drive the stock price higher. A front page article in *The Wall Street Journal, Investor's Business Daily,* or any of the other financial publications will bring buyers into a stock.

How can you tell if the information has been fully disseminated? If the stock is running in the afternoon, and the news story that is driving the stock higher was not in the newspaper that morning, the news has not been fully disseminated. The ideal situation is to buy a stock that is strong in the afternoon and sell into a gap opening the next morning after the stock makes the front page of *The Wall Street Journal.* Conversely, if the good news has already been in the newspaper that morning, you should not hold the stock overnight. Why? Because the news moving the stock is already out. That is the difference.

Please note that this is the exact opposite of the trading strategy of buying on bad news that we discussed earlier in the chapter. When buying on bad news, you want to make sure the bad news is fully disseminated before you buy. If it is not, more selling pressure will be placed on the stock. When buying on good news, you want to make sure the news is not fully disseminated to the investing public, so that buyers continue to flock to the stock, thus causing it to trade higher.

THE APPLE COMPUTER TRADE

Every so often, the forces of the market align in such a way that a profitable trade is inevitable. I know from experience that this kind of opportunity does not come around often, so when it does, you must jump all over it. Following is a real-life example that occurred in Apple Computer (AAPL) in July 1998 that is relevant to the principles of holding a stock overnight.

There are many variations of the overnight trade, but the underlying recipe for success is the same: You want to buy before the news fully reaches the investing public and sell the instant it disseminates. In other words, you want to buy on rumor and sell on fact. Let me show you precisely what I mean, using Apple Computer.

On a summer night in 1998, CNN was going to air its weekly financial program *CNN/Fortune Magazine.* The main story of the show for that week was about the incredible turnaround at Apple Computer, and its return to profitability among dominant computer companies. This was a very positive news story, and I was convinced that the millions of viewers across America and around the world would inevitably bring buying interest into the stock the next morning.

Most of the time, when a company is featured in the media, you do not have the luxury of knowing ahead of time. If you did, you could make a substantial amount of money, because good publicity always moves the stock higher. But this case was different. CNN was advertising the lead story on Apple Computer's newfound prosperity several days in advance of the show.

On the eve of the show's airing, trading in Apple Computer was heavy. The stock was up 1½ points by the close, undoubtedly moved up by traders anticipating exactly what I was anticipating: that the favorable news coverage would move the stock higher. Chances were that the stock would gap higher the following morning, as the investing public who saw the show would enter their buy orders in AAPL at the market on the stock's opening trade the next morning.

As it turned out, I was right. The news story delivered exactly what it had promised. The stock opened for trading up ¾ the next day, and I sold on the opening print. The buying momentum created by the favorable story was simply too strong. And I could see it coming for several days in advance. This was one of the market's rare gifts.

The situation in Apple Computer sheds some light on the nature of momentum trading. To be profitable, you need to be on the right side of the momentum, ride the stock higher, and sell into the buying climax. In a sense, this is what I mean when I say that day traders make money by being buyers when the market needs buyers and sellers when the market needs sellers. But that is only half of the equation. The other half is that you have to be alert enough to spot these opportunities and to know the difference between buying on rumor and buying on fact. In this case, I bought on the rumor that the story would be favorable, and sold immediately after the fact. How did I make a profit? Simply by being one step ahead of the investing public. That is the key to success.

BUYING STRONG STOCKS ON PULLBACKS

The other trading strategy that I have found works very well on NASDAQ stocks is buying strong stocks on *pullbacks*. A pullback occurs when a stock opens high, but falls back slightly in the 10 to 15 minutes after the open. Why do strong stocks pull back? It has to do with how the market makers react to a flood of buy orders. Remember, the market makers, like the specialists, are forced to be sellers of last resort if they cannot find true sellers to match with buyers. If good news comes out on a stock and the stock is inundated with buy orders at the market, the market makers are in a peculiar and dangerous situation. They will be forced into having to fill the influx of buy orders themselves, even if it means having to short the stock. Imagine a buying frenzy in a little-known and thinly traded stock. What if the stock only trades 50,000 shares per day on average, but on this day it has buy orders totaling over 1 million shares at the market that have to be filled when the stock opens? What are the market makers to do? Remember, every buyer has a seller. Someone always has to be on the other side of the trade. The market makers will be forced into shorting the stock to the investing public. Like the specialists, the only way the market makers can protect themselves is to open the stock as high as possible. Keep in mind that the market makers are setting the price at which the opening trade occurs. In whose best interests is that price determined? Yours or the market makers'? You know the answer to that question by now.

OPENING THE STOCK ABNORMALLY HIGH

If you are shorting stock, the higher the trade occurs, the better your chances of covering the short for a profit. It is the exact opposite of going long the stock. You are selling the stock before you buy it, so naturally you will want to sell high and buy low. The market makers will protect themselves and open the stock abnormally high when there is a buying panic by the investing public. The result? The stock may never again trade higher than it does on the opening trade, when the buying pressure is strongest.

There is no better example of this than a stock called EntreMed Inc. (ENMD). In May 1998, there was a small article in the Sunday edition of *The New York Times* that hinted that this company had discovered a possible cure for some forms of cancer. The next morning, the stock was inundated with buy orders. Everyone wanted a piece of the company. The greed was overwhelming. What did the market makers do? They opened the stock at a ridiculously high level. That was the only thing they could do to protect themselves. After closing on the previous Friday at 12⅟₁₆, the stock opened on the morning of May 4 at 83, up 71 points!

THE DANGERS OF BUYING A STRONG STOCK ON THE OPENING TRADE

Why did the stock open so high? That was the only price at which the market makers felt comfortable in shorting stock to the investing public. What happened next is a textbook example of the dangers of buying a stock on good news on the open. In the next several hours of trading, the stock proceeded to drop like a rock, hitting an intraday low of 40¾, over 40 points lower than where it opened! And remember, there was not bad news on the stock, there was good news; yet the stock still sold off after the opening trade. Why did it sell off so violently after the gap opening? Because the market makers manipulated it lower after they got their short positions off. The market makers made a substantial amount of money on this trade, at the expense of the investing public. They shorted the stock at 83 and covered their positions at lower prices, buying back the stock to cover as it dropped. How would you feel if you were an investor who bought the stock at the market on the open of trading? After being filled at 83, you would have seen your investment cut in half by noon. That is a very dangerous situation.

This is proof of the tendency that strong NASDAQ stocks typically drift lower after the high opening trade. The reason? Once the marker makers have filled the influx of buy orders by taking the other side of the trade, they are short the stock. The lower the stock drifts, the more money they will make when they attempt to cover their shorts by buying the stock back. All of a sudden, after the opening trade, the market makers have a vested interest in moving the stock lower. The stock is manipulated lower immediately after the open. That is the name of the game.

INFLICTING HEAVY DAMAGE ON THE MARKET MAKERS BY ATTACKING THEIR VULNERABILITY

Here is where the alert day trader can participate in a buying spree that can level substantial monetary damage on the market makers. Once a strong stock begins to drift lower for a bit after opening high, day traders will typically attempt to inundate the stock with a second wave of buying. Why? Because the day traders know exactly how the game is played, and they are attacking the market makers at their weakest point. The day traders are certainly not foolish enough to buy the stock at the market on the open. They are well aware of the trap the market makers have set, and they are not about to step right into it. They know what the market makers' intentions are: opening the stock high and letting it drop like a rock after the opening print.

The day traders will strike when the market makers are at their most vulnerable. This is a very important situation to comprehend: The alert day traders are aware that the market makers are short the stock. As you know, the market makers are short because they were obligated to take the other side of the influx of customer buy orders on the open. They were forced into being sellers of last resort. Their only defense was to open the stock high in the hopes of covering their shorts (i.e., buying) as the stock drifted lower. The market makers will now try to cover their short positions at a profit. That is why they try to let the stock drift lower. But the day traders will not let them; instead, they bombard the stock with a second wave of buying.

MAKING A PROFIT AT THE EXPENSE OF THE MARKET MAKERS

The result? The market makers, instead of covering their short positions, are now short even more stock at lower price levels. This is a very dangerous situation. If all goes according to plan, the day traders will make a substantial profit on this kind of trade at the expense of the market makers. How? Because the market makers are forced to join in on the buying to cover their short positions. Thus, the stock runs higher as the market makers cover their shorts. In essence, by buying, the market makers become their own worst enemy. Alert day traders will capitalize on the situation by selling stock into the upsurge, hopefully making a nice profit in the process.

This situation did not work in our Entremed example because the stock opened so high. But it should be noted that this tendency is exactly the reason the stock did open at 83. The market makers were very fearful of the potential for a second wave of buying sparked by day traders. Imagine if, after the stock opened at 83, the day traders waited 5 or 10 minutes and then began to bombard the stock with buying before the market makers were able to cover their first set of short positions. Now, instead of covering their shorts, the market makers would be short even more stock. That is how the stock could easily go to 100 in the blink of an eye, as the market makers would become buyers in a buying panic.

PLAYING THE CNBC TRADE

There is another interesting situation that I have found is a good trade from a risk/reward standpoint. I call it the *CNBC trade*. The CNBC trade, if done correctly, is a high-percentage trade. Spending the better part of the last two years observing how stocks react to news events has shown me that this is one of those rare times when the odds are in the day trader's favor.

CNBC, as you know, is the leader in providing up-to-the-minute news on the financial markets. Each trading day, I have CNBC on my television for the entire day, from before the open of trading to the closing bell. Throughout the day, the network features in-depth news stories and interviews CEOs about market rumors and events that influence stock prices. This coverage will always affect the supply and demand in the stocks that are featured. And, as you know, when there is a supply-demand imbalance, there is the chance for quick profit.

The way to work this trade is to buy a stock that is being talked about favorably on CNBC the split second the stock is mentioned. It doesn't matter if it is a NASDAQ- or NYSE-listed issue. However, there are two conditions necessary for the trade to work:

1. *The Favorable News Coverage Must Occur During the Trading Day, Not Before the Market Opens.* The reasoning behind this trade is that, because all of Wall Street and millions of investors are glued to CNBC all day, stocks will typically get a quick pop after they are mentioned favorably. Why? Because good news brings buyers into the stock. As you know, if the stock is mentioned before the opening bell, the trade will not work, because the good news will be priced into the stock when it opens.

2. *It Must Be a Smaller, Thinly Traded Stock, Not a Large, Liquid Issue.* The stock must be thinly traded so that a small amount

of buying will move it higher. Remember, you are not looking to get greedy. If you can make ¼ or ⅜ on the trade, that is plenty. If it is a thinly traded issue, so long as get in early, the slightest buying pressure will take the stock higher by at least that amount. If it is a large, well-known stock, it will be more difficult for a small group of buyers to move the stock higher.

THE SYBASE TRADE

Let me show you a real-life example that occurred in the fall of 1998. I remember seeing the announcement on television. At about 12:30 P.M., the CEO of Sybase was going to appear live on CNBC. I wasn't too familiar with the company, but that didn't matter one bit. My rule of thumb is that, when you hear that a company's CEO is going to do an interview, that is all you need to know. You do not hesitate a single second, especially if the stock has performed poorly. You do not wait for the interview to see what the CEO has to say. You buy immediately.

The stock was unchanged on the day. So I bought a few thousand shares at 6¾ on a market order. The interview was to begin on the other side of the commercial break. When the CEO finally came on, my hunch was right. This was going to be good news. No CEO in his or her right mind will ever say bad things about his or her company on national television. That is not CEOs' job. They are salesmen, and to them the glass is always half full, no matter how bad the prospects. I knew Wall Street and the rest of America would react positively. But for this trade to work, it is necessary to be one of the first people in. Luckily, this time I was. The stock began to move, slowly and deliberately. By time the interview was over, the stock was at 7⅛ as investors began to move into it. I was tempted to hold on. *Stick to the game plan,* I told myself. *Get in, make a profit, and get out. There will be plenty of time for second-guessing later.* So I sold. I had played this one right. I had been in and out in five minutes, making $1,000 in the process. And by 2:00 P.M., the stock was right back at 6¾.

That is exactly how this trade works. You hope that, by reacting fast, you can buy the stock before the investing public can get their buy orders in. Your intention is to get in before them and sell into the rally minutes or seconds later. The strategy on this trade is to hold the stock only briefly, because the buying pressure will usually subside within a few minutes after the news story is over. That is why many times the stock will trade back down to where it was before the news story began. Keep in mind that as a day trader, you are nothing more than a middleman. This trade only works because you are fulfilling a temporary need in the market. You make a profit because you are smart enough to sell into the buying climax. In other words, you follow the golden rule: You are a seller when the market needs sellers.

CHAPTER 13

The Day Trader's Ticket to the Poorhouse

How I Managed to Lose $12,000 in Less Than 24 Hours

Losses are a part of trading. No one is immune to them. What separates good traders from bad traders? Good traders are able to handle losses, learn from them, and move on. Bad traders, on the other hand, are not able to do this. Keep in mind that trading performance is affected by your state of mind. If your confidence is shattered, you will be doomed to fail. Always remember that the markets are filled with opportunity. But they are also filled with danger. If you trade long enough, you will learn this the hard way. Large losses are a rite of initiation, because until you have experienced one, you will not know what it truly means to call yourself a trader. For it is only in losing money that you come to appreciate the two most important things an experienced trader can possess: an understanding of the nature of risk and a respect for the power of the market.

Eventually every trader will face his or her own demons. I faced mine in an afternoon of terror in the fall of 1998. For almost two years, I had compiled a profitable track that I was extremely pleased with. This was achieved by trading for ¹⁄₁₆s, limiting my losses, and refraining from trading stocks caught in downdrafts. In the last week of August and the first few days of September, I had weathered a nasty correction in the overall markets that saw the Dow drop more than 500 points in a single day. I actually turned a profit that day. That week was easily one of the most volatile in the markets' history. I was able to survive in the midst of this volatility by keeping a level head, maintaining my composure, and not getting greedy. Then came my day of reckoning.

As is obvious by now, I don't like to take big risks. I only like to trade when I feel the odds are in my favor. However, this was one opportunity I couldn't pass up. What I learned was a very valuable lesson on how *not* to trade. I broke every single cardinal rule I've ever set for myself. In the process, I proceeded to lose over $12,000 in the blink of an eye. In hindsight, I completely lost my composure.

For the better part of two months, I had watched Citicorp (CCI) stock with amazement (as you know, the stock is now Citigroup after the merger with Travelers). I had made a few profitable trades in the stock over the previous year, but I usually found them to be difficult trades. This is probably the most volatile stock in the Dow. On many occasions I had witnessed the stock swing 10 points within the course of a single day. But this situation was different. The stock had been in a continual free fall from about 180 to 100 over the course of a couple of weeks. It seemed to be due for a huge upsurge. Analysts and portfolio managers alike were claiming that this stock would be a 200 stock in a year. Yet, day after day, it kept going lower. There were worries about Asia, a currency devaluation in Latin America, and rumors that the high-profile megamerger with Travelers was about to go bust.

As the stock broke through 100 earlier in the week, I kept weighing the pros and cons of taking a stab at it. I thought for sure the stock could easily move 5 to 10 points in a day or two. I knew that if I did commit trading capital, this would not be a short-term trade. I would have to hold the stock overnight and hope I was right. I wasn't comfortable with this strategy. It seemed to me that buying a stock on a severe dip with a plan of holding it for a day or two was a form of short-term investing, not trading. And I was a trader, not an investor. So I decided not to get involved.

Over the next day and a half, to my dismay, the stock went up 13 points, to 113, apparently on a recommendation from a Morgan Stanley Dean Witter analyst. I felt sick to my stomach that I missed what was undoubtedly the opportunity of the year. I kept thinking about the 2,000 shares I would have bought. That would have been a $26,000 profit in about 36 hours, if only I had had the guts to do it.

THE PAIN OF MISSING A TRADE

I had always said to myself that, if the situation ever arose again, I would be willing to stray from my trading strategy and take on added risk to hit a home run. I kept questioning my own motives and my lack of initiative. Why didn't I just trust my instincts? I knew the stock would eventually come back, yet I didn't do anything about it when I had the chance. Words cannot describe the feeling of misery I felt. In trading, there is nothing more painful than missing a trade. So I swore to myself that if the stock ever dropped back below 100, I was going to throw caution to the wind and jump all over it.

To my surprise, the stock did make its way back down. When I missed it the first time, I was convinced Citicorp would never again trade below 100. The day the stock broke back through 113, it sold off and closed around 108. The next day, after opening down 3 at 105, it continued to go lower and hovered around 101. I felt like the gods of trading were on my side. I had been given a second chance! This time, I was not going to let opportunity slip by. For the first time in my trading career, I didn't care about the risks. I had to act. The impulse of greed was simply too strong. The moment of truth had arrived.

HOW COULD THE STOCK GO ANY LOWER?

So I took a leap of faith and bought 1,000 shares at 101½. I had thought about buying 2,000, but I wanted to play it safe instead. Visions of huge profits began to dance in my head. This was going to be a $20,000 month. I would hold the stock for a day or two, if need be, and sell it up 10 points. Indeed, this would be a $10,000 day. The upsurge was inevitable. Over and over again I kept reassuring myself that this was going to be a huge windfall. The stock had lost 12 points in 24 hours, so how could it go any lower?

Within about 10 seconds after my order was filled, the stock began to break below 101. To my horror, the stock continued to fall. 100⅞ . . . 100⅝ . . . 100¹⁄₁₆ . . . in less than five minutes' time, I was already down $1,500. And $1,500 was about my loss threshold. I should've sold right then and there, taken my loss, and moved on. But I didn't. Breaking every rule I have ever set for myself, I was riding a loss into the ground.

THE TERRIFYING FEELING OF GETTING CAUGHT IN A DOWNDRAFT

The stock continued its free fall for about 25 minutes. $100\frac{1}{16}$ . . . $99\frac{7}{8}$ . . . $99\frac{1}{4}$ . . . 99. In the blink of an eye, I was now down over $3,000. This is a very dangerous time for any trader. When you start to lose large sums of money in a very short time, it becomes very difficult to maintain your composure. I was beginning to fall apart. Irrational thoughts were entering my head. I was angry. My brother Peter was in the room and I was even mad at him. I got a phone call from a friend and I practically hung the phone up in the middle of the conversation. It finally reached the point where the mental anguish was so great that I had to sell. It was simply too painful to continue. I entered a sell of 1,000 shares at the market. I got filled at 98.

In a little over 30 minutes, I had managed to lose $3,500. In the grand scheme of things, $3,500 is not that much money. I should have stopped right there. But greed is a very powerful force. I was not done yet. I felt that the stock owed me something. The stock had taken my hard-earned profits, and I wanted them back. After taking such a large hit, my worst fear was that I would watch the stock finally move higher while I was sitting on the sidelines. That would be a fate worse than death. I knew that in trading, Murphy's law is alive and well. The second I sold the stock, it was going to rebound! I was not about to let this happen. I had to be long the stock.

A FEELING OF IRRESISTIBLE GREED

The stock drifted lower, and I bought it back at 97. This was the second cardinal rule I had broken: Never go back into a stock after you have just lost money in it. Then, the stock started to move higher! It closed at $98\frac{1}{2}$, and I was still long the stock. I refused to sell for a small profit. I wanted to make all of my money back. This time, however, I had only bought 500 shares instead of 1,000. I should have bought 1,000, but my confidence was shaken. So, to get back even, I had my work cut out for me. I was forced into holding the stock overnight.

Something really strange occurs when you hold a volatile stock overnight, especially one you have just been on the losing side of. You have a tendency to do all you can to convince yourself your actions are justified. For me, it meant watching CNBC and *Moneyline* that night in the hopes someone would say something good about the stock. It also meant checking the news wires every few hours in the hopes of a positive press release by the company.

Finally, it meant going on the Internet to the Yahoo! Finance message board on Citicorp in search of moral support. This Web site is where investors and traders can express their opinions about a given stock. Each actively traded stock has its own message board. Usually, it is where people who share the same opinions on a stock commiserate about why they haven't made any money in the stock recently. These message boards are filled with rumors and speculation. This can be very dangerous, as it tends to reinforce stubborn bullish beliefs about a stock that is tanking. You can always find someone else who thinks a stock is going higher, no matter how bad the situation is. There was one message on the board that claimed that the stock was headed to 120 by the end of the next week. So much for message boards.

I find that when I hold a volatile stock overnight I have trouble sleeping. I toss and turn all night worrying about what the next day will bring. It is a matter of hoping for the best and fearing the worst. This is no way to trade, nor is it any way to make a living. When you depend on profits to make a living, you will be surprised how your body reacts to stress—which is exactly why I don't like to hold volatile stocks overnight in the first place. The mental toll it takes is too great.

After a lousy night's sleep, I got up early to check how the S&P Futures had done overnight. A large-cap stock like Citicorp will usually trade with the momentum of the overall market. If the S&P Futures were up overnight, there was a good chance Citicorp would open higher. The S&P Futures, to my relief, were up fractionally. I was hopeful that Citicorp, after closing at 98½, would open up at 100 or more. The last piece of the puzzle was to watch *Squawk Box* on CNBC. In the final few minutes before the opening bell at 9:30 A.M., Maria Bartiromo reports live from the floor of the New York Stock Exchange. This is the nerve center for the day's trading action. Maria usually mentions in which direction the financial stocks are indicated to open. On this day, she said Citicorp would open higher.

With this in mind, with two minutes to the opening bell, I was preparing my strategy. Should I sell on the open or hold out for more?

One of the most profitable strategies in trading is to sell into a gap opening. This is because the specialists will usually overshoot the market intentionally. This means that if there is an influx of buy orders on the open, the specialists will open the stock high to protect themselves. They are obligated to fill the buy orders even if they have to short the stock. They are more likely to open the stock higher if forced into a large short position. On many days, this opening trade is the high print of the entire day.

THE NEED TO BREAK EVEN

The main problem I faced that day was the need to break even. I felt that unless I recovered the $3,500 I had lost the day before, this day would not be a success. In fact, I refused to take a small profit in the stock. I was greedy and felt that Citicorp owed me the $3,500 it had taken from me. The only problem with this is that, because I only owned 500 shares now and not 1,000, I would need to make twice as many points on the upside as I had lost on the downside. I would need to sell the stock at 104, 7 full points higher than where I bought it. This was a recipe for disaster. But the stock was due for a run. So I decided not to sell on the open.

The stock opened at 100⅛ and ran up to 101. I felt like things were finally going my way. The stock was 4 points higher than where I bought it, and I needed another 3 to make back $3,500. If I could just break even! Then things took a turn for the worse. To my dismay, the stock started to sell off. 101 . . . 100½ . . . 100 . . . 99½ . . . 99. Like the day before, it was dropping like a rock. The last thing I wanted to do was take a loss on this stock two days in a row. If it got below 99, I was going to lock in my profit. I saw it trade below 99, and immediately entered a sell at the market. I got filled at 98⅜.

In hindsight, this was a very bad day to trade. The market was in the midst of a major correction, currencies around the world were collapsing, and Citicorp was right at the forefront of this chaos. To make matters worse, it was the Friday before the Labor Day holiday. The markets would be closed on Monday. There is always selling pressure going into long weekends, as traders like to lighten up their positions. Did the market know something I didn't? How could the stock go any lower?

BUYING THE STOCK FOR THE THIRD TIME

This is when things began to unravel. I was angry. I should have sold on the open at $100\frac{1}{8}$. Instead, like the day before, I rode the stock lower. Even after I sold at $98\frac{3}{8}$, the stock continued to trend lower. $98\frac{3}{8}$ . . . 98 . . . $97\frac{5}{8}$ . . . 97. If it got below 97, I was going to jump all over it again. But this time, it was not going to be for 500 shares. I was convinced I could make back more money. The lower it got, the more tempted I was. Then, I made a huge mistake. In total greed, instead of buying 500 or 1,000 shares, I bought 2,000! This was the beginning of the end. Here's how the rest of the day went:

Tarred and feathered—an example of how not to trade

Bought 2,000 at $96\frac{1}{4}$
Sold 2,000 at $95\frac{1}{8}$ for a loss of $2,250
Bought 2,000 at $95\frac{1}{8}$
Sold 1,900 at $94\frac{1}{2}$ for a loss of $1,187.50
Bought 2,000 at $94\frac{15}{16}$
Sold 2,000 at $93\frac{3}{4}$ for a loss of $2,375
Bought 2,000 at 92
Sold 2,000 at $90\frac{3}{8}$ for a loss of $3,250

In less than 24 hours, I had managed to lose over $12,000—weeks worth of hard-earned profits down the drain in the blink of an eye. To add insult to injury, the stock did manage a small rally right after I sold out the final time. I remember sitting in my home office in a state of total shock. This was easily the worst 24 hours of trading I had ever had. Since I began trading, I had managed to turn a profit almost every single day I traded. Now, I was sitting on a $12,000 loss for less than 24 hours' work!

MURPHY'S LAW

As if losing that amount of money wasn't painful enough, watching how the stock performed the next trading day was torture. The stock opened the very next trading day at 104, up over 11 points! I was right, but I was too soon. I knew the stock was ripe for a pop, but I had been caught on the wrong side of it. I calculated that I would have made $27,000 if I had held the stock overnight on my final trade. The problem was that it would have entailed holding the stock over the long Labor Day weekend, something I did not want to do. Murphy's Law is alive and well in the markets. My instincts were right, but I was right at the wrong time. Some situations are not meant to be.

A FEELING OF DEVASTATION

I recall a feeling of total devastation that lasted for several days. What an absolute disaster! Even as I write this, I sit in disbelief. I can only now begin to put the pieces of the puzzle back together about what happened during that reign of terror. I had disregarded every rule I have ever lived by in trading. What was I thinking? In hindsight, there were several factors that contributed to this debacle. If anything, it sheds some light on the dangers of day trading stocks like Citicorp during volatile periods. I would like to share these insights with you.

Abnormally Wide Bid-Ask Spreads

The first problem with trading a stock like Citicorp over the Internet in a downdraft is the size of the bid-ask spread. Typically, in a large sell-off, bid-ask spreads become abnormally wide. This is because the specialists are unsure of which direction the stock will trade next. They keep the spread wide to protect themselves. As liquidity dries up, they are forced to take the other side of every trade. This wide spread is devastating to you as a day trader because you won't be able to play the spread. If you try to buy on the bid or sell on the ask, I guarantee you will miss the market and leave money on the table.

Yet you will leave even more money on the table by placing market orders when the spreads are so wide. That's exactly the problem. I don't know if there's really any way to make good money trading momentum stocks over the Internet when this happens. In volatile situations, when bid-ask spreads are wide, the only time the specialist will ever let you buy the stock cheaper than the ask price is when the stock is heading lower. Thus you are forced into a situation where, if you think the stock is running, you must enter a market order to buy the stock. This is the only way to get a fill in a rising market. I would have to say that, as in a poker match, when spreads are wide, the day trader holds the weakest hand. Weak hands should not bluff; they should fold. I'll show you what I mean.

Here's how Citicorp looked after I bought it for the sixth and final time. After trading as low as 91, the stock appeared to make a quick upsurge. The problem is that this upsurge was exaggerated by a wide bid-ask spread. It only takes a few buy orders to make a stock appear to be moving higher, when in fact it is not.

The market was:

$$91\text{--}91\frac{1}{2} \quad 10 \times 10$$

Stock traded at 91½, then again at 91¾. I reacted by entering a buy of 2,000 at the market, thinking the rally was sustainable. At the time my order was entered, the market was:

$$91\text{--}92 \quad 10 \times 10$$

Can you imagine buying at the market when the bid-ask spread is $1 wide! There is essentially no way to make money on this stock unless it really begins to run. It is a losing trade from the start. But there is no other way to buy the stock if it is running. If you enter a limit order to buy cheaper than where the stock is for sale, one of two things will happen:

1. You will miss the stock as it goes higher.
2. You will only buy the stock if it is on the way down and headed lower.

That's the problem. Volatile stocks move higher because offers are lifted. Market orders are the only way to play this game. To make matters with my Citicorp stock worse, if I were to turn right around and sell seconds after I bought, I would have lost $2,000 because the highest bid was $91. And there was no middle ground.

In my case, after I got filled on 2,000 shares at 92, the stock began to trail off. I had stepped right into a trap. The sell orders began to inundate the stock. This was about the 10th wave of selling that day. A seller hit the bid at 91 and offered more there. The market changed from:

91–92   10 × 10

to:

90⅜–91   5 × 50

Just like that, I was down over \$3,250 on paper. I couldn't afford to lose any more money. My only exit would be to hit the next lowest bid, which to my horror was at 90⅜. The liquidity in the stock seemed to dry up. If I tried to get cute and offer the stock out between the spread, I was sure I would only get filled if the stock was heading higher. It was a no-win situation: Hit the bid and get creamed on the spread, or offer the stock out and only get a fill if it was trading through my price. And, if I didn't act, the stock could easily be at 89 in no time. I was forced to sell. I got filled at 90⅜, losing \$3,250. This put my two-day loss total at over \$12,000. This is exactly why I hate trading volatile stocks.

Trading on Old Information

The second problem with trading Dow stocks during volatile periods is that in times of extreme price movement and high volume, your online real-time quote screen will be slightly delayed. This delay might only be a fraction of a second, but it means you are seeing the trades print before the bid-ask spreads are updated. For instance, the bid-ask spread might read 90⅜–91, but you might see the stock trading at 90$\frac{1}{16}$ or even 89$\frac{15}{16}$. This is not because the specialist is trading the stock below the market. It is simply because the bid-ask spread you see is a fraction of a second old and the market changed before the online quote system could pick up on it. If the volume is extremely heavy, it could also mean that the specialist is so inundated with sell orders that he or she is forced to print the stock before updating the market. This is a dangerous time for the day trader. I absolutely hate to trade when this happens.

The Dangers of Attempting to Short-Term Invest instead of Trade

In addition to getting hammered on the bid-ask spreads, and getting lousy executions, there were a few tactical errors I made that led to the

$12,000 loss. In hindsight, what I was trying to accomplish was a form of short-term investing, not trading. After losing $3,500 the first day, I was determined to make the money back the next day. I had unrealistic expectations, thinking I could hold the stock for 7 points. I normally trade for ¹⁄₁₆s, so to think I could make 7 full points was preposterous. Taking small profits is the key to day trading. It is far easier to make 7 points by making ¹⁄₁₆s over and over again than to make it all on one trade. Never, ever stray from a short-term trading strategy that has made consistent money to try to hit a home run. The nature of trading is such that you earn your profits by making ¹⁄₁₆s, and if you are not careful, you will lose them in whole points. There is no such thing as easy money.

Refusing to Cut My Losses

Another error in judgment occurred in my refusal to cut my losses. When the bid-ask spread is so wide, you absolutely must cut your losses the second the stock goes against you. If the spread is wide, and the stock begins to go against you, you must sell. As you can see, if you don't, the losses can be devastating. The problem is that the wider the spread, the more difficult it is to sell, because in the back of your mind you know how much money you are leaving on the table. But you don't have a choice, because that is what you face when you trade a volatile stock.

Going Back into the Stock after Losing Money in It

Perhaps the biggest lapse occurred when I decided to go back into the stock after I had lost money in it. In my case, I went back five separate times! If this isn't an emotional attachment, I don't know what is. Never go back into a stock after you have lost money in it. The stock does not owe you anything.

Buying Twice as Many Shares

Along those same lines, if going back into the stock was bad, buying twice as many shares was even worse! One thousand shares were no longer enough. Instead of 1,000, I had to own 2,000. As the losses mounted, I was determined to make back the money. If you are stupid enough to go back into a stock after you have just lost money in it, never, ever buy more shares than you did the first time.

Choosing to Trade a Volatile Stock on the Afternoon before a Holiday Weekend

Last but not least, going long a tanking stock on the Friday afternoon before the Labor Day weekend was a recipe for disaster. Traders typically lighten up on positions going into long weekends, and they usually do it in the afternoon. Refrain from buying volatile stocks on Friday afternoons before long weekends. The market is more likely to go down than up during this time.

LEARNING FROM THE MISTAKE AND MOVING ON

It is my hope that you remember this example if you ever find yourself in a similar situation. If you trade long enough, it is bound to happen at least once. But, as I did, you will learn from the mistake. It is not the end of the world: It is a bump in the road and nothing more. It took a few days, but I was able to recoup the profits I lost in that 24-hour span. The point is that, no matter how much experience you have, there are going to be certain times when your self-discipline is going to be put to the test. Composure is hard to maintain and easy to lose. The forces of fear and greed can destroy you if you are not careful. I was lucky I didn't lose more than $12,000 during this debacle. But I made sure it would never happen again.

A FOOL AND HIS MONEY ARE SOON PARTED

Online trading is not something I do for fun, for entertainment, or for the rush I feel after a good trade. I enjoy what I do, but that is secondary to the task at hand. If I want a cheap thrill, I go to Las Vegas. Trading is my livelihood, and I take it very seriously. If you are going to make a living at this game, you must have respect for the power of the markets. This respect will keep you out of harm's way, because if anything, it will teach you that you will not be able to outsmart the market day in and day out.

You are not smarter than the market. There will be times when you will get lucky, but luck will not put food on your table. If you blindly throw your life savings at every trade, eventually you will have nothing left. Over time, the market will take your money away from you. Remember, a fool and his money are soon parted. Where will the money go? Out of your pocket and into the pocket of the person who took the other side of your trade. How did that person get your money? By being smart, by knowing the risks, and by only trading when the odds were in his or her favor.

So, we have reached the end. I hope you have enjoyed this journey as much as I have. You are now on your own. I wish you all the best in the uncertain times that lie ahead. Be careful, stay alert, and remember the things you read here. Good luck, and may the gods of trading be with you.

INDEX